THIS NEW AGE BUSINESS

Set your mind on God's kingdom and his justice
before everything else,
and all the rest will come to you as well.

Jesus of Nazareth (Mt. 6:33)

Other books by Peter Lemesurier

Published by Findhorn Press:
The Cosmic Eye

Published by Element Books:
The Great Pyramid Decoded
Gospel of the Stars
The Armageddon Script
Beyond All Belief
The Great Pyramid: Your Personal Guide
The Healing of the Gods

THIS NEW AGE BUSINESS

The Story of the Ancient and Continuing Quest to
Bring Down Heaven on Earth

Peter Lemesurier

Findhorn Press

© 1990 Peter Lemesurier
First published 1990 by
Findhorn Press, The Park, Forres IV36 0TZ, Moray, Scotland

ISBN 0 905249 72 0

Set in Palatino on Mackintosh SE via Amstrad PCW
Design and layout by Philip Mielewczyk, Bay Area Graphics
Cover photo © Andrew J Zito, Image Bank
Printed and bound by Billings, Hylton Road, Worcester

Contents

Acknowledgements

I am grateful to Oxford and Cambridge University Press for their kind permission to reprint numerous quotations from the New English Bible (2nd ed., 1970) and to Element Books for allowing me to reproduce the laws of prophecy on page 207-8, which are taken from my own *The Armageddon Script*. The extracts on page 31 taken from pages 61-2 of Juan Mascaró's translation of the *Bhavagad Gita* (Harmondsworth, 1962; copyright © Juan Mascaró, 1962) and on page 97-8 taken from pages 75 and 77 of Geza Vermes's *The Dead Sea Scrolls in English* (Harmondsworth, 1968; copyright © G. Vermes, 1962, 1965, 1968) are reproduced by permission of Penguin Books Ltd. The photograph of Raphael's *The School of Athens* on page 128 is reproduced by courtesy of the Mansell Collection.

I should like to take this opportunity to express my thanks to all the friends and colleagues who have kindly read the manuscript and offered advice and criticism, or who in a variety of other ways have helped to make the book possible — among them Brian Adams, Rhiannon Hanfman, Ken Llewellyn, John Major, Michael Mann, Alun Owen, Liz Price, Nick Rose, Richard Thomas and Frank Ward. Finally the list would not be complete were I to neglect to record my gratitude to Sandra Kramer, whose editorial collaboration, support and sheer good sense have been indispensable throughout.

P. L.

Author's Foreword

In the course of this book I have used the traditional English generic term 'man' and its associated pronominal forms 'he', 'his' and 'him' wherever clarity and sense demanded. The use of this familiar linguistic convention naturally has no implications whatever for the relative position and value of women and men in society, though it does have certain historical implications that are, as it happens, by no means irrelevant to my theme.

It could be said, after all, that it was not the feminine in us (the biblical tale notwithstanding) that brought about our race's expulsion from whatever Eden it may once have enjoyed, or that banished heaven to the back of beyond in the first place . . . .

Prologue: The Changes

Extraordinary things are happening. Great and far-reaching changes are afoot. A strange, autonomous transformation is spreading like some irresistible virus through society.

It all started back in the 1960s and 70s, when a veritable social and spiritual revolution seemed to be in progress. All over the affluent West the children of perfectly well-bred and well-to-do families were flocking to join 'alternative' communes and communities which promised them neither status nor respectability, neither wealth nor career prospects. Some of them were shaving their heads and donning outlandish robes to roam the streets as virtual beggars and outcasts. Others, equally berobed, were abandoning themselves to unrestrained orgies of self-expression and self-indulgence under the approving eyes of inscrutable gurus. Yet others were committing themselves with naive intensity to all manner of occult movements and groups whose claims about the nature of reality were so astonishing as apparently to defy all reason and science.

Some of these things still happen. Young drop-outs still drop out, though more often 'one by one and silently' than in the former lemming-like droves. Gurus are still two-a-penny and as inscrutable as ever, even if most of the 'grand gurus' have retired, discredited themselves or simply faded from the media picture out of sheer public over-familiarity. Reason and science are defied no less intensely now, if perhaps in different ways, than in that former 'alternative' heyday before the scientific establishment finally got its act together and set up its own jealous groups and committees — a kind of latter-day Dominican Order in white coats — to preserve the integrity of the faith.

Bliss was it in that dawn to be alive . . . .

But the former children have grown up, as children will. Alternativism has given way to the rat-race, the rat-race to bored materialism, bored materialism to the second thoughts and agonising retakes of midlife.

And so the scene has changed.

In a thousand suburban sitting rooms, often amid the glow of candles or the reek of incense, it is groups of frustrated housewives and newly sceptical yuppies, of determined divorcees and refugees from Christianity, of older and now much wiser nurses and teachers, of questioning shop-assistants, maverick medical doctors and secretly seditious civil servants who are assembling to pursue little-known techniques of group therapy, inner exploration or oriental meditation. In old barns, converted churches and abandoned schoolrooms others with equally (and often newly) open minds are deeply engaged in various forms of yoga, 'growth games', magical rituals and so-called sacred dances. In locations as diverse as Berlin and Tokyo, the Highlands of Scotland and the west coast of the USA whole families and groups of people from all walks of life — many of them noticeably more mature and level-headed now — are nevertheless blithely forging new forms of living and being that owe allegiance to none of the traditional gods of respectable middle-class society and to all of the gods of a new, alternative pantheon characterised by self-exploration, voluntary simplicity, ecological lifestyles, anti-consumerism and deeply-felt global awareness.

But things have not stopped there. The associated ideas and attitudes have actually succeeded in infiltrating the Establishment itself. Traditional church luminaries who twenty years ago would have dismissed devotees of other faiths as mere misguided heathens and condemned their activities as black magic now themselves join the berobed leaders of those same religions in multi-faith services and conventions on a basis of total parity. The established medical profession conducts serious investigations into the formerly scorned 'traditional' approaches, and shows signs of welcoming some at least of them as useful adjuncts to their own skills, if not always yet as valid alternatives. High-powered business executives are regularly sent by their firms on 'de-stressing' weekends involving not only physical exercise and wilderness-experience, but a whole range of 'alternative' psychological and emotional therapies too. In the fields of cosmology and quantum physics, pure science shows every sign of taking on board conclusions every bit as irrational and bizarre as those of the occultists — and sometimes remarkably similar to them into the bargain. At the same time Green politics — another name, perhaps, for the ancient cult of the Earth Mother — is starting to become respectable even in the most right-wing circles. Third World charity, with all its implications of global thinking, is rapidly becoming big business, and even an arm of government policy. And royalty itself is, it seems, not only (like many much more ordinary folk) increasingly ecologically-minded, but quite prepared to sit quietly in meditation or talk to plants.

What does it all mean? What strange mutation of the human psyche is afoot? Where is it all leading? And, perhaps above all, what basic conviction (if any) underlies this weird kaleidoscope of apparently irrational behaviour that has been in growing evidence now for something like a generation?

As it happens, the answer to the last of these questions is also in large measure the answer to all the rest.

For underlying all of these activities (however unconsciously) is the conviction that, to quote the celebrated words of the singer Bob Dylan, *the times they are a-changin'*. Whether founded on factual evidence or merely on a desperate rejection of the idea that things can possibly go on as they are, the word is out that a new age is upon us, a new dispensation ready to begin, a revolutionary World Order about to supervene.

The idea may not yet have struck the Establishment itself in so many words. Yet in our own time, no further ahead than the dawn of the 21st century — so the rumour has it — Earth's long-lost Golden Age of peace and love, justice and plenty is to be restored in all its glory and splendour.

And from that single belief — whether stated explicitly or merely assumed — flows the whole phenomenon of modern 'alternativism' in all its varied forms.

* * *

The conviction itself seems, if anything, even more astonishing than its results as I have listed them above. Indeed, in the light of the current world situation it may well be seen as thoroughly crazy. The prevailing wisdom, after all, is that the present world is on a downhill slope. Crises of AIDS, pollution, food shortage, population growth and social disintegration stare us in the face. For all the talk of abolishing it, the threat of imminent nuclear annihilation still hangs over all our heads. The more the politicians work to overcome the problems, the more the problems seem to multiply. The old idea that progress is inevitable and the Millennium just around the corner is all but dead, for all the virtually universal approval that it enjoyed only a few years ago.

Which makes all the stranger and more remarkable that idea's latter-day resurgence in the form of the so-called New Age movement.

Yet even that idea — that determined creed of perennial optimism — was not always the accepted wisdom. In fact 'progressism' is of fairly recent origin. Prior to the Renaissance a much bleaker and more pessimistic view reigned, in Europe at least, under the aegis of mediaeval Christianity — a view which, it has to be said, had much more in common with today's somewhat jaundiced popular view than the comparatively optimistic outlook of more recent centuries. An eventual Millennium there would be, admittedly, but there was no telling when, nor who would be here to enjoy it when it came. For it was to be preceded by a universal conflagration, a period of hell on earth which few living creatures could hope to survive.

The idea went right back through Christianity to Judaism, and through it in turn to the ancient teachings of the Persian prophet Zarathustra. Yet even it was new in its day. And before it there reigned an entirely different paradigm — a circular vision of the ages which saw the good times and the bad times as returning on an eternal, cyclic basis geared to the stars and planets and the seasons of the cosmos. Even the very breathing of the Creator was, in the Hindu tradition at least, encompassed and measured within the framework of this vast conception. And under its terms humanity was seen to be in eternal decline, the universe destined to repeated destruction, even the Creator himself doomed to extinction on a regular, cyclic basis.

And the only hope lay in the periodic, almost magical renewal that was destined to befall all three.

* * *

From all these various traditions New Age enthusiasts have drawn constant encouragement and inspiration. Most of them readily admit to borrowing various Hindu magical and religious ideas, to adapting for their own use Buddhist psychological techniques and philosophical assumptions, to appropriating a variety of Christian mystical, eschatological and scriptural traditions. Yet few of them ever realise that even the fundamental utopian conviction to whose service they devote such borrowed ideas is itself far from new or original. At one time or another, indeed, it has been regarded as only common sense by large parts of the Earth's population. 'New Ageism' — or millenarianism in its broadest sense — is in fact one of the oldest and most widespread ideas known to humanity. And to this day it remains (as the writings of Mikhail Gorbachev explicitly make clear) every bit as basic to the official outlook of the Marxist East as it does to that of the capitalistic and science-orientated West — even if it has now fallen largely out of favour, on the basis of bitter experience, with the sceptical masses of both hemispheres.

This basic ignorance by many New Agers of their own roots and ideological kinships, combined with an associated lack of clarity about their ultimate objectives, has various consequences. Most of these show up in a general failure of communication. To 'outsiders' (or 'Old Agers') the real nature of the New Age movement is for the most part shrouded in mystery and rumour. Even 'insiders' — most of whom are much more concerned with doing their own particular group thing than with achieving a broad overview — generally find it extremely difficult to explain to others what 'this New Age business' is all about. And this very largely because neither outsiders nor insiders have, for the most part, much idea at all of the movement's real origins or philosophical background.

For the insiders especially, this last fact can be a source of grave misapprehension, not to say actual danger. Part of the movement's main attraction, after all, lies in the word 'new' that is part of its very name. The implication is that it somehow represents an approach that has never been tried before — and which for this very reason offers real hope for the world.

In fact, nothing could be further from the truth.

There is thus a real need for the New Age movement and its ideas to be placed back in their true historical perspective. Not only is this likely to reduce the delusion by scotching the false idea of novelty; it may also help insiders to achieve a truer idea of what it is they are about, while outsiders, too, may be helped to gain a clearer 'angle' on the movement, and thus to relate it more successfully to the corpus of existing knowledge and assumptions.

And by seeing more clearly where it has come from, both may gain a better idea of where it is likely to be going next.

Such, consequently, is the main theme of this book. Starting with the earliest times, the notion of a once-and-future Golden Age is traced from its likely origins in the development of primeval human language and thought, first to the most ancient oriental religions and philosophical traditions and thence, via the apocalyptic religions of the early Middle East and even further afield, to the more secular hopes and aspirations of the European Renaissance. From there the story is pursued through the rise of rationalism and science, via the consequent Industrial Revolution and Romantic movement, to the Victorian era's ill-fated confidence in its own future and the subsequent disillusionment of our own day.

And so to the latter's inevitable result in the quest for alternative sources of hope.

Eventually, then, the story reaches the present day with the rise of the modern New Age movement — the same movement against whose manifestations Christian fundamentalists have recently taken to fulminating so loudly. Who were its founders? What are the real sources of its most typical manifestations? What are its devotees really up to behind the scenes — unknown, perhaps, even to themselves? And what, in the light of what has gone before, are their prospects of ultimate success?

The questions are many, the answers not always easy to find or half as simple as we might wish. Yet at least there is some hope that, by conducting our enquiry across so broad a historical canvas, we may gain a truer perspective on what is really at stake, and so assess more accurately the extent to which we ourselves can — or indeed should — become involved.

PART I
THE LAND
BEYOND TIME

1
Not Now . . . .

The world's great age begins anew,
The golden years return.
Percy Bysshe Shelley

Now is never a good time. The past, if we are to believe our elders, was always better. Their own elders traditionally said the same thing to them, and so on far back into antiquity. The logic is therefore obvious.

The further back, the more idyllic.

Edwardian gaiety, Victorian values, Renaissance idealism, Classical perfection, nomadic wisdom, even savage bliss. The story of humanity comes to be seen as the tragedy of a fall from grace, a long descent from a former Golden Age of supreme harmony, happiness and perfection.

A Garden of Eden that was lost to us at the very beginning of time.

How, then, to restore that long-lost state of grace? How to bring heaven back down to earth again? Here, too, the logic is obvious. Since now is always nasty, all hope of humanity's redemption has to be relegated to an unknown future — perhaps a far-distant future, or possibly one that is much nearer than we think.

For all we know, the evangelicals are right, and the Kingdom of Heaven is at hand.

And so the whole of human history comes to be seen as a cycle of fall and redemption, a ritual round-dance from bliss to despair and back to bliss again. It is a symphonic movement in A-B-A form, a trio section designed to lead on to an ultimate, triumphant finale.

* * *

Now it has to be said that this view of existence has a certain aesthetic elegance about it. Its symmetry is satisfying, even reassuring. Possibly it is that very symmetry and balance that has enabled it to endure for as long as it has.

For the fact is that its foundations are distinctly shaky.

The initial premise, you will recall, is that now is always a bad time. Life, in other words, is hell. But why do we take such a view? How, indeed, can it possibly be true? The cows in the field give no sign whatever that their 'now' is the slightest bit less satisfactory than the 'now' of two thousand, four thousand or even six thousand years ago. The cat stretching itself in front of the fire presumably does so with all the primal ecstasy of its forebears of a million years ago, and there is no reason whatever to suppose that the cat of a million years hence will do so with any greater sense of joy.

'Ah,' you may say, 'but today's domestic animals don't remember that once upon a time their ancestors were wild and free. And the cows in particular are blissfully unaware that they are going to end up amid the horrors of the slaughterhouse.'

'Blissfully unaware' — the words are revealing. They put the finger squarely on the point at issue. For it is indeed our awareness — our conscious awareness — that has to be the cause of our present unease and dissatisfaction. And this because it is an awareness that deals exclusively in terms of memory and anticipation.

It is precisely because we — no less than our elders — selectively recall moments of intense pleasure from the past that yesterday always seems so rosy. It is precisely because so much seems to stand between us and the gleaming future for which we all hope and pray that the present often seems so desperate and threatening.

Our conscious thoughts are so firmly locked into the past and the future, in other words, that we actually forget to live today. The present passes us by almost unnoticed. Such joys as we experience we attempt to hang on to, fearing to lose them tomorrow. Such disappointments as we experience are due very largely to our persistent measuring of today's experiences against our joys and anticipations of yesterday. To this extent we are yesterday's people, imprisoned in yesterday's ideas. And so, as Lewis Carroll's Looking Glass wisdom has it, it is jam tomorrow and jam yesterday, but never jam today.

The essence of the problem, then, is that we have become incapable of living in the present. We refuse to Be Here Now.

No such accusation, it is clear, can be levelled at the average cow or cat. And so there does indeed seem to be a close link between our state of awareness and our capacity for happiness.

And it is the specifically human capacity for conscious thought that seems to constitute the proverbial fly in the ointment.

* * *

The true state of affairs, then, is almost the exact reverse of the idea I posited at the beginning of this chapter. Our belief in a former Golden Age and our faith in a future New Age, or Kingdom of Heaven on earth, are not, after all, the result of our realisation that now is hell.

Now is hell precisely because we insist on projecting the Golden Age into the past and the Kingdom of Heaven into the future.

* * *

At least part of the basis for the persistent 'Golden Age' tradition, then, seems to lie in a distortion of our perception brought about by the way in which we habitually think. We may refer to this explanation as the perceptual approach to the phenomenon.

And it seems to be intimately related to what we might term the psychological approach.

Here memory is still seen to lie at the basis of the process, but in this case it is a memory of a personal, rather than a racial, Golden Age.

Namely our own childhood.

Possibly the idea of the 'lost Eden', in other words, is a distilled memory of a childhood state of grace which each of us experiences in his or her own life before the world and its language and thought start to crowd in on us, much as Wordsworth describes in his celebrated ode entitled *Intimations of Immortality from Recollections of Early Childhood*:

> There was a time when meadow, grove, and stream,
> The earth, and every common sight,
> To me did seem
> Apparell'd in celestial light,
> The glory and the freshness of a dream . . .
> But yet I know, where'er I go,
> That there hath pass'd away a glory from the earth.

Even ignoring the begged question of Wordsworth's belief in spiritual pre-existence as expounded later in the poem, it may be that in our infancy we do indeed experience reality as it actually is, or at least as our limited senses perceive it, in all its heavenly hereness and nowness, and with little or no modification either by subsequently-imposed expectations or by conscious thought itself.

* * *

Yet might the story of the former Golden Age have some real, historical basis too? There are, after all, persistent traditions — many of which claim to be true accounts — that once upon a time there was an actual era on earth, before humanity had lost its innocence, when universal bliss and harmony reigned and evil was unknown. Almost every folk-tradition tells of such a time. In many a religion, in fact, its description forms a vital part of the scriptural canon.

And if such an era *did* ever exist, then there might be real grounds for suggesting — as the New Agers constantly do — that it can somehow be restored.

Paradise lost. Paradise regained.

The thought is a seductive one. Yet it relies heavily on one initial premise — namely that the traditional accounts are as historical as they claim to be.

What, then, is the factual evidence for this?

Sadly, it is non-existent. There is absolutely no direct evidence that people at any time in the past were, on average, any happier than people today. There exists, after all, no independent index of happiness by which anything of the kind could possibly be measured. As to the future, any statement in this regard has similarly to be treated as the purest speculation.

Unless the legendary accounts are to be taken totally on trust, then, what might be called the anecdotal approach seems to be a complete non-starter.

Related to it, however, is an approach which seems to be a good deal more hopeful. We could describe it as the historico-deductive approach. And it runs something like this . . . .

Granted that we today suffer from a sense of 'loss of grace' thanks to the distortion of consciousness to which we have already referred — a distortion which seems to be typical of virtually the whole of modern humanity — must there not have been a time before consciousness became so distorted?

Assuming, in other words, that modern humanity evolved from more primitive ancestors — as is now accepted by almost everybody apart from the most rabid biblical fundamentalists — must there not have been a time when human beings shared the perfect equanimity which we observe today in the proverbially contented cow or cat?

Conscious thought, after all, is highly dependent upon the human capacity for conceptualisation, and specifically upon the development of language. It is language that enables us to divide the world into objects, time into 'then' and 'now'. It is language that enables us to handle such abstract ideas as 'yesterday' and 'tomorrow' in the first place. And there has to have been a time when language first developed in primitive humanity — and a time before that when it did not yet exist at all.

Identify that time, then, and we have uncovered the original Golden Age.

The problem is that we necessarily have no records of such a time, since those records (unless entirely pictorial, with all the difficulties of interpretation which that must involve) would themselves have to be cast in the very language whose absence they would be purporting to reveal. To expect such records to exist would be rather like expecting to discover dark corners by the light of a torch.

But what would happen if we extended the word 'records' to include not merely written accounts — which in any case go back, at most, only some five thousand years or so — but orally-transmitted accounts as well? Inevitably, exactly the same difficulty would apply. Indeed, this very suggestion serves to reveal how daunting the sheer scale of the historical problem is.

For oral traditions necessarily depend upon the existence of spoken language, and spoken language goes back a good deal further than we sometimes realise. It is all very well for Welsh propagandists to claim that their language is 'the oldest in Europe', or for Hindus and would-be New Age esotericists to assert that all languages derive from ancient Sanskrit. Both assertions, as it happens, are wildly wrong. In fact Sanskrit and its latter-day cousin Hindi, along with Iranian and all modern European languages apart from Basque, Finnish, Estonian and Hungarian, can themselves be shown to derive from a single, far more ancient precursor which was probably spoken in an area of south-eastern Europe not too remote from the Danube basin and the Caspian Sea.

This language was, quite literally, prehistoric. In other words it antedated the invention of writing. Consequently what we know about it derives exclusively from a fascinating piece of detective work by philological researchers who, by tracing related words and structures across these more recent languages, have established what single, spoken original must over the course of time have given rise to each form in question. Modern philologists generally preface these presumed 'originals' with an asterisk (*) to indicate that they are hypothetical, or reconstructed, forms. And the presumed parent language they refer to (for obvious reasons) as 'Indo-European'.

What we have deduced about that language tells us a good deal about the people who spoke it. Merely by analysing the remnants of its vocabulary in the various present-day Indo-European languages we are able to establish that they cleared woodland for agriculture and used wheel-less ploughs and harrows to cultivate grain which they ground into meal. They had already domesticated dogs, horses, cattle, pigs, goats and sheep. Their wheeled carts were hauled by draught-oxen, their boats propelled by oars. They manufactured clothes, shoes and pottery (though not on a wheel). They fought with spears, swords, bows and arrows. They already knew the use of copper. They lived in patriarchal clan-villages and practised both a dowry-based marriage tradition and a highly developed form of polytheism.[61]

In short, they were already civilised. They had a good command of technology. They already thought and behaved as perfectly social human beings. And so we have to assume that they were almost as far removed in consciousness from the presumed original 'state of grace', the mythical condition of bliss and sheer animal innocence, as we are ourselves.

And this, it should be remembered, was long before the original parent tribe or tribes split up, some to move westwards into Europe, others south-eastwards into India.

The start of this latter migration is generally dated to around 3000 BC. In fact it was the Indians' word for their former nomadic ancestors — the *Arya*, or 'noble ones' — that was first applied by the mid-19th-century Oxford philologist Professor Max Müller to the ancestral language and the presumed race who originally spoke it. Avidly taken up and elaborated by the occultist Madame H.P. Blavatsky and her late-19th-century Theosophical movement (one of the prime sources, as we shall see, of today's New Age movement), the idea of the lordly 'Aryans' subsequently found its way into the German Nazi party's official mythology, so giving rise to Hitler's infamous doctrine of the *Herrenvolk*, the race of lordly ones, or 'Master Race'.[42]

The result, as everybody knows, could not have been further from the blissful world-Millennium that the Third Reich (surprising as it may seem) was actually intended to be.

Which is one good reason why philologists nowadays avoid the term 'Aryan' like the plague, sticking instead to the totally uncontroversial term 'Indo-European'.

But I digress. If the prehistoric Indo-Europeans of the fourth millennium BC were apparently little nearer conceptually or psychologically to the presumed original Golden Age than we are today, just how far do we have to go back before we encounter such an era? How old, in other words, is the most ancient evidence of the existence of specifically human culture and civilisation, and thus for the use of language which seems always to have been the potential fly in the ointment of human consciousness?

Archaeology has revealed that the ancient city of Jericho, in Palestine, was already flourishing as early as 10,000 BC. The celebrated cave-paintings of Lascaux and Altamira show a sophistication which suggests that the Cro-Magnon inhabitants of southwestern Europe were perfectly social and cultured beings — even if their culture appears primitive in our own eyes — well before 18,000 BC. The palaeontological work of the Leakeys in East Africa[39] has revealed sufficient social organisation and technological skill in our ancestors even of some two million years ago to suggest that a measure of language may have been in use even at this early date.

We should have to travel back in time even further than this, then, before we came to a point at which the ancestors of humanity could be said to be living in a truly wordless state. And only at this point is it likely that their consciousness still corresponded to the state of blissful nowness which we have already attributed to the cow, the cat and, by implication, the rest of the animal kingdom.

By the same token, however, the logic of the evidence would seem to suggest that such an era did indeed exist once upon a time. The tradition of a former Golden Age, in other words, may not be founded wholly on illusion. A grain of historical truth may underlie this almost worldwide conviction, a spark of flame lie hidden beneath the billowing clouds of anecdotal and largely spurious smoke.

* * *

Yet it seems unlikely, on the face of it, that the 'Golden Age' tradition could itself represent an orally-transmitted memory of a state of grace so extraordinarily remote from us in time. The feat of memory and oral transmission involved would be altogether too great to be credible. And what, in any case, would there be to be transmitted? Certainly nothing that could be expressed in words, since words, by definition, did not exist at the time being described. And so the most that language could be expected to convey would be a vague expression of some (necessarily) contentless nostalgia.

True, there *is* something of this feeling about the persistent 'Golden Age' tradition. And yet the enormous timespan involved still makes it seem a good deal more reasonable to surmise that the tradition refers, if at all, to a much more recent era when language-based consciousness was already well-developed, but had not yet assumed the all-pervasive nature which today cuts us off not only from a full and uninhibited appreciation of our present experience, but also from each other, from the world around us and — it has to be said — from our own deeper selves.

There was a time still within the reach of oral transmission, in other words, when language was able to do its job of facilitating people's capacity for focused consciousness without falsifying their immediate and instinctive appreciation of reality as a whole.

A time when now was not nasty, nor even nice, but merely reality as it was and as it had to be — purely because there was no other reality, whether past or future, with which it could possibly be compared.

* * *

Language being, it seems evident, the key to the whole problem, it is of course tempting to imagine that, merely by tracing our ancestral languages back to their primitive beginnings, we might be able to discover a time when the very idea of past and future had not yet appeared. At such a time, after all, 'living in the now' might reasonably be assumed to have been the norm.

And true it is that the present tense is, in every known language, clearly the most basic of verb-forms — after the simple command — with past, future and other 'oblique' aspects merely variants on this standard.

Yet, surprisingly perhaps, however far back we search in time, or in whatever remote corners of the present-day globe we seek, we never discover the slightest sign — other than in recently developed pidgins and creoles — of a language that is in any way more primitive than our own. Adapted to different assumptions, certainly. Appropriate to different forms of society, inevitably. But in complexity, range of expression or grammatical sophistication the most ancient languages, like the most far-flung indigenous tongues of today, are every bit as well-developed as present-day English.

So-called 'savages', it seems, just do not speak in so-called 'grunts'.*

And so, in searching for a stage in linguistic development when past and future were as yet unknown concepts, we are clearly barking up the wrong tree. Might there, then, be other pointers to the existence of a comparatively recent Golden Age of present bliss — pointers based on some sphere of investigation other than language itself?

Curiously enough, the answer seems to be 'yes'.

* * *

It has long been recognised among archaeologists that the ancient Egyptians, like other ancient peoples, were not given to what we would regard as abstract thought. Even their religion was decidedly concrete in its approach. What we today regard as mere symbols were seen by the Egyptians as concrete actualities every bit as real as whatever we now see such symbols as representing. The *ankh*, or *crux ansata*, was no mere symbol standing for long life; it *was* long life. The god's image *was* the god. The pyramid-capped obelisk in the temple of Ra at Heliopolis *was* the descending rays of the sun. The dome-shaped symbol for bread (◠) had every bit as much 'breadness' about it as the rather gritty lump of baked dough of similar shape which came out of the oven and, as we now know, played so much havoc with the Pharaohs' teeth.

Much the same could be said about the pre-classical Greeks. Merely on the basis of their use of language, it is clear that they made no distinction between the sky and the god whom later generations were to see as personifying or inhabiting it. Both were simply *ouranos*. The same applied to crops, air, sea, sun and even Earth itself. What we today often see as a superstitious tendency to turn ordinary physical realities into fictitious gods and goddesses was originally nothing of the kind. It was purely a natural and spontaneous recognition that what you experienced was what

* Indeed, it could actually be argued that modern English is a good deal *less* sophisticated and discriminating than many of its 'primitive' forebears in a remarkable number of ways. The former noun and adjective case-system is virtually dead, the dual (as opposed to merely singular and plural) number category exists only in a few residual examples ('both', 'between'), the subjunctive (doubt-oriented) and optative (wish-directed) moods of the verb have virtually passed into oblivion, and all but the simple past and present tenses have long since been replaced by much clumsier and more long-winded 'constructed' variants ('I have eaten', 'she will be arriving' and so on). The future tense, indeed, has all but ceased to exist in popular spoken usage.

you experienced. Our obsessive — and, as it now increasingly appears, scientifically dubious — tendency rigidly to divide what is 'in here' from what is 'out there' had scarcely yet seen the light of day.

The fact is important. For what it suggests is that, even as recently as the late Stone Age and the beginning of the Bronze Age, our forebears may still have been able to see existence in a single light, to experience reality as they experienced it, rather than measuring it against the imagined reality that they thought they ought to be experiencing. Because there was no conflict between the 'in here' and the 'out there', there was no conflict, either, between stored memories and immediate perception, or between immediate perception and future expectations. Or, at very least, that conflict had not yet reached anything like its present almost obsessive pitch.

From which it might seem to follow that the blissful state of Being Here Now was an almost everyday experience for our late Stone Age ancestors, much as it still is for every growing infant. Now was not nasty for the simple reason that now was truly alive, and therefore needed no evaluation in terms of past memories or future expectations in order to make it live. This attitude contrasts starkly with our own, in which 'now' tends to be merely a dead husk entirely divorced from the vivifying world of ideals which we insist on consigning to the past or relegating to the far-distant future.

The Kingdom of Heaven, in short, was truly spread abroad upon the earth for a humanity which, conceptually at least, was indeed — as the Bible would have it — like a little child.

Possibly, then, it is to the racial memory of that time, or even to the orally-transmitted tradition of it, that we owe the ancient story of the paradisical Garden of Eden. The biblical account, you will recall, is quite clear in placing this state of former bliss just before the historical development of agriculture — which would date it at the latest to around the end of the Old Stone Age and the beginning of the New.

Putting actual dates on the presumed former Golden Age is thus a matter demanding some flexibility, even if we tentatively accept as a working hypothesis the not entirely unreasonable biblical order of events. Its demise would appear to have spread in a disordered progression across the globe, rather than taking place everywhere simultaneously. In the Middle East the rot may have started to set in as early as 10,000 BC or so. By 5000 BC it had probably reached Western Europe. Yet it was only during the last century of our own era that the Australian aborigines started to suffer the resulting psychological and social traumas — and there are some remote tribes in South America and New Guinea particularly who even today have still to be finally expelled from their ancestral paradise.

And so it is striking — and encouraging for our present theory — to note that the oral tradition of the Australian aborigines still wistfully recalls what they refer to as the Dream Time — a comparatively recent Golden Age when animals and plants, sea and sky, gods and human beings had not yet been separated into their several kingdoms. A time before the coming of the white man when language had not yet intruded on the world of directly-experienced reality to divide past from future, man from nature, man from man, man from himself.

And humanity, as the ancient tradition has it, could still converse at will with all the natural kingdoms.

* * *

Such, then, might be the gist of what we have termed the historico-deductive approach.

But in this case how did our subsequent fall from grace come about? What precisely was it about language that was so destructive — if we are right — of humanity's former state of bliss? And what was the presumed flaw in human consciousness that permitted this disintegration to come about in the first place?

Like the whole of the mammalian kingdom, humans are blessed with a brain (or, to be more accurate, a cerebral cortex) which is divided into two distinct halves. Or rather, just as we each have two arms, two eyes, two legs and two kidneys, so we have two brains as well. At basis, this characteristic seems to be part of an early insurance policy on nature's part, an example of the time-honoured strategy of belt and braces. If one brain were accidentally injured, especially during early infancy, the other could take over all its functions. This ability is still known to persist today.

Unfortunately, humans in particular also have a tendency towards lateral preference. That is to say, most of us are predominantly right- or left-brained, and consequently have also become right- or left-handed, rather than truly ambidextrous. Moreover, that preference subsequently leads to a specialisation of roles. Thus, in Arab countries even today, the right hand is traditionally reserved for eating and social functions, the left hand for personal ablutions. In 'polite' British circles, on the other hand, the left hand is reserved for eating, the right for shaking hands.

The lateral brain-specialisation underlying such traditions seems already to have applied in the most ancient times — indeed, possibly it is a characteristic of all mammalian predators. In the case of *homo sapiens*, the right brain has generally taken on the entire burden of generalised consciousness, while the left brain has been assigned the specific task of developing the highly focused awareness necessary for efficient hunting and gathering. This arrangement is apparently reversed only in the case of fifty per cent or so of left-handers — and specifically those whose mothers were also left-handed. Bear in mind, however, that this specialisation predicates no actual split. The two halves of the cortex have merely arranged themselves into a cooperative and mutually supportive team whose interaction is potentially to the benefit of the whole organism.

Thus, even though the cat's brain may also work in the same way, there is clearly no conflict of interest. Merely to watch a cat's eyes and ears reveals the two types of awareness in action. For most of the time it is clearly the calm, contented, generalised consciousness that reigns. The moment there is a sudden movement of bird or mouse or insect, however, the specialised, hunting mode of awareness cuts in. Then, as soon as the chase is over, the generalised mode resumes, and the cat becomes once more a picture of quiet contentment. Any temporary psychic maladjustment which this switch of modes may cause is subsequently ironed out during sleep, when simple observation suggests that the hunting responses are often reactivated, possibly so as to permit their reintegration into the psyche's more generalised overall activity.

Such a condition of dynamic psychic equilibrium, we may assume, is the ideal state of affairs. Certainly it seems to do the cat no harm. Yet it is a state of affairs which, in humanity's case, has long since ceased to be. And this because the brain's left hemisphere, intent on its function of focused awareness, at some point in the ancient past developed the remarkable ability of attaching words and concepts to the various objects of its awareness. In a word, it took over responsibility for the development of *language*.

And from that moment the conscious mind as we now know it started to stir into action.

In the early stages, admittedly, this new development posed little threat to humanity's over-all consciousness — which, by contrast, we have recently taken to designating (paradoxically enough) as the 'unconscious'. It merely made even more efficient our ancestors' efforts to hunt game and to devise shelter for themselves.

Later on it enabled them to learn the skill of controlling fire and to make a somewhat halting start on the business of primitive agriculture.

Possibly it was when this new development started to draw together larger and larger numbers of people into communes, and then villages, and then small towns, that language's tendency to 'fix' a largely illusory outer reality started to pose its main threat to humanity's formerly harmonious state of consciousness. Suddenly it became vitally necessary as never before to use language for distinguishing 'I' from 'you'. The result may well have been the birth of self-consciousness — i.e. true consciousness as we nowadays regard it — but it was also the birth, necessarily, of both inner and outer conflict. For, thanks to language, 'I' and 'you' were now taken to be everlastingly fixed and immutable entities, forever at war with each other. And since, in practice, neither 'I' nor 'you' *are* fixed and unchanging, a great gulf inevitably started to yawn between theory and practice, between ideal and reality — to the point where even the newly-invented 'I' now started to feel as though it were at war with itself.

As clans and villages, similarly, began to claim specific territory for their own agricultural use, inevitably they too came into conflict with the parallel claims of other communities. Ideas soon arose about what was 'right' and 'wrong', what was 'mine' and 'yours', what ought and ought not to be, what used to happen and what threatened to happen in the future unless something were soon done about it.

Language started to tear human inner consciousness apart, in other words, at roughly the same time as the new technological achievements to which it had largely given rise were also threatening to tear the outer world apart. For the first time war had entered the picture, not merely in the everyday physical world, but within the human psyche as well. Humanity had truly tasted the fruit of the Tree of the Knowledge of Good and Evil.

And it is that moment, with its final sundering of left and right brains, of conscious and unconscious, that seems to correspond to the proverbial Fall.

* * *

Yet it would be easy to let ourselves be side-tracked and even blinded by the historical aspect of the question. The actual evidence for a historical Golden Age for humanity as a whole, it needs to be re-emphasised, remains cloudy at best. Deduce though we may that something like it may have existed as late as neolithic times, the only age of total, primal bliss of whose existence we can be virtually certain — and then only on logical, not on evidential, grounds — clearly came to an end long before *homo sapiens* ever became truly *sapiens* in the first place.

Any attempt to re-establish such an age in the historical context thus amounts to a kind of death-wish, a would-be return to the racial womb. It implies a future return to some ape-like state which would seem to betray both our essential humanity and the universal process of evolution which seems to have produced it.

Even, that is, if it were shown to be possible for human consciousness deliberately to abandon itself in any case.

Much more to the point, then, is the general question of *human awareness*. For if anything is clear from our investigation so far, it is that the nature of human perception underlies all the explanations of the 'Golden Age' tradition that we have so far examined and found to be viable. In a sense, they are all variations on what we described initially as the perceptual approach. The fact that we look both backwards and forwards to a longed-for Golden Age goes back directly to the way in which we view our world, obsessively using language to divide 'then' from 'now', 'this' from 'that', 'good' from 'bad', 'you' from 'I' — and even 'I' from 'me'. The historical approach to the argument merely attempts to establish when this fatal and — it seems — self-perpetuating process started to happen, and contributes little to creating a new situation in which it can be brought under control once more.

The fault, then — if fault there is — lies in our view of the world. In Albrecht Dürer's words, 'The lie is in our understanding.' Our use — or rather our misuse — of human consciousness and the language which makes it possible lies at the root of the problem.

And so it is by modifying our consciousness and the ways in which we apply it that we are most likely to bring about a New Age for humanity.

* * *

This task, consequently, is central to a good deal of contemporary New Age endeavour, and we shall have more to say about it in due course. In the meantime, however, the various 'Golden Age' myths and traditions continue to exert their spell.

And it is a highly potent spell.

For the result is that virtually all of us have a fixed view of the future that is conditioned largely by whatever version of the millenarian tradition we grew up with or have come to adopt. Such views in turn affect our present actions. Indeed, we live as we do today largely because of the particular form of the myth to which our society or particular social grouping currently chooses to subscribe.

In religion, it is the millenarian conviction that often provides the sole foundation for the whole massive edifice of ritual and morality which characterises the faith in question. In politics, it has been the mainspring of virtually every reform and revolution that the world has ever known. In science and technology, it continues to provide the chief motivation not only for unlocking the secrets of nature, but also for applying that knowledge for the benefit of humanity as a whole.

And of course it is absolutely basic to the modern New Age movement and all that it stands for.

No longer, consequently, is the future exclusively the result of the present — if, indeed, it ever was. Instead, the present is largely the result of the future that we carry about with us in our heads.

And so it is truly vital for us to understand the ideas which shape that imagined future, and to appreciate the extent to which our myths, our utopian traditions, our social and scientific expectations condition the perceptions with which we approach the world. For it is those perceptions which, as we shall see in due course, actually *create* that world in the most literal sense.

What we shall be dealing with in the following chapters is the very stuff of our civilisation, the very life-force which powers our communal endeavour. Understanding ourselves demands above all that we understand the perennial New Age myth.

It behoves us, then, to study its manifestations with the utmost care, and in particular to trace the development of our millenarian convictions from their earliest beginnings, so that we may be the better equipped to detect their continued influence behind the scenes even on what we suppose to be our most factual and rational assumptions.

Including, as it turns out, our very worship of reason itself.

And once we have laid bare the extraordinary extent to which the associated perceptual distortions have repeatedly waylaid us throughout our history, we shall perhaps be sufficiently motivated by our new-found awareness to set about tackling the problem at source, so finally opening up the way for the real New Age to dawn.

2
Now and Again

For everything its season, and for every activity under heaven its time . . . . Whatever is has been already, and whatever is to come has been already, and God summons each event back in its turn.

Ecclesiastes 3: 1, 15

If there is one thing on which nearly all of the world's most ancient prophetic traditions agree, it is that things have to get worse before they get better. There is scarcely one of them that takes an optimistic view of human progress, or even believes in it in the first place. If there is to be a future Millennium, or Golden Age, then humanity is going to have to approach it through a chasm of fire, a total collapse of existing civilisation, a period of hell on earth.

The conclusion is actually far from illogical. As we have already seen, human civilisation is founded almost entirely upon our use of language, which is in turn the exclusive preserve of the left brain. Thus, present-day civilisation reflects directly the typical outlook of the left brain. It divides in order to rule. It sunders reality into discrete concepts, separate activities, unrelated fields of endeavour, competing interests, warring factions, rival nations and — above all — human beings who themselves are divided down the middle. Not only do we see life in terms of right and wrong, of 'us' and 'them', of 'being on the right side', but we extend that attitude into confrontation politics and (often unconscious) racial assumptions. Falling prey to rampant dualism, we divide our very planet — no less than our brains — into opposing hemispheres, whether militarily in terms of east and west, or economically in terms of north and south.

It is through the agency of our language, in other words, that we have created most of our present problems. It is through over-concentration on left-brain activity that we have given birth to the hell through which we now seem to be passing. And if we are eventually to come out again on the other side, it therefore follows that this over-concentration — together with the civilisation which is its exclusive progeny — will have to go.

Thus far, then, the ancient traditions are virtually — and it seems, rightly — united.

Where the various traditions disagree, however, is over the exact framework within which this system of collapse and restoration is expected to operate, the precise mechanics of damnation and redemption. Broadly the division is between those which conceive of human history as a once-and-for-all straight-line graph, and those which see it as an eternally-recurring cycle or spiral. Of the two concepts, the latter seems to be by far the older. Moreover, whereas the straight-line view is a typically Western phenomenon, the circular or spiral view is almost archetypically characteristic of the Far East, as well as of the more ancient traditions of other parts of the world such as the Americas.

It seems logical, therefore, for us to consider first of all this more ancient point of view, and only then to go on to consider the transition — if transition there was — to the more 'modern' Western model of things.

* * *

Quite why the circular model of history — the so-called myth of eternal recurrence — arose in the first place we shall possibly never know. Could it have been a notion drawn from direct observation of nature, of day and night, life and death, winter and spring? If, after all, nature worked in this way, almost obsessively eschewing straight lines, then surely it was reasonable to assume that similar considerations applied to the child of nature which was the human race? All the while, that is, that humans could still seriously consider themselves to *be* children of nature. And so, just as no new day could dawn until night had had its way, no spring airs waft in until winter had laid bare the landscape, no new generation of children grow to adulthood without knowing the death of older relatives, so any future Golden Age would have to be preceded by an age of destruction, a winter of despair, an era of universal death and decay.

The only alternative explanation to a tradition based on analogies of this kind, after all, would have to be based on factual knowledge. And such knowledge in turn would have to depend upon some kind of record of former eras going back almost unimaginable distances into the past. For such cycles — if cycles they are — must operate not in terms of decades or centuries (even though a whole variety of cycles of fashion, culture and social psychology can of course be observed in the short term), but of multi-millennia.

Even our quite extensive present records, after all, contain no reliable description of any previous Golden Age, whatever inferences we may care to draw from our inherited mythologies.

Yet such periods of time were clearly well beyond the ability of the ancient civilisations to conceive of in the first place. Almost throughout the ancient world, a period of a mere thousand years was traditionally taken to be equivalent to eternity. Indeed, the tradition is most obvious of all in respect of the expected Millennium itself. For the world 'Millennium', it is quite evident, originally meant no more and no less than a period of a thousand years. That is precisely how long venerable Jewish tradition allocated to the anticipated Kingdom of Heaven on earth, and exactly how long Adolf Hitler expected his own twisted travesty of the idea — the German Third Reich — to exert its baleful influence over the earth's peoples.

And yet it is quite evident that the term 'a thousand years' was never intended — or interpreted — as any kind of restriction. Once God's Kingdom was firmly established on the earth — once, in other words, the will of God was universally and wholeheartedly done by the whole of humanity through the priestly or even coercive agency of the Jewish people who had been 'chosen' specifically for this purpose — there could be no question of the Kingdom's collapse or failure. For just as God himself was eternal, so his Kingdom too must inevitably be a 'world without end'.

The scriptural basis for this whole tradition seems to have been the celebrated passage from the Ten Commandments (Ex. 20: 5-6) in which Yahweh warns:

I punish the children for the sins of the fathers to the third and fourth generations of those who hate me. But I keep faith with thousands, with those who love me and keep my commandments.

The expression 'with thousands' has sufficient ambiguity about it in the original Hebrew to permit not merely the interpretation 'for a thousand years', but also 'for a thousand generations' — which was the reading given the passage by the celebrated Essenes of the Qumran monastery, authors of the Dead Sea Scrolls, during the last century or so BC.[81]

But then they had good reason for feeling the old 'thousand year' interpretation to be somewhat inadequate. For by this juncture Middle Eastern ideas of time, and indeed of number generally, had started to be greatly extended.

And the fault, if fault it was, lay with the Hindus.

Not that the Hindus had originally been any more far-seeing temporally than the rest of the peoples of the orient. Here, too, 'May you live a thousand years!' would never have been interpreted as meaning anything other than 'May you live for ever!' Things were no different, either, where number in general was concerned. The best that the great Indian epic, the *Mahabharata* could do to describe a godly weapon of infinite brightness, for example, was to describe it as 'brighter than a thousand suns'. The perceptive Chinese sage Lao Tsu, similarly, was restricted by his ancestral conceptual tradition to describing the infinite diversity of the world in his celebrated *Tao Te Ching* as 'the ten thousand things'.[38]

An improvement by a factor of ten, admittedly. But then even the relatively primitive Hebrews of similar date were managing retrospectively to reckon up the numbers of their tribesfolk at the time of the Exodus in terms of hundreds of thousands. Not that there is anything very surprising in this, since, for a start, when you are counting a mass of human beings they are indubitably there to be counted. Moreover, once given the concepts of 'hundred' and 'thousand', there is nothing to stop you putting the two together and counting hundreds of thousands. The Hindus, too, were up to this trick. And by looking back at the mass of people you have been counting, there is even some prospect that you might manage vaguely to gather what such vast concepts actually mean.

With years, however, it is a different matter. Hardly anybody, after all, has ever had first-hand experience of a period much longer than a hundred years. And if written records, ably assisted by a fertile imagination, can extend this experience back by proxy to the extent of a handful of generations — even though, in the nature of things, each preceding generation tends to become increasingly foreshortened in the mind — the extent of that retrospection is necessarily curtailed, in the end, by the fact that written records go back, even in our own day, no more than five thousand years or so.

It was, of course, considerably less than this in the case of the ancient Hindus — who thus had no prospect, other than by highly unlikely magical means, of seeing back the enormous distances into the past which were necessary if the details of some former cycle were to be descried, and the process of human evolution thus mapped out on the sort of timescale which later Hindu writers were to describe with such evident gusto.

Whence, then, did the conceptual revolution come which, it seems, suddenly extended the Indian view of time in or after the

4th century BC? What was the source of the extraordinary mathematical ideas which have surrounded the oriental concept of cyclic evolution ever since, and in particular the datings of both the original Golden Age and the eventual Millennium?

The source, it has to be said, was literally a mere nothing. It lay in the sudden realisation that you could actually have a written symbol which stood for nothing at all. The result was the zero.

Curiously enough, this conceptual bombshell was reportedly invented not by a mathematician, but by the grammarian Pānini, the great formaliser of classical Sanskrit grammar in the 5th century BC. A fact which makes the whole business even more extraordinary. For classical Sanskrit, like classical Latin, was a language which nobody actually spoke, other than in the performance of public ceremonies and rituals. Apart from this, it was exclusively a written language — whence, of course, the need to formalise its grammar in the first place. And it was while doing so that Pānini realised that he needed a symbol to represent the case where a word lacked the ending which it might normally have elsewhere. His reaction was to draw a circle around the resulting space.

The result was the zero.

And from that unlikely beginning a whole panoply of human speculation and mathematical endeavour eventually ensued, from Hindu calculations about the overall timetable of human social evolution on the one hand to modern calculations of the distances of the stars and the dimensions of subatomic particles on the other.

The possibilities were almost endless. Suddenly a comprehensiveplace-based system of numbers became feasible. Merely by adding a little circle to the end of the number you first thought of, you could multiply it by whatever factor your particular system of numbers was based on. In the case of the system that we ourselves have inherited from the Hindus via the Arabs, that number is ten. In the case of the digital computer (which by its very nature can only count up to one) it is two. Yet even in this case it is sufficient to follow the number one with a mere thirty-three zeros to arrive at a number that is greater even than the total number of human beings alive on our planet today by a good three thousand millions. In the case of a ten-based number system the possibilities are of course almost incomparably vaster. And so the Hindus could start to indulge in a fine frenzy of speculation into the lengths of past and future ages, manipulating their new mathematical tool rather like a magic wand.

And secure in the knowledge that neither they nor anybody else at the time could check up on their figures — or, for that matter, could ever have more than the haziest of notions as to what the figures actually meant.

This legacy of general fogginess in respect of very large numbers is, of course, still with us today. It is what lies behind the astronomer's somewhat cowardly resort to the concept of the 'light year' (which is merely a shorthand for 5,880,000,000,000 miles), as equally behind the particle-physicist's use of the Ångström (which is a unit of measurement equal to a 100,000,000th part of a centimetre). It also underlies the general woolliness of economists and politicians when talking about billions of pounds or dollars: generally there is no attempt to establish whether the billions in question are American ones (1,000,000,000) or British ones (traditionally 1,000,000,000,000) since, as far as anyone can have the slightest inkling about what such figures mean, it would clearly be pointless even to attempt to make the distinction.

Or does anyone really have the slightest idea of what a heap of a thousand million, or a million million pound coins or dollar bills would actually look like?

The Hindu speculators seem to have been totally unworried by such considerations, however. Rather like modern high-energy physicists and students of Einsteinian relativity, they seem to have assumed that if the figures were there they had to mean something, even if you could not put your finger on it. In a sense, the true meaning was in the figures themselves, and there was no guarantee that you could ever translate it into common-sense terms that could be understood. In effect, the result of the whole exercise was to place its revelations firmly in the realms of the 'sacred', where questions as to the how and what and why were ruled firmly out of account, if not condemned as downright heretical.

And the eventual outcome was the truly mind-boggling set of figures that has come down to us as the definitive Hindu word on the seasons of the cosmos, the outline of history, the changing paradigm of human consciousness throughout the ages.

* * *

The universe, according to the resulting Hindu mythology, goes through an unending cycle of seasons of being and non-being known as the Days and Nights of Brahma (the Hindu Creator). Each Day of Brahma — each outbreath of the Creator, so to speak — lasts no less than 4,320,000,000 years; which means, of course, that each turn of the cycle lasts twice that amount of time, or 8,640,000,000 years. (The fact that this period corresponds remarkably closely to half the presently fashionable estimate of the universe's age among Western cosmologists may *seem* impressive, but may equally indicate no more than that both sets of speculators are equally prone to whistling in the dark. The same could no doubt be said about the remarkable similarity between the presumed length of the Day of Brahma and current Western estimates of the age of Planet Earth itself, at about 4,700,000,000 years. A mere 380,000,000 years' difference may seem peanuts in the context of the figures involved, but it should still not be forgotten that even 380,000,000 peanuts are quite a lot of peanuts.)

This vast cycle, it is alleged, goes on for ever, with Brahma eternally breathing out the universe and then reabsorbing it. Indeed, the process is not confined merely to the physical universe. Brahma too undergoes the same cycle of being and non-being — a notion which would of course tend to associate Brahma, or God, with existence itself, rather as the tribal god of Moses likewise defines himself in Exodus as EHYEH ASHER EHYEH, 'I am that I am'.

Before we allow ourselves to be carried away on the wings of metaphysical speculation to make comparisons with the hypotheses of quantum field theory, however, perhaps we should come back down once again rather closer to earth, and remind ourselves that such flights of fancy are apt to lead us into the common trap of using words about words as though they had meaning, and numbers about numbers as if they had tangible value.

A trap to which our Hindu speculators were by no means immune.

Possibly we owe it to them, however, at least to trace out their general ideas as to how things were liable to develop during each Day of Brahma, even though here, too, the periods of time involved are still too stupendous to be capable of any clear comprehension.

For the Day of Brahma — i.e. the total evolutionary lifetime of the universe, and presumably of the Earth with it — is said to comprise a thousand *Mahayugas*, or 'Great Ages', each of which is in turn made up of four lesser ages called respectively the *Satya* (or *Krita*) *Yuga*, the *Treta Yuga*, the *Dvapara Yuga* and the *Kali Yuga*. On mathematical grounds alone, then, each of these sub-ages has to average well over a million years in length. But things are not quite that simple. For each age in the sequence, it is claimed, is much shorter than the one which preceded it. In fact their respective lengths are supposed to stand to each other in the ratio 4:3:2:1 — so that the length of the overall *Mahayuga* of 4,320,000,000 years works out at exactly ten times that of the last, and shortest, of its component ages.

In terms of human evolution the first of the four ages, the 1,728,000-year *Satya* (or *Krita*) *Yuga* naturally corresponds to the 'Golden Age' of the cycle, and thus to the legendary Garden of Eden. This is followed by the beginning of the *Treta Yuga*'s 1,296,000-year-long decline in human nobility, piety and morals — which possibly we could associate with the initial development of separative thought and language — leading to an even steeper decline during the third age, the 864,000-year *Dvapara Yuga*. Possibly we could make an association here with the formation of the first organised nomadic communities, whose smooth running necessarily demanded the formulation of clearly understood rules of conduct and notions of 'right' and 'wrong'. With the invention of the idea of law, in other words, it became possible to sin against it, and the increasingly widespread realisation that nobody was entirely faultless in the eyes of that law could in turn give rise to the conviction that the community as a whole had somehow 'fallen from grace'.

The last age in the great cycle is that of Kali, and by all accounts this age, while shorter than any of the others, is also inevitably the worst of all. During it, according to the Hindus' *Vishnu Purana*, religion and spirituality are abandoned and the earth is swept by fire, drought and famine. There ensues a century of worldwide death and destruction, followed by a further planetary drought and a great holocaust which finally wipes out all vestiges of humanity from the Earth. Indeed, at the end of the last cycle in the sequence the Earth itself, together with the entire universe of which it is part, likewise disappears in a vast whirlpool of fire, leaving only a silence and an emptiness during the whole of the succeeding Night of Brahma.

Until, at some inconceivably distant point in the future, a new dawn arises and a new universe begins.

You may feel, on reflection, that the above description of the Age of Kali is a remarkably apt account of our own times, at least in its initial stages. Before you credit the ancient Hindus with magical powers of foresight, however, you would do well to remember that it was in many respects an equally apt account of their own. As, indeed, it had every right to be, since even this comparatively brief age, according to their own computations, is still quite long enough to encompass both us and them.

For its duration is said to be no less than 432,000 years (the equivalent, interestingly enough, of three times 144,000 — a 'magic' number which, as we shall see in due course, was to be taken up again by the much later author of St. John's Revelation in a similarly 'end of age' context). Its inauguration was marked by the death of the god Krishna, which is alleged to have taken place in 3102 BC. Since this date corresponds fairly closely to the start of the Aryan invasions of India, we may thus take Krishna's death (however historical or otherwise) as a remarkably apt symbol for the death of the Aryans' former nomadic life in favour of the new, settled, agricultural life of the Indian plains — a new era of villages and towns, of cities and politics, of inter-state rivalries and wars, and so of the progressive decay of what were seen as the former nomadic virtues of the *Arya* or 'noble ones' (the term which, as we saw earlier, was in due course to be borrowed by Hitler for his infamous concept of the *Herrenvolk*, or Master Race).

Krishna, incidentally, was only one of a long line of avatars or divine incarnations who are said to appear to inaugurate each successive age, and even specific stages within each age. As the much-loved *Bhagavad Gita* or 'Divine Song' puts it:

> *When righteousness is weak and faints and unrighteousness exults in pride, then my Spirit arises on earth. For the salvation of those who are good, for the destruction of evil in men, for the fulfilment of the kingdom of righteousness, I come to this world in the ages that pass.*[48]

And so the god Vishnu, preserver of the universe, appears successively as fish, tortoise, man-lion and dwarf; then as Rama-with-the-axe, then as Rama-Chandra, then as Krishna himself. Since then there has been, it is said, at least one other divine incarnation — though Hinduism, with its extraordinary ability to tolerate a whole variety of spiritual traditions, is undecided as to whether that avatar was the Buddha (for all his opposition to official Hinduism) or Jesus of Nazareth (for all his apparent ignorance of it).

Moreover, there is still one great avatar to come. He is Kalki, the final avatar of Vishnu, who will appear as a giant with a horse's head. Wielding a fiery sword like a comet, he will finally put an end to the wicked — and which of us is perfect? — to bring to a close the 'Age of Iron'.

So, at least, the ancient traditions maintain.

Only then, following the destruction of all human life (for that, as we saw above, is what it actually amounts to), will the future Golden Age finally dawn — and then not for humanity as we know it, but for a new humanity altogether. That blissful event, in other words, lies not just around the corner, but all of 427,000 years in the future.

Not something, you could say, worth holding your breath for, even if you were likely to be still here to hold it.

On the face of it, the whole scheme seems fanciful in the extreme, and far too neat mathematically to be at all likely as a description of what really happens in the untidy world of real events. And yet it does offer some striking parallels to the findings of modern palaeontology.[39]

On the basis of the figures proposed by the Hindu tradition, after all, the ancestors of present-day humanity are supposed to have been in their state of primal bliss from around four million years ago until some two million years ago — a period which corresponds remarkably closely to that identified by palaeontologists with the earliest, pre-linguistic forms of hominid. The 'decline' which is supposed to have ensued around two million years ago corresponds with a fair degree of accuracy to the changes in the shape of the human cranium which, as it now seems, first allowed the development of language as we know it in *homo erectus* — a development whose results, as we saw earlier, may well have precipitated the initial 'fall from grace'. The even steeper decline which allegedly set in around 800,000 years ago antedates by only a few hundred thousand years the appearance of the first remains of the even more linguistically oriented and culturally developed *homo sapiens*. And while the appearance of *homo sapiens sapiens* (i.e. modern man) some 50,000 years ago is not signalled by the Hindu canon, the date of 3102 BC for the onset of the final, and ultimately fatal, phase of human decay and degradation offers quite a good fit in terms of the beginning of the move towards the more settled life of agriculture and eventual civilisation, despite isolated evidence both of earlier and of later transitions.

That date, after all, is extraordinarily close to the official 'Year One' both of dynastic Egypt (c.3200 BC) and of the apparently unrelated Mayan civilisation of Central America (c.3113 BC).

The Hindu paradigm, in short, represents a remarkable piece of guesswork, if not of actual clairvoyance — a fact which could in turn be seen to suggest that the apparent similarity between the length of the proposed 'Day of Brahma' and the age of the Earth (as currently reckoned, at least) may not be so entirely accidental as we may at first have supposed.

Even so, we can take little comfort even from this apparently inexplicable bullseye on the part of the ancient Hindu speculators. For its upshot, if the scheme is projected into the future, remains as unpromising as ever — namely that we have very nearly half-a-million years yet to wait for the next Golden Age, and that even then we are unlikely to be the ones who finally inherit it.

Which can hardly be a cause for much optimism, whether individually or collectively, let alone a justification for proclaiming an imminent New Age . . . .

* * *

Like Hinduism, Mahayana Buddhism sees the history of the human race and its universe as cyclic in form and similar in timescale. Quite how Buddhists can maintain such a view in the light of their founder's insistence on the illusory nature of the perceived universe is something of a conundrum, unless one sees the whole thing as the history, not of the universe, but of an agreed illusion.

But the fact that Buddhism echoes Hinduism in this way is not particularly surprising in view of the fact that the Buddha himself was originally a Hindu, and that his new philosophy was merely one of a number of contemporary revolts intended to reform the religion and free it from institutional and intellectual corruption. Consequently the two movements have many techniques and ideas in common — even extending, as we have seen, to a widespread Hindu acceptance of the Buddha himself as a divine (if archly inscrutable) avatar, not to mention a tendency in Buddhism's more popular Mahayana school to worship the Buddha very much along the lines of the Hindu gods whom he had been at such pains to dethrone.

And so in Buddhism the history of the universe is widely held to be in thrall to the same vast tyranny of ages, each of them worse than the last, leading to ultimate extinction. And here too each age is inaugurated by a larger-than-life leader of supreme enlightenment, its creaking wheels oiled at intervals by other figures of only slightly less distinction. In this case, however, the Hindu avatars are replaced by a whole succession of Buddhas ('Awakened Ones'), of whom Gautama, the 6th-century prince and ascetic to whom we nowadays attribute the name, was merely the most recent. Or rather, they are replaced by a *single* Buddha who repeatedly reincarnates for the salvation of humanity. As in Hinduism, there remains one such figure yet to come — the so-called Buddha Maitreya — but his advent is no more imminent than that of Kalki, still lying as it does some hundreds of thousands of years in the future.

As for the lesser figures, these are the so-called Bodhisattvas — human beings well on the way to becoming Buddhas, but who voluntarily renounce their final entry into *nirvana*, or total and undifferentiated being-and-knowing, until such time as all other sentient beings shall have attained the same pitch of enlightenment. Once again, the tradition fails to explain how it is that a being on the verge of total and undifferentiated being-and-knowing can possibly think in terms of 'other beings' in the first place, let alone of his or her own entry into such a state as an isolated individual. Nevertheless, such is the tradition, and the Bodhisattvas have come to play a role in popular Buddhism not unlike that of the Christian saints in Roman Catholicism, many of them fulfilling an important historical role as teachers and missionaries.

Whatever their efforts, however, and however exalted the spiritual state of the lamentably infrequent Buddhas, the fact remains that the actual historical prospects for humanity remain decidedly bleak in the light of the overall Buddhist view of universal evolution — just as bleak, in fact, as it does from the Hindu point of view. Both chronologies suggest that looking either to the past or to the future for the Golden Age is, for all practical purposes, a total waste of time. It is already too late to return to whatever Golden Age there might once have been, and humanity (or, at least, the humanity we know) has no hope at all of surviving to enjoy whatever Golden Age may dawn at some indescribably remote time in the future. Behind us lies only regret, in front of us only hopelessness. There is nothing to look forward to but common physical extinction.

This view, it has to be said, is the exact reverse of that gleaned by most modern New Agers from their Hindu and Buddhist studies. Astonishingly, perhaps, it seems to be generally assumed within the movement (though with a marked reluctance to quote chapter and verse) that Hindu doctrine actually anticipates an imminent World Millennium. Genuine Hindus who are naive enough to insist otherwise tend to be given a distinctly frosty reception. Equally, it is widely bruited that the Buddha Maitreya is close at hand to inaugurate the Millennium, if not already infiltrating the consciousness of contemporary humanity.

Such views, it hardly needs saying, are generally based not on the Hindu and Buddhist scriptures themselves, but on secondhand accounts by Western Theosophists[30], or bowdlerised ones by émigré Eastern gurus, most of whom are in practice only too anxious to adapt the original teachings to the favourite preconceptions of Westerners — and particularly to those of lapsed Christians in search of alternative sources of hope.

This particular tendency (conscious or otherwise) is often quite blatant. The Scottish New Age propagandist Benjamin Creme, for example, has gone so far as to insist — in line with the writings of the post-Theosophist Alice Bailey[42] — not only that Maitreya is already with us in the flesh (and living, it is said, in the Brick Lane area of east London), but that this numinous figure and the returning Christ so long expected by Christians (to say nothing of Krishna and the Muslims' Imam Mahdi) are in fact one and the same.

The real teachings of Hinduism and Buddhism, by contrast, are much less familiar to most New Agers in the West. And this for the very good reason that the oriental purists — unlike the by-now notorious 'missionary gurus' who have become so fashionable in the West since the 1960s — tend to stay determinedly at home. The Hindus among them, in particular, tend to look down their noses at the proselytising efforts of their peripatetic brethren, whom they regard for the most part as disreputable layabouts and charlatans. Money and prestige, they insist, is the main motive behind such activities. And in this they merely see further proof of what their religion actually teaches — namely the raw, unvarnished assertion that humanity, far from being on the brink of a New Age, is actually on a downhill slope, and doomed to inevitable annihilation.

Perhaps it is understandable that such a conviction should be unpopular among New Agers in the contemporary West — especially as the current world situation makes it seem only too close to reality. Yet for all its bleakness there is, as we shall see, cause for great hope in such a view. By placing heaven beyond our reach, the ancient cosmologists effectively contrived to throw humanity back on itself, forced it to look at itself as it is and as it has to be.

And in doing so they may yet — if unknowingly — have rendered us an inestimable service.

3
Heaven Only Knows

The fault, dear Brutus, is not in our stars,
But in ourselves.

William Shakespeare: *Julius Caesar* I, 2

Even while the after-shocks of Pānini's conceptual earthquake
were starting to reverberate around the citadels of Hindu thought,
the ancient subcontinent was sent reeling by yet another major
upheaval. But this time it came not from within, but from outside
Hindu civilisation.

Suddenly down out of the same Khyber Pass through which the
Aryans themselves had once entered India swept an extraordinary
army of battle-hardened Greeks. And at their head, resplendent in
golden corselet and silver helmet, rode the swashbuckling Alexander, then all of 29 years old, still intent on his heroic mission of
marching to the edge of the world. With the upper Indus valley
secured, however, his war-weary and increasingly homesick veter-
ans reminded him that many of them had wives and families to
think of back in Macedonia, and refused flatly to go any further.
Alexander did his best to work the old, idealistic magic on them,
but they were obdurate. And so the long homeward trek began
via the southern desert — a journey during which Alexander himself only just survived an arrow in the lung, and many of his men
died of thirst and exhaustion.

It had been only a brief encounter, but one which was to have
profound effects on both sides. In Alexander the Indians saw a
hero almost of the stature of their god Rama himself, while in
India Alexander and those who attended and followed him found
new philosophical ideas, new views of the purpose and meaning
of life — and a venerable civilisation whose sheer antiquity was in
itself a marvel.

The result was an opening of the floodgates of culture, a cross-
fertilisation which was to some extent to revivify both East and
West. In the sphere of philosophy, for example, the ancient Greek
doctrine of metempsychosis, or reincarnation, which possibly
dated back as far as the original Orphic Mysteries, and certainly as
far back as Pythagoras and his school, was given a new impetus.
And the Indians, for their part, were introduced to Greek ideas on

a range of topics — and notably the art, or science, of astrology.

Now it has to be said the astrological ideas in question were by no means the Greeks' own copyright, any more than were a good many of the ideas and traditions for which they are conventionally given credit today. Just as the majority of the geometrical techniques and propositions attributed to Pythagoras and Euclid were known in Egypt a good two thousand years before their time (that supreme example of advanced three-dimensional geometry known as the Great Pyramid of Giza, for example, contains at least one clear example of the supposedly 'Pythagorean' 3:4:5 triangle[44]), so Greek astrology was largely the product of its Egyptian antecedents, which in turn derived from the Chaldaean astrologers of ancient Babylon — and who knows what sources before that.

Not that the ideas of the fledgling science remained unchanged throughout all that time, however. The Babylonian astrologers used the stars simply as a form of divination, much as modern psychics might use tea-leaves or Tarot cards.[20] The Egyptian idea that the stars and planets actually exercised some kind of *influence* over events on earth would have caused them no little astonishment. But once the somewhat mystical idea of sheer synchronicity had been replaced by the much more mechanistic cause-and-effect interpretation, the new view rapidly took on. By the time the system had been adopted in Greece itself, the notion of celestial influences (a notion which survives, even in modern medicine, in the name of the influenza virus) was in full swing. This, consequently, was the form in which the tradition arrived in India during the years following Alexander's invasion — and for those who were plunged into understandable depression by the vast vistas of traditional Hindu and Buddhist cosmic chronology it was to prove something of a godsend.

* * *

It was the very randomness of the stars in the night sky that originally qualified them for use as a divinatory tool. It is in the nature of such tools, after all, that the diviners should be able to make out of them any picture they wish, following the promptings of their deeper consciousness. The process is, in effect, a kind of objectivisation of those wordless processes of the unconscious which the conscious mind is often only too anxious to censor and filter out.

Now the times when such insights are most highly valued and

thus most likely to be sought by society at large are, in the very nature of things, times of crisis or tension. And for any ancient agricultural society those times were associated, above all, with the phases of the agricultural year — and particularly with the end of the old year and the beginning of the new. Unfamiliar as the idea may nowadays seem to us, that time, for any truly agricultural society, is the time of harvest, when the old year's labours are at an end and the soil is about to be prepared for the next year's crops. And there, for the ancient astrologers, were the symbols of their divination, standing in all their splendour above their heads. Representing the old year's ripened fruit, the golden glory of the Harvest Moon. Representing the new year's scattered seed, the minute dust of the stars. The astrologers had merely to read the position of the full moon's disc relative to the stellar backdrop to obtain their divination for the fortunes of the coming season.

And so it came about that the position, relative to the stars, of the full moon nearest to the autumn equinox came to be regarded as of paramount importance in assessing the temper of the times.[43]

And in case it should be objected that it was the position of the *sun* at the *spring* equinox that was of first importance — as it has nowadays become in modern astrology — perhaps the simple fact should be borne in mind that you cannot see the stars when the sun is shining.

Now it goes almost without saying that the full moon of harvest does not always coincide with the date of the autumn equinox. In fact, it very rarely does. The simple mathematics of the case mean that the full moon in question may occur anything up to fifteen nights on either side of the equinox itself. Consequently the Harvest Moon's position relative to the stars varies correspondingly. There being roughly as many days in a year as degrees in a circle — as the Babylonians has been very careful to see that there should be — it follows that the Harvest Moon's 'arc of possibility' covers a total band of about thirty degrees of the heavens. Possibly it was for this reason that the stars behind the moon's track were subsequently divided into twelve 'signs' of thirty degrees each — one, as it happens, for each month of the year.

Now this particular band of the heavens had long been a source of particular interest for the ancients. Through it passed not only the moon, but also the visible planets: indeed, whether or not the early astrologers realised it, so did the sun itself. As a result, this band — which we nowadays refer to as the 'ecliptic' — had long since had its shimmering stellar dots joined up with imaginary lines to produce a whole succession of animals and fabulous

creatures. Zōon being the Greek for 'animal', this projected celestial frieze soon became known as the 'zodiac'. And, while its original purpose seems to have been primarily to serve as a clock at
night for wandering herdsmen, it cannot have been long before its
ready-made symbols were called into the service of astrological
divination.

There things might have rested, had it not been for the fact that,
as the years and centuries passed, it gradually became clear either
that the moon was starting to 'break bounds', or alternatively that,
contrary to all expectations, the eternal stars themselves were
actually moving. Painfully slowly, to be sure, but there could be
no doubt that the moon no longer visited one end of what had formerly been its 'arc of possibility', while on other occasions it was
starting to encroach on new and unfamiliar star-fields.

It was no illusion. What the ancients had observed, but could
not yet satisfactorily explain, was an effect produced by the fact
that the Earth does not stand upright as it revolves about the sun.
Canted over at an angle of some 23½ degrees, the planet behaves
rather like a spinning top in the same situation.

It wobbles.

In the case of the Earth, it is a slow wobble, taking nearly 26,000
years to complete one revolution. But it is a wobble none the less.
As a result, the Earth's North Pole points at a whole succession of
different Pole Stars. This fact failed to impress itself upon the
ancients, however. Since, for any given generation, the same old
Pole Star presides over the northern sky every night of the year, it
presents little cause for special interest. There are no auguries to
be read in a pattern which always stays the same.

It was a different matter where the equinoxes were concerned,
though. For the second result of the Earth's slow wobble is that
the two points in its orbit at which it stands square-on to the sun
themselves slowly revolve. And these points are, of course, the very
points at which day and night are, uniquely, of equal length all
over the globe — i.e. the equinoxes. Observing the stars which
stood behind the sun on such occasions, then — or, since this was
optically impossible, those stars opposite them which stood
behind the corresponding full moon — would reveal a slow
change of relative position. And from that change of relative position, that mutation in the apparent stellar backdrop, new auguries
could be read.

Quite how early the ancients realised that this slow precession
of the equinoxes could be used as the basis for a new cyclic theory
of ages is a moot point. Given a shift of the Harvest Moon from

one star-sign into the next, it clearly demands little imagination to deduce that, given time, it might eventually complete the whole circuit of twelve signs. The question of just how long that circuit might take, however — and how long, in consequence, each sign's reign might last — must have taken a good many centuries to settle with any accuracy.

Certainly it seems clear from the early bull-cults that the Middle-Eastern civilisations of roughly 4000 to 2000 BC were well aware that the Harvest Moon's territory was currently that of Taurus, the Bull. That realisation may equally well lie behind the choice of the bull's head to lead the alphabet which seems to have started its development somewhere in Phoenicia during this same period (turn the first letter of the next paragraph upside down and the connection will immediately become apparent).

After its long spell in Taurus, the Harvest Moon next migrated backwards (relative to the normal nightly procession of the zodiacal signs across the sky) into Aries, the sign of the Ram. And, sure enough, we find that most contemporary religious cults placed correspondingly greater emphasis upon the Ram as their sacred symbol. In Egypt, for example, the cult of the ram-god Amun became all-powerful, as witness the very names of the pharaohs dedicated to him — most memorably Tutankhamun himself — while the tribes of Israel were likewise weaned by Moses from their worship of the Golden Calf in favour of a sacrificial cult based on the Passover Lamb.

From about 150 BC a further change occurred in the heavenly hierarchy, as Pisces, the Fishes, took over. And so it comes as little surprise to find Jesus of Nazareth taking on fishermen as his chief followers, expounding his teaching in terms of fishes and 'fishers of men', and bequeathing to posterity a movement which took as its rite of entry a form of ritual drowning and recovery from the water, and as its secret symbol the sign of the fish.[43]

By this time, of course, the general shape of the procession of the astrological ages must have become abundantly clear to those in the know, and so we may reasonably assume that ideas had already started to crystallise about which ages were likely to be propitious for humanity and which were not. In view of the almost universal tradition of Golden Ages both past and future, we may therefore imagine that definite 'Golden Age' links had by now been made with given astrological ages. The fact, for example, that the Great Sphinx, guardian of the sacred places of the Giza necropolis, was hewn out of the soft desert limestone in the form of a lion — albeit with the head of a man — might suggest that the Egyptians who carved it regarded the age of Leo (from about 11,000 to 8800 BC) as the original Golden Age, as indeed the lion's own colour could be taken to hint. The design of the circular carved zodiac (dating from the 1st century BC) discovered in the temple of Hathor at Dendera near Luxor, and now in the Louvre, can be seen as adding credence to this view.[43] There are some, indeed, who claim that Leo's was the actual age during which the Sphinx — and with it the Great Pyramid itself — was created.[44]

As for the presumed future Golden Age, this has a marked tendency to be associated by each age's commentators with the next age — or even the one currently dawning — however apparently unpropitious its symbolism. Symbols, after all, have a marvellous way of allowing themselves to be interpreted in almost any way which suits the interpreter's purposes, or indeed his or her unconscious needs — a familiar fact which has long been of inestimable value to diviners and psychotherapists alike.

In the case of Jesus of Nazareth, for example, there is clear evidence[41] that he and his followers expected what they called the 'Kingdom of Heaven' or 'Kingdom of God' to be inaugurated just forty years after his prophesied survival of crucifixion and his subsequent anointing as the Jewish King-Messiah. St Paul, too, clearly shared this view, as his celebrated 'We shall not all die . . . ' proclamation in his first letter to the church at Corinth makes perfectly plain. With the coming Last Judgement the dead would indeed be raised, but 'we (i.e. the living) shall be changed'. And then would ensue an imperishable Kingdom during which the entire universe would take on a new, spiritual nature and present itself in an entirely new light.

And possibly, as we shall see later, there is a sense here in which the ever-perceptive Paul, thanks largely to his early training in Pharisaic esoterics, comes very close to the probable truth of what is likely to be involved in any such 'New Age'.

A Golden Age commencing early in the Age of Pisces — such, then, was the clear expectation both of the original Nazarenes and of their successors, the early Christians. And it was this expectation, perhaps above all, that gave them the extraordinary courage and disregard of personal safety for which they have since become almost legendary. But events, as it turned out, were to let them down badly. The year 73 AD produced not the promised kingdom, but the final extinction of current messianic hopes in Palestine, with the fall of the fortress of Masada and the mass suicide of almost a thousand Jewish freedom-fighters *almost exactly on the fortieth anniversary of the crucifixion itself.*[41] It may, indeed, have been the failure of the Kingdom to materialise on time that prompted that mass suicide in the first place. All the hopes of the Jewish people — or at least those of them who supported the Nazarene cause — had, it seems, been cruelly dashed. The expectations and prophecies had been wrong. The whole idea, possibly, had been a mirage in the first place.

The feeling was understandable. And yet no faithful Jew could ever really accept that the scriptures and the prophecies they enshrined were so much hot air. Inevitably, therefore, what followed was not so much an abjuration as a drastic re-think. The Kingdom had been postponed. Or rather, human fallibility had been responsible for a misreading of the texts and a foreshortening of the timescale.

The results are there for all to see in the New Testament record. The author of the Revelation of John defers the Kingdom to some unspecified future epoch when the number of the Jewish redeemed shall have reached the magic total of 144,000 (compare page 32 above). Whoever wrote the two letters attributed to Peter, on the other hand, makes clear his conviction that the current time of tribulation might last not a mere forty years but anything up to two thousand.

Alongside the ancient 'forty-year' expectation derived from the Old Testament, after all, Jesus himself had made a number of veiled references (equally derived from the Old Testament) to a 'three-day' interim period. And God being God, and humans humans, there was no guarantee that the word 'day' meant the same to both parties: indeed, there was clear Old Testament authority for equating the Divine 'day' with a thousand earthly years.[41] 'On the third day', then, could perfectly well mean not — as the current Hebrew idiom dictated — 'the day after tomorrow', but 'during the millennium after next' — i.e. sometime after the year 2033 AD . . . .

This, of course, would place the expected Golden Age firmly in the age of Aquarius — which, astronomically speaking, is due to start anytime after the year 2010 AD. The symbolism — as is the way with symbols — seems perfectly apt. The Fishes, admittedly, had suggested an age of comparative freedom, of wild creatures in their element, even of a further, vertical dimension added to the previously two-dimensional world of the Arian flocks. But the image of Aquarius pouring out his pitcher of water is redolent of nothing less than the bursting forth of the waters of the womb, and thus of some great rebirth.

So, at least, it could be argued.

And, curiously enough, the gospel-records attribute to Jesus a number of what — in the event — seem to be verbal and practical hints of just such an Aquarian Millennium.[43] Most notable among them, perhaps, is the extraordinary secret sign by which he indicated to his followers where his final Passover meal — the so-called Last Supper — was to be celebrated. Going into the city, they were to follow a *man carrying a pitcher of water*. Given, then, that the meal itself stood for the anticipated messianic banquet — the never-ending Divine bean-feast foretold by the prophets for the coming Kingdom — the symbolism of the Water-Carrier could now be interpreted as a clear reference to the astrological age which was to usher in that Kingdom.

Not, it has to be said, an interpretation favoured by present-day Church circles, but not at all a surprising one in an age riddled — as much among the Jews as elsewhere in the ancient Middle East — with astrological symbolism.

And by now, we may assume, the astrologers had managed to set their house sufficiently in order to realise — if only on the basis of their circular charts — that the celestial position of their meridian (and thus, notionally, of the full moon) at midnight of the autumn equinox must correspond more or less exactly to the *noon*-position of the sun itself at the preceding and succeeding *spring* equinoxes. Certainly this would accord with the fact that a number of attempts were made at around this time to substitute solar calendars for the old and notoriously inexact lunar ones — not only by Julius Caesar with his celebrated Julian calendar, but also by the Essenes,[81] an important Jewish religious group who may well have been responsible for producing Jesus of Nazareth in the first place.[41] With a solar take-over of the formerly lunar astrological regime, a much more exact assessment of the current celestial situation was, of course, possible. And it is this system which modern astrologers use to this day.

Quite how inevitable it is that the Aquarian age should turn out to be an Age of Gold, however, is open to question. Its symbolism, certainly, can be taken to refer to some kind of reborn world — and indeed, Matthew's gospel uses just this expression (generally translated into English as 'the world to come') to refer to the awaited messianic Kingdom.[70] Equally certainly, the goat-symbolism of Capricorn is hardly an obvious candidate for identification with the Millennium. Yet the imagery of the following age — that of Sagittarius — has an almost overwhelming millenarian feeling about it. The picture of the great Archer, half horse and half man, launching his arrow into the cosmos, bespeaks a humanity whose animal instincts and higher consciousness have at last become one, just as they had apparently been once before during the age symbolised by the equally-composite Great Sphinx. It also suggests a common endeavour to penetrate the heart of reality and achieve unity with the universe itself.

Truly a picture of the Golden Age ideal.

* * *

Such, at all events, were the elements of the zodiacal system bequeathed by the Egyptians to the ancient Greeks, and in turn passed on by them to the Hindus following Alexander's annexation of north-west India. In the process, however, the system had undergone further modification at the hands of the Greeks themselves.

For Greek mythology, long before the influx of such ideas, had been insisting that whatever happens on earth is decided and ultimately controlled by the gods of Mount Olympus. And that being so, it was difficult to see how everything could also be the responsibility of the stars in the sky. The inevitable compromise followed. True it might be that the signs of the zodiac delineated the outlines of each succeeding age, but its temper was still dictated in its essentials by the gods themselves. And so it followed that not only earthly events, but also the zodiacal signs themselves, were under the direct control of the Olympians.

Unsurprisingly, therefore, a kind of celestial carve-up followed. Each cage in the celestial zoo was allocated, so to speak, to a godly keeper who imparted something of his or her own nature to the sign in question. But exactly who was responsible for which sign long remained a source of some controversy. That Aphrodite (Venus) was the guardian of Taurus, and Ares (Mars) that of Aries seems to have been generally accepted. But exactly who was responsible for Pisces and Aquarius seems to have been less certain, as subsequent changes of 'rulership' reveal.[20]

At all events, the result was a system not merely of star-signs, but of controlling gods as well. The introduction into the zodiacal equation of the divine variable brought new possibilities into the process of interpretation. Thus, the age of Aries, for example, could now be seen not merely as an age of wandering flocks of humanity, but also as a truly martial age, an era of repressive warlords — much as it was indeed turning out to be, not least in the case of Alexander himself.

The truly astrological lobby was still strong, however. And it seems to have been less than happy with this Olympian dilution of the former zodiacal purity. Before long, therefore, a move was afoot to link the gods with the wandering planets whose sojourns in each sign had long been heralded as of great divinatory significance. And so to each divinity was allocated one of the seven known 'wanderers' (which included the sun and moon). They duly became known (to use the later, Latin names) as the planet of Mercury, the planet of Venus, the planet of Mars, and so on. Eventually mere ownership turned into identification. The planet of Venus *was* Venus, that of Mars *was* Mars. (The fact that, in at least one classical list, the ruler of Pisces was listed as Neptune — as it has once more become in our own time — thus necessitated a hurried rethink, as no actual planet was available to be given that name until 1846. It was only some sixty years before that date, similarly, that the newly-discovered Uranus, nowadays regarded as the ruler of Aquarius, first received its name.)

And the upshot was the familiar system of signs and rulers much as we have it today. Complicated, however, by the fact that the twelve theoretical 'signs' have long since become separated by the Earth's precession from the very constellations after which they were named — so that the position of the sun at the spring equinox is still known, by astrologers and astronomers alike, as the 'first point of Aries', when in fact it has already migrated all the way through the constellation Aries and most of the way through Pisces, and is due to enter Aquarius in, at the latest, a few centuries' time.

Whence, of course, the concept of the 'Age of Aquarius' which is currently being associated in New Age circles — if a little previously — with an imminent millennial era.

* * *

Certainly the resulting system of astrology figures large in such circles. Indeed, it has long since become big business among the New Agers. It is regularly used by them both as a source of personal insights and as a guide to communal action. By a good many it is seen as a means of linking humanity with the overall process of the cosmos, microcosm with macrocosm. Its very circularity seems to proclaim the end of the old Judaeo-Christian dualities of black and white, good and evil, salvation and damnation, and to offer instead a truly holistic paradigm of experience in which time is without beginning or end and everything is interrelated.

At the same time — New Agers being human beings just like

everybody else — there are a good few who are only too anxious
to co-opt the techniques of astrology as tools for personal self-
aggrandisement, obsessively pigeon-holing others by their birth-
signs and insistently offering advice and dark warnings to all and
sundry on the basis of what is often the most superficial knowledge of the subject.

Perhaps this is no more than should be expected.

True enlightenment is often no more evident, either, in the
underlying view on which these activities are based. Although the
astrological outlook of an increasing number of New Age
astrologers is based on an understanding of the subject which
might be described in terms of 'holistic synchronicity', there are a
good many (especially at the fringes of the movement) for whom
the popular cause-and-effect theory of celestial influences is still
axiomatic. The stars and planets are held to *bring about* what happens on Earth, rather than merely reflecting common universal
developments. Latter-day Egyptian mechanicalism, in other
words, has in such cases triumphed over the Babylonians' original, purely divinatory approach.

And so astrologers of this latter type, being unable, in the
nature of things, actually to demonstrate the alleged celestial
influences or to identify any medium of transmission, run the risk
of bringing astrology as a whole into disrepute. Ignoring its
remarkably enlightened founding principles, they persist in bam-
boozling the public with a long-outdated nineteenth-century view
of how the universe works. The scientific model necessary to support that view has a good deal in common with the pre-Einstein-
ian conception of the cosmos about which the former Theosophists[542] were so enthusiastic — a picture of the universe as a kind of
mechanical clock in which every part was separate from every
other part, and could operate on it at a distance only through a
process of mechanical linkage.

That model, it has to be said, has long been superseded. The
current, relativistic view sees every part of the universe as an inte-
gral function of every other part. Without it, indeed, the rest of it
could not even exist. Far from proceeding through Newtonian
cause-and-effect, the universe is seen to operate on a basis that is
much closer to that described by the already-mentioned Jungian
term 'synchronicity'. Every happening is a universal event. Every
movement is reflected in all parts of the cosmos at once. Transmission no longer necessarily lies at the root of the process.

Which means, of course, that astrology is no longer even needed to link an earthbound humanity with a supposedly separate

universe 'out there'. Microcosm and macrocosm are one, and have been all along.

As above, so below.

To the extent that astrology is seen still to have a purpose at all, then, that purpose now becomes merely to act as a symbolic catalyst, to objectivise — albeit in largely illusory form — the processes of our own being and awareness. At the popular, 'birth-chart' level, it becomes a perceptual tool to help us become more sensitive to where we stand in relation to the world about us. At the planetary level, it has the potential to symbolise and help us understand the universal processes that are afoot as the world moves slowly out of the Age of Pisces and into that of Aquarius.

As, indeed, the more perceptive of the New Age astrologers already realise.

And in becoming truly aware of such things we actually become free of the very influences and determinisms which traditional astrology seeks to impose on its more credulous devotees. We become conscious, no longer of the astrology, but of the underlying reality that it masks at the very same moment that it symbolises it. Casting aside the mumbo-jumbo, we stumble upon the truth. And the truth, in the event, is seen to contradict the traditional astrological assumptions.

And so what price the Golden Age promised by that self-same astrology? What price the long-cherished millenarian hopes? Especially as the astrological logic itself actually undermines, as we shall now see, much of what is confidently expected by New Agers in this regard.

* * *

For the ancient Hindus — and even for some Buddhists — the astrological paradigm in general had, as we saw earlier, very obvious attractions. Where previously people had been condemned to a cycle of ages so vast as to be virtually meaningless in practical terms, now they had at their disposal a cycle of ages that seemed to offer some hope — if not to anybody living, at least to their descendants, or even to themselves in some future incarnation. And this, in particular, because it did not predicate a worldwide holocaust before the onset of the next Golden Age. Hard times there might be, certainly, but at least there was some hope that humanity might survive them to enter upon its long-promised earthly reward.

The prospect was alluring. Yet there was a difficulty. A difficulty so great that it actually had — and still has — the effect of scuppering the whole utopian edifice of astrologically-based millenarianism, at least in earthly terms.

And it was this.

Whichever age was identified as the future Golden Age, the very nature of the system limited its duration to a mere two thousand years. Thanks to Pānini's bombshell, that period could no longer be equated with eternity. And so, almost by definition, no astrological age could, after all, be identified as the definitive Millennium, the everlasting Kingdom. The best that could be hoped for was that it might offer a period of relative earthly bliss, a season of grace prior to yet another descent into further earthly decay.

Thus, the age of Aquarius must be superseded, after a mere twenty-one centuries or so, by that of the humble Goat. Even the supremely hopeful era of Sagittarius must eventually give way to the more ominous dispensation of the Scorpion. And eventually, after what appears to be a final Libran 'age of judgement', a new age of Virgo must arise (theoretically in around 12,800 AD), apparently presaging the start of a whole new precessional cycle.[43]

The implications of this realisation were various.

Among the more myopic of Hindus and Buddhists, as among the more myopic of their modern New Age counterparts in the West, it had little real effect, even if it was taken on board at all. The Golden Age was the Golden Age, and once it was here the whole system on the basis of which its arrival had been predicted could be forgotten, cast to the four winds.

To those who bothered to think the thing through, on the other hand, there was real cause for renewed despair, and a consequent tendency to deduce that earthly bliss was a contradiction in terms, a mirage to which the only logical reaction must be total world-denial, asceticism, mortification of the flesh and a general withdrawal into isolated contemplation — for which ample precedent was, of course, already to be found in ancient Hinduism.

In short, the astrological paradigm, originally a potential source of great hope, soon turned sour on all but the more simple-minded.

The stars had let us down.

But then few of the ancient civilisations which believed in stellar links with human destiny ever assumed otherwise. For it should be remembered that the astrological tradition which the Hindus inherited from the Greeks, Egyptians and Babylonians was by no means the only such tradition known to world history.

And most of the others have a similar tale to tell.

4

Tomorrow and Tomorrow
and Tomorrow

The days were numbered for them to experience the blessing of the sun.
The days were numbered for the lattice of the stars to look down on them,
and for the gods confined within the stars to watch them through it and
stand guard over their safety.

The Mayan 'Chilam Balam of Chumayel'

Astrological cyclism is, of course, only one particular application
of the more general cyclic model of universal evolution. That
model has not always been linked specifically to the stars, let
alone based on them. As we saw earlier, its foundations may well
lie in any one of a number of cyclic events in nature.

Among New Age philosophers in particular a cyclic — or even
spiral — view of human destiny has long been fundamental, quite
independently of any astrological considerations. Philosophical
straight lines, it seems, are anathema. Thanks especially to the
work of Helena Petrovna Blavatsky and her later German protégé
Rudolf Steiner[5,42] — of whom more later — it has for some time
been taken to be virtually axiomatic that humanity, like Planet
Earth and the universe itself, is involved in a whole range of ever-
recurring cyclic processes, and not least that which from time to
time tends to produce ages of dross or of gold.

And it is the process that is important, rather than where it is
leading.

To an extent, this view can be seen as contradicting the evident
one-shot millenarianism whose fire burns bright within many a
New Age breast. But then New Agers are far from alone in personifying the spirit of contradiction. Nor is their characteristic
concept of universal cyclism particularly new to Western civilisation, for all its ostensibly Hindu origins.

Even in Greece itself there seems to have been a very early tradition of a vast cycle of ages not dissimilar to that propounded by
the Hindus, though without the latter's claimed mathematical precision. The ancient Greek poet Hesiod, for example, writing as
early as 700 BC or so, advanced the view that world history takes

the form of a continuous cycle of five ages — those of Gold, Silver, Bronze, Heroes and Iron — each of them representing a further step in a universal decline from joyful innocence to guile, misery and corruption. The resemblance to the Hindu scheme of things is striking enough to pose the question of whether both traditions might have had their origin in some ancient and now-forgotten piece of prehistoric Aryan tribal lore, possibly incorporating elements of actual social and metallurgical history.

We have no record of whether this particular doctrine was linked in any way with the stars and planets, but we do know that a similar theory, advanced some two hundred years later by Hesiod's compatriot Heraclitus, was based specifically upon the supposed rotation of the eight 'planetary spheres' — concentric firmaments, or heavens, within which each luminary was thought to be embedded. His notion of the 'Great Year' — like the astrological 'Great Year' of the earth's precession, which lasts some 26,000 normal years — refers to the time taken for the whole system to revert to its initial state. And as a result of it the world is periodically dissolved into flame and then reconstituted.

A notion which once again knocks firmly on the head any hopes of our ever enjoying a permanent Golden Age on earth.

Meanwhile Hesiod's scheme of things finds a further, somewhat astonishing echo in the Hebrew scriptures, where the prophet Daniel is described as decoding a dream by Nebuchadnezzar, king of Babylon, which has distinct symbolic affinities to the Greek poet's tale of cosmic decline. The dream was reportedly of a mighty statue whose head was of gold, whose breast and arms were of silver, whose belly and thighs were of bronze, whose legs were of iron and whose feet were 'part iron and part clay'. In the dream, a mighty stone struck the statue's feet and it crumbled to smithereens, while the stone grew into a mountain as big as the earth itself.

Not unexpectedly, perhaps, Daniel interprets the dream as referring to a series of world-empires, each imperial age inferior to the last, which will eventually be shattered and superseded by the millennial Kingdom of God.

Once again the familiar image of periodic decline, destruction and ultimate rebirth.

How far the story is to be relied on as a pointer to current Babylonian beliefs is a moot point. The book of Daniel, it is now generally accepted among biblical scholars, is something of a fake, having been composed as late as 165 BC to boost national morale at a time of savage Greek repression.[41] Consequently it may be reflective more of current Greek mythology than of its former Babylonian equivalent. Which is a pity, as it might have been intriguing to speculate on how the already mentally unstable Nebuchadnezzar, fresh from a session on cosmology with his gloomy, doom-obsessed priesthood, had subsided into a fitful sleep after some over-rich banquet, only to awake sweating out of a screaming nightmare of toppling, monolithic, metal figures . . . .

But then Nebuchadnezzar was in any case king of Neo-Babylonia, not of the truly ancient Babylonian empire in which Middle Eastern astrology seems to have come to birth. Of the beliefs current during that earlier period before the precessional paradigm took over as arbiter of the ages we know very little. Nevertheless, the Roman philosopher Seneca does report an account by the Babylonian historian Berosus which, although written in Greek, and as late as the third century BC, may give some flavour of the earlier scheme of things.

According to this account, the earth passes periodically through general cataclysms caused by fire and water. The dates of these cataclysms, moreover, are determined by the positions of the stars and planets. The periodicity in question, in other words, is governed by astrological considerations, but not necessarily an astrology based on precessional ages — a fact which might indicate that the ideas in question are of fairly early date.

And the conclusion? That the earth will next undergo a general conflagration when all the planets are aligned in Cancer, while the next world-flood will occur when a similar conjunction occurs in Capricorn.

This story of world-deluges and conflagrations is not exclusive to the Babylonian records. The Babylonian flood-legend involving the building of an ark by one Utnapishtim is merely a later version of an ancient Sumerian original, and was itself evidently taken over by the Hebrews as the story of Noah's flood. Indeed, such flood-legends are, for perfectly sound climatological and hydrographical reasons, to be found reported world-wide in ancient folk traditions. Greek mythology records as many as three of them, notably that of Deucalion. Ancient Egyptian tradition likewise records such cataclysms as a regular feature of terrestrial existence. So, at least, we are assured by Plato (whose pupil Aristotle subsequently became the young Alexander's tutor). In his *Timaeus* he has the Greek sage Solon report the Egyptian priesthood as claiming, in a now-celebrated statement, that wholesale destructions of humanity regularly occur as a result of a variety of causes, the major ones being fire and water and the rest a whole range of other agencies. The legend of Phaëthon, he continues, is mythical in character, in reality referring to a periodic declination of the heavenly bodies relative to the earth, and to correspondingly periodic major conflagrations.[31]

A mechanistic concept of cause-and-effect which, it has to be said, is not merely astrological, but borders on the astronomical.

And indeed, we now have ample geological and climatological evidence that the very precessional cycle which gives rise to the apparent movement of the equinoctial point against the stars does result in massive and even catastrophic changes on Earth. According to what is now known as the 'Milankovitch model', after the scientist who first proposed it, one of the results of our planet's precessional wobble as it follows its somewhat eccentric orbit about the sun is that the amount of solar radiation received by each hemisphere varies considerably over the familiar period of some twenty-six thousand years — enough to raise and lower the world's sea levels *by some three hundred feet* during that period.[18,43] At the time of the last minimum, some seventeen thousand years ago, the northern hemisphere underwent its last ice-age. The subsequent thaw, with its rising sea levels, would have been more than sufficient to account not merely for the drowning of Atlantis and any other low-lying civilisation, real or imaginary, which may have existed in around 10,000 BC, but for the whole host of still-surviving flood-legends.

Though the case remains to be proven whether, as the astrological paradigm would have it, certain epochs within that cycle are more likely than others to produce times of depravity or ages of gold.

Social effects there must necessarily be, however, as human beings are forced to devise new technologies to beat the cold, or else to migrate to new lands to escape it. Yet today's high sea-levels have so far failed to produce a Golden Age. Could it be, then, that the Golden Age tends to dawn at the other end of the pendulum-swing? Might the Ice Age, with its scattered populations of shivering, cave-dwelling hunters, have been the true Garden of Eden, at least as far as northern Europe was concerned? In terms of our analysis in Chapter 1, this surprising possibility cannot be dismissed. Or possibly it was the great thaw during the astrological age of Leo, when the new lands of the northern hemisphere were at last opening up for human habitation, which more truly merits that accolade — a possibility to which we have already referred.

At all events, changes in the heavens do seem to be reflected in changes on earth, and so it is not entirely surprising to find a number of ancient civilisations basing their notions of human history on the fact.

And not merely in the Old World.

* * *

It seems somewhat doubtful whether the Hopi Indian tradition that the current age is shortly to be terminated by a great 'purification'[78] is based on observations of the stars. Indeed, it is by no means clear how old this particular tradition really is. The possibility cannot be excluded that the Hopi beliefs may have been contaminated by those of the early white settlers of North America. Certainly the Hopi expectation of a subsequent Golden Age, when the Great Spirit will return to preside over a new era of universal natural harmony, has much in common with Christian expectation.

Which could be one reason why the various North American native traditions, and particularly those of the Hopi, are nowadays proving increasingly popular among New Agers, with their essentially *post*-Christian outlook and philosophy.

Yet we should not be in too much of a hurry to assume mutual contamination merely on the grounds of similarity. Just as certain archetypal dreams, as the great psychologist C.G. Jung pointed out, occur the world over without any suspicion of extra-cultural influence, so it may equally be that there are good and universal psychological grounds for the expectation of a coming period of destruction followed by a Golden Age — or even reasons founded, as we suggested earlier, in simple observation of nature.

But if that nature, in the case of the early Hopi of Arizona, was other than astronomical or astrological, then it was certainly not so in the case of the Maya or Aztecs.

Admittedly the traditions of these two great Central American peoples have so far had little influence upon New Age thinking, possibly because they seem so alien to the ancient European and Asian traditions. And yet both nations took a view of cosmic evolution that was just as inexorably cyclic as that independently proposed by the Hindus before them, and just as self-consistent. Nor did that view prove any less capable of nourishing, and sustaining for several centuries, the civilisations that had produced it.

In the event, however, it was to lead them to utter disaster — a racial and cultural cataclysm of the first order whose story is fascinating enough to be well worth recounting in its own right. It is also a story which, by virtue of its very remoteness from us, enables us to take a 'Martian's-eye view' of the dangers implicit in the sort of over-reliance on cyclic models of cosmic destiny to which many New Agers have themselves been more than a little prone in the past.

The danger, in particular, of assuming that a New Age will automatically dawn merely because a given date has arrived — or, equally, that no New Age can be immediately in prospect merely because it has not.

The Maya in particular were skilled in astronomy, devoted to astrology and obsessed with the mathematics which supported both. So much so that their public monuments are nothing so much as a series of mathematical statements in stone. Not merely does each feature itself have a mathematical significance — the height of a building, the number of steps in a stairway and so on — but the masonry positively bristles with overt calendrical inscriptions in high relief.[24]

The point is that the calendar was of overriding ritual importance to the Maya, as also to the Aztecs who were later to take it over virtually intact. The very survival of society was held to depend upon the priests' ability to identify correctly just which gods should be prayed to and ritually appeased on any given day, as well as at any given hour of the day or night.[79] And this piece of arcane lore depended implicitly on the mechanics of the calendar.

The Mayan Calendar had a marvellous complexity of its own which was more than sufficient to qualify it — rather like a deck of cards or the starry heavens themselves — as a constant source of oracles. It was based on a month of twenty days (for the Maya, roping in all the fingers and toes they could muster, counted in twenties, not tens) and a sequence of thirteen numbers, possibly associated with the thirteen lunations in each year. In consequence, they observed not only a solar year of 365 days and six hours, but a ceremonial year of 260 (20 x 13) days — not to mention a synodic *Venus*-year of 584 days.

Now every so often, necessarily, the beginnings of the solar and ceremonial years corresponded. Once every fifty-two years, in fact, the two great celestial rhythms were at one. Moreover, at the end of every *second* fifty-two year cycle the Venus-count also fell into synchronisation with the others.

The fifty-two year cycle, in consequence, acquired enormous cosmic significance. If, after all, the very sequence of numbers governing the days of the year predicated a fifty-two year cycle, then it seemed to follow that the entire universe must be governed by the same cycle. For its very parameters had been determined in the first place not merely (as it would seem) by the thirteen annual appearances of the moon, but by the cycle of twenty days, each of which was sacred to one of the gods. Moreover, the whole thing was clearly validated by the synodic cycle of the planet Venus, which for the Aztecs was the very soul of Quetzalcóatl, one of the greatest gods of all.

And the gods, it went without saying, were the driving force that powered the universe itself.

But precisely what did the end of one fifty-two year cycle and the beginning of another signify? Clearly there could be no suggestion that each cycle represented a whole age of human history, or that the universe was destroyed and regenerated on such a short-term basis. People, after all, had parents and grandparents who could remember a good deal further back than fifty-two years. Moreover, thousands of people successfully survived the awful transition every time it happened — even if only by dint of frenzied penance and sacrifice.

Yet at the same time it was clear to the Mayan and Aztec cosmologists — i.e. the respective priesthoods — that if the end of the present world were to come, then it was most likely to happen at this particular juncture. The present universe, after all, must presumably have started at the beginning of the cycle. What more natural, then, than that it should finish at its end?

The cusp between any two cycles, in other words, was rather like that sinister hour in the early morning when, with human resistance at its lowest, most deaths occur.

And so the cosmologists turned their mathematical attention to the likely shapes and contours of the ages, much as the Hindus had done long before them. For this the Mayan vigesimal system of counting was, of course, ideal. Moreover, the Mayan mathematicians had, quite independently of Pānini, invented the use of the zero. On this basis the cosmologists (in all probability one and the same) could now proceed to devise a whole series of symbols, each standing for twenty times the value of its predecessor, which enabled them to calculate theoretical dates millions of years in the past. One symbol alone, *alautun*, stood for a period of no less than sixty-three million years.[24]

The upshot of all this was that the world was held to pass regularly through a whole series of ages, rather after the ancient Eastern model. Already, according to Aztec tradition, there had been four previous 'worlds', each of which had been destroyed when humanity had grown too big for its collective boots. These destructions had been brought about by wild jaguars, hurricanes, fire and flood respectively. The present 'solar' age, the fifth in the series, had started in the year 3113 BC (give or take a scholastic disagreement or two over the exact correlation between the Mayan and Christian calendars), and was destined to meet its end by earthquake, ably assisted by a marauding army of skeleton-like monsters from out of the west.

The cosmologists seem to have been much more cautious than the Hindus, however, over the matter of extending their calculations into the future. The gods, after all, had a will of their own. And while it was they who had, in a sense, sanctioned the calendar, they were not above changing it. As a result, while projections into the future were made on the basis of a cyclic understanding of past history, the precise date when the present world-order might be expected to come to an end was a cause for worrying uncertainty. All that could be said was that it was likely to occur at the end of any given fifty-two year cycle.

And it was at this point that the astrologers as such came into their own.

For the gods were not merely associated with the days of the month. Like their Greek counterparts, they were also associated with the stars. And not merely associated with them, but — to use a term from the Mayan *Chilam Balam of Chumayel*, 'confined within' them. The stars, in fact, were embedded, as in the ancient Middle Eastern model, in a series of heavens, or firmaments — in this case thirteen in number. Of these, the outer one was the preserve of the fixed stars, and each of the others was devoted to one of the planets, the sun or moon, and such intangibles as the clouds, the lightning, the heat and the rain. Possibly, then, the term 'confined' suggests that the gods were somehow seen as restricted to their own particular spheres of operation.

On the whole, however, it seems more likely that the term merely indicates that each star contained within it the *soul* of a god. Certainly the Aztecs regarded all the stars and constellations as divine. Thus, the oldest of the Aztec gods was Ueueteotl (Old Old God), the fount both of fire (and thus of life) and of the destruction of used-up things, and his seat was the Pole Star, the pivot of the universe. Quetzalcóatl, on the other hand, the god of the sky and of learning, was associated, as we saw earlier, with the planet Venus. The sun embodied the god Tonatiuh — the word actually *means* 'Sun God' — and Metztli was the Moon God. All the stars and planets, likewise, were associated with gods and goddesses, who — under the terms of the Aztec notion that the entire universe was engaged in a perpetual war between light and darkness, heat and cold, north and south, east and west — were divided into the 'Four Hundred Southerners' and the 'Four Hundred Northerners', not to mention the *Tzitzimime*, the Monsters Descending from Above.

Thus, while not all the gods were specifically stellar divinities, it was clear that the stars and planets exercised enormous powers over the universe for good or ill. And so their movements were scrupulously studied, their periodicities minutely calculated with all the care that a modern researcher might observe while studying some highly unstable explosive substance.

And never more so than at the approach of the dreaded end of each cycle.

As the fateful year approached, indeed, omens were sought wherever they could be found. Divination of all kinds abounded. And the astrologers in particular, having calculated the positions of the heavenly bodies, proceeded to interpret them in terms of the sojourns of the gods in the thirteen houses of their zodiac, with all that each house portended of doom or good fortune.

During the few years leading up to the Aztec change of cycle in 1507 AD, it was the earthly omens that firmly upstaged the astrological ones. For during this period worrying reports started to come in of strange, winged vessels prowling off the eastern shores of the empire. There were even stories that exotic, godlike beings had alighted from them and come ashore. The now highly-sensitised priests were, quite naturally, thoroughly alarmed at the news. Nothing so extraordinary had been reported for generations. Earthquakes, volcanoes, hurricanes, comets, thunderbolts — all these, certainly, had been endured and survived. But *winged vessels bearing godlike entities* — and so close to a change of cycle? What could it all portend?

Bad news, almost certainly, but not, apparently, the imminent extinction of humanity. For the present age was destined to end — it was well known — at the hand not of eastern gods, but of skeleton-like monsters from the west, and accompanied by cataclysmic earthquakes, at that. Earthquakes there had been, admittedly, along with a variety of other disturbing omens, yet their scale did not seem to warrant the assumption that the present world was about to be destroyed.

Accordingly, orders were given for the great ceremonies of transition to go ahead as planned. As the dreaded night approached which signalled the end of the current cycle, all fires were extinguished, including those that burned perpetually atop the sacrificial platforms of the great temple-pyramids. The people fasted and lamented. All household furniture was destroyed, pregnant women shut up in granaries, children marched continually up and down to keep them awake lest they turn into rats.[79]

And then came the final night of the cycle. As the people kept constant vigil in the darkness below, the priests ascended the temple on the summit of Huixachtecatl, the Hill of the Star, to await the rising of the Pleiades. For some hours the anxious watching and waiting continued, until at last the twinkling star-cluster reached the zenith. Now was the critical moment. Would the stars suddenly go out, and the world disappear amidst tremendous earthquakes?

We may imagine the scene. As the seconds dragged by, the tension first built up . . . and then, almost imperceptibly at first, started to subside. There was an almost audible release of pent-up breath. And then, as the priests kindled the fire of the New Cycle in the breast of a newly-slaughtered human sacrificial victim, shouts of joy and jubilation broke out. Soon the temple-pyramid was lit up by a veritable cascade of points of light, as runners bearing flaming torches sped on their way towards the other sacrificial centres, rekindling at the same time the local temple-fires at every intervening town and hamlet.

Thence the people rekindled the fires in their own hearths, joyful with the symbolic promise of renewed life. And, as dawn broke, they set about the task of refurbishing their houses, renewing their household utensils and preparing special celebratory meals, as well as the more serious ritual requirements of personal blood-letting.

In the temples, too, there were the solemn rites of sacrifice to be performed in gratitude to the gods, and plans to be laid for adding new casings to the temple-pyramids. And, in particular, there were captives to be immolated in order that their blood and their hearts — torn, still beating, from their living breasts — might revivify Tonatiuh, the sun, whose age had so miraculously been renewed.

So pressing, indeed, was this requirement in the Aztec view that the provision of suitable captives to satisfy it had long since become the major purpose of their foreign policy. Increasingly racked with anxiety lest their world should come to a sudden end, they continually embarked on bigger and better wars in order to provide the captives who would be sacrificed, first in their hundreds, then in their thousands, and eventually in their tens of thousands. And so it is hardly surprising that, with their temples literally awash with human blood, the Aztecs were hated and feared not only by their neighbours, but by most of their subject-peoples too.

Nevertheless, the dreadful magic seemed to have worked yet again. The omens from the east had not, after all, betokened the end of the world. Yet what *did* they mean? Somewhere in the backs of the priests' minds faint bells were undoubtedly ringing. Was it not from the eastern coast that the god-king Quetzalcóatl had disappeared on his raft of serpents all those years ago at the beginning of the age, promising that one day he would return to reclaim his kingdom — the same Quetzalcóatl whose name and symbol was the *plumed* serpent? And if the connection were a significant one, what might his return betoken — always assuming that something of the kind might be in the offing?

A new dispensation, certainly. A new Golden Age, equally certainly. But at the same time it had to spell the end of the present hierarchy, perhaps of the whole current social order. In all practical respects, indeed, it had to mean the end of the world as the reigning priesthood knew it.

There was thus cause — and urgent cause — for a new bout of speculation and omen-watching. And particularly in view of the fact that the year One Reed, which was sacred to Queztalcóatl — indeed, during which his original departure was sometimes said to have taken place — was due to recur only twelve years in the future (for the Aztecs simply named each year after the name and number of its first day).

As the critical date approached, the omens duly materialised. Indeed, they became increasingly insistent. The emperor Montezuma — himself no mean dabbler in witchcraft — not only lost a ritual ball-game with a neighbouring chief, but also had a worrying vision in which the stars in the heavens turned into a multitude of armed men. A column of fire set the sky alight every night for a year. Two temples were destroyed by fire and lightning. A comet appeared by day, while sudden waves came up as though by magic on Lake Texcoco. And a disembodied woman's voice was heard crying, 'My children, we are lost.'[79]

Then came the portentous year One Reed itself (AD 1519 on our calendar). And with it the sudden and truly apocalyptic news that more godlike beings had come ashore from their winged ships on the south-eastern coast. With them were strange, four-legged monsters with human bodies sprouting out of their backs. In their hands the strangers carried murderous weapons that could kill at a distance as though by magic. And at their head, encased in a kind of shiny carapace every bit as exotic and intricate as the symbolic accoutrements of the bearded Quetzalcóatl, the equally bearded . . . Hernando Cortés.

The priestly hierarchy, inevitably, was racked with all the panic and despair of men whose pigeons of religious belief and dogma had finally come home to roost. As for Montezuma, he could only welcome the new arrivals with copious gifts. What could he possibly do, he was heard to remark, in the face of the gods themselves?

Only when Cortés subsequently placed Montezuma under house-arrest and one of his commanders allowed himself to be panicked into ordering a massacre of a huge crowd of peaceful citizens did the scales start to fall from the Aztecs' eyes. But by then it was too late. Once hostilities commenced, the Aztecs' methods of ritual combat proved no match for the sophisticated military techniques of the Spaniards. Even their enormous numerical advantage proved of little avail when their hitherto brutally subdued subject-peoples started to throw in their lot with the strangers. And their cause was not helped, either, by their obsession with trying all the time to take prisoners to sacrifice to their war-god, rather than exterminating the enemy wherever he was to be found.

The outcome was inevitable. Within a matter of a couple of years, Cortés's small band had succeeded in bringing the Aztec empire crashing to the ground. And for this they had ultimately to thank not so much the natives' relative military incompetence, still less any cowardice on their part, as the blindfolds of superstition, astrological speculation and cosmic fatalism which the Aztecs insisted on wearing even in the thick of battle.

Possibly there is a lesson here for today's New Agers, as for all of us. It is, after all, no means beyond the bounds of possibility that our own particular superstitions and cosmological beliefs may likewise lead not to heaven on earth, but to eventual disillusion and failure in the face of stark reality. Which is a cue, if ever there was one, for checking all our favourite beliefs and assumptions against the claims of fact and reputable scholarship and genuine, first-hand investigation, constantly bearing in mind that honest reality will always have the last laugh.

For the Aztecs, certainly, it was the end of an age.

And not only for the Aztecs. A new era of European colonisation was now to sweep across the whole of the American continent. And this at least in part because Europe, too, was — as we shall see — in the throes of embarking upon an equally new era.

To an extent, then, the Aztecs' omens had been right. The former age *had* come to an end. In its place a new era had dawned for humanity — though whether it was the expected Golden Age must, even then, have been open to doubt.

Yet it was not the *astrological* omens that had had this limited success. The stars, it should be remembered, had apparently indicated that all would be well as the new cycle dawned in the year 1507 AD. The Pleiades had successfully risen and passed the zenith. The sun had duly risen the following morning. All was set, it seemed, for another successful new cycle.

But the stars had been wrong. Once again, they had let humanity down. For the Aztec nation, indeed, it was the end of the road. And the new era, as it turned out, was to be based firmly on the unheard-of European notion that the Golden Age, if Golden Age there was to be, lay in the gift not of the stars, but of the human race itself.

It was a new and remarkable idea, and one which (as I shall go on to explain) was eventually to have profound repercussions even within the modern New Age movement. It predicated a constant upward slope, in place of the former conviction of an ever-lastingly-repeated downward slide into depravity. In placing humanity's destiny in its own hands it seemed almost to turn *homo sapiens* into a god.

And for this reason it came into direct conflict not only with the former Aztec doctrine of cyclic inevitability, but with another paradigm of great antiquity and power which had hitherto held sway, almost unquestioned, throughout Europe itself, not to mention North Africa and the Near East.

Namely the alternative, straight-line view of history, with its one-way ticket to damnation for the many or eternal and final salvation for the few.

5

One Fine Day

For upon us the fulfilment of the ages has come.
St Paul (1. Cor. 10:11)

Every people at some time or other imagines that it stands at the centre of the universal stage. Every generation at some time or other assumes that its age is the culmination of world history. In the case of the Jews, the surprise is therefore not that they adopted such views, but that those views were to persist for so long.

Why should this have been? And what was it about the Jewish outlook which produced that extraordinary elitist phenomenon, the 'chosen people' syndrome, which has endured to this day, bearing with it the constant promise of an imminent and final Millennium?

This whole complex of ideas is, as we shall see, so fundamental to the assumptions of the modern New Age movement that we should do well to look very carefully into its origins.

* * *

No doubt the most ancient and primitive Israelites — whoever they were and wherever they came from — assumed, as most of us do from time to time, that they themselves were ultimately responsible, barring accidents, for whatever happened to them, whether for good or ill. The feeling is understandable — and certainly it seems just and right that this state of affairs should be so.

At an early stage, though, the realisation seems to have forced itself upon them that reality was far from just and right. There were altogether too many accidents, and most of them were distinctly nasty. Consequently some more direct cause — some particular outside agent — had to be discovered, or invented, to explain this parlous state of affairs.

On the one hand there was a whole chapter of tribal calamities to explain, yet on the other the extraordinary fact that the tribe had still managed to survive them all. (This last thought is of course related to the well-known How-strange-that-the-world-should-be-as-it-is idea, which blithely ignores the fact that, if the world were not as it is, you wouldn't be there to appreciate its strangeness in the first place.)

The result, almost inevitably, was the invention of a supervising and controlling tribal deity who had obscure but decidedly grandiose plans for his protégés, and was prepared to resort to almost anything to ensure that they were fulfilled.

Not that there was anything very new about this notion. Other tribes, too, had invented such gods. But where Yahweh scored over his rivals was in his invisibility and intangibility.

Quite why he acquired these characteristics is a matter for some debate. Possibly it had to do with the fact that he was originally a sky-god, and the sky-god of a nomadic people, at that. Like the Egyptians' falcon-god, Horus, and the original of the Greeks' Zeus — as equally of his counterpart and successor, the Jupiter of imperial Rome — his dwelling was placed firmly 'in heaven', i.e. in the sky. And just as Horus, in the ancient Egyptians' essentially non-symbolic way of thinking, *was* the sky, and both Zeus and Jupiter derived their names from an Aryan root which *meant* 'sky', so 'heaven' became, to the Jews, a synonym and euphemism for the name of Yahweh in an age when merely to pronounce the sacred name had been decreed a form of blasphemy.

Thus it was that, by the time of Jesus, their own version of the expected earthly Millennium, previously described as 'the Kingdom of God', could equally well be referred to as 'the Kingdom of Heaven'.

As if this were not enough, we continually find Yahweh's priestly and prophetic representatives ascending mountains to meet him in the clouds. From Abraham, through Moses and the prophet Elijah, to Jesus of Nazareth himself, it is on the hilltops that Yahweh seems most ready to contact his leading human spokesmen. The very bargain, or covenant, whereby Yahweh pledges himself to regard his chosen people as 'my kingdom of priests, my holy nation', and to protect and preserve them accordingly, is struck with Moses on the summit of the holy mountain, Mount Sinai.

But the site of Sinai seems curiously indeterminate. The mountain described in the book of Exodus is clearly a volcano, yet the current Mount Sinai, near the southern tip of the Sinai peninsula, has not been volcanic for many thousands of years. Moreover, the texts frequently refer to it by the alternative name of 'Horeb'. Even granted, then, that tradition has come to assign this name to Sinai's north-eastern peak, the curious fact needs to be borne in mind that 'Horeb' seems to be a direct transliteration of the Egyptian expression *Hor-'ib*, meaning 'heart of Horus' — i.e. 'heart of the sky'.

There seems to be a distinct possibility, then, that the name 'Horeb' was indiscriminately applied by the migrating Israelites to *any* mountain which their leaders ascended in order to speak with their sky-god, Yahweh.

And I use the word 'leaders' advisedly, since the name 'Moses', equally, is merely a form of the Egyptian word *ms*, meaning 'boy' or 'son', which is found as part of the pharaonic names Rameses ('son of Ra' or 'Ra-is-born') and Thothmes or Tuthmosis ('son of Thoth' or 'Thoth is born'), and which is still commonly used (in the form Mâose) as a boy's name in Egypt to this day.[34] 'Moses', in other words, could represent a folk-memory of a whole series of tribal leaders who led various groups of Israelites out of slavery in Egypt (for even the notion of a single, grand-slam Exodus is itself nowadays doubted by a good many biblical scholars). Or possibly it was a hereditary leadership, with father giving way to son (*ms*), and son to grandson — which might account for the relatively short journey's extraordinary duration (reportedly forty years) and the equally extraordinary longevity (120 years) which the texts attribute to its leader.

(The direct distance from the Nile Delta to the reported entry into the land of Canaan, or Palestine, is some 250 miles. The roundabout route described by the text is nearer six hundred. Even in the latter case, then, the Israelites' average speed was no more than seventy-five yards a day. If true, this would seem to indicate that, once clear of Egypt, the leadership had no definite idea of where it was going, and that the assembled tribes spent far more time 'trying out for size' a variety of possible new home-lands — presumably the forty-two different camp-sites reported by tradition — than in actual travelling. This in turn would suggest that there may in all have been only some forty-three days of travelling, and that on each of them the tribes covered the perfectly normal distance of some fourteen miles.)

At all events, it comes as no surprise to find that the Israelites, once they had succeeded in identifying and occupying what they regarded as their God-given promised land, gravitated to one or more holy mountains as the centre of their worship of Yahweh. Under King David it was Mount Zion in Jerusalem that took on that sacred role and was duly crowned by his celebrated son with the fabulous temple for which Solomon is still remembered today. The later religious reactionaries of Samaria, for their part, preferred to construct their own temple on the summit of Mount

Gerizim, while prophetic 'outsiders' such as Elijah seem to have founded other mountain cult-centres — in his case in the far north, on Mount Carmel.

In all this we may see the Israelites worshipping not a mere mountain-god, still less the god of any particular mountain, but the god whose heavenly dwelling might most closely be approached by climbing to the most lofty summit available. It was often a strenuous, even dangerous undertaking (for it should be remembered that nobody but a madman ever dreamed of climbing mountains for fun, let alone for Romantic reasons, until about the middle of the nineteenth century). But at least it maximised the chances of contacting, and if possible winning over to their side, Yahweh the god of the sky.

Yet for the very reason that he *was* the god of the sky, it was clear to as essentially nomadic a people as the early Israelites that he was always with them. Indeed, there was no escaping him. Moreover, any attempt to make a gross physical image of him would clearly be to misrepresent him, to demean the sheer splendour and breadth and limitlessness of his heavenly presence. To attempt to confine a god who 'takes the clouds for his chariot' to any fixed temple made by humans, as the Egyptians and Canaanites were prone to do, was to the early Israelites clearly pointless. Even to limit him with a name had its dangers — whence, presumably, the stern Mosaic command 'You shall not make wrong use of the name of Yahweh your God' (which, in effect, eventually came to mean a total taboo on pronouncing it at all).

For it followed that, with Yahweh as the sky-god, he was totally intangible, totally impossible to pin down. The sky was not even a thing. Not only did it perpetually change colour, but it faded, became transparent and, at night, was totally transformed. What you could see, in other words, was not the sky, still less Yahweh himself, but a continual process. The sky was not so much a noun as a verb.

And Yahweh, in consequence, was essentially the sum of his acts.

That, presumably, was why the deity was reported as having identified himself to the enquiring Moses in terms of the enigmatic, but essentially verbal expression EHYEH ASHER EHYEH — 'I am that I am'.

* * *

Now it goes without saying that the sky does not always shower humanity with nice things. It is all very well for churchgoers to carol forth the words of the familiar harvest hymn:

He sends the snow in winter,
The warmth to swell the grain,
The breezes and the sunshine,
And soft refreshing rain.

'All good gifts around us,' the chorus goes on to explain, 'are sent from heaven above' — but it pointedly draws a veil over all the nasty things that descend upon us as well. For it is clear that the 'snow' in this verse is seen by its author as a delightful decoration pertaining to some pastoral idyll, and not as the farmer's bane that it truly is. And as for hail, tempest and lightning — not to mention the biblical 'fire and brimstone' — all these are studiously ignored.

For the early Israelites, however — for whom life was certainly pastoral, but hardly idyllic — there was no ignoring such things. Yahweh, it seemed, sent equal measure of the good and bad things down on his people, to the point where it had to be assumed that, if he really did have a plan for his chosen flock, then he was subjecting it to a pretty severe form of training — a training typical, it could be said, of a particularly stern parent. 'Take this lesson to heart,' Moses is reported as saying of the tribulations of the exodus in the book of Deuteronomy, 'that Yahweh your God was disciplining you as a father disciplines his son.'

Possibly it was out of this thought that the idea arose that Yahweh was indeed not merely the god, but the spiritual father of the nation — which meant that, by the same token, the nation was literally his collective son on earth.

But at this point the question naturally tended to be asked, 'What is the purpose of such a parental up-bringing?' Pursuing the family analogy, the answer had to be that Yahweh had it in mind to train his collective offspring to grow into an 'adult' like himself, just as any normal father would do. Which logically had to mean that the Israelites were destined to become the physical counterpart on earth of Yahweh in the heavens — the arms and legs of God, so to speak.

At which point a further consideration insisted on obtruding into the argument. Namely that Yahweh was manifestly the earth's 'top god'. There he was in the sky, after all, lording it over all the other petty tribal deities who were mere blocks of wood or metal or stone imprisoned in human-made sanctuaries. In the

words of Psalm 115, 'Our God is in high heaven; he does whatsoever pleases him' — whereas 'their idols are silver and gold, made
by the hands of men. They have mouths that cannot speak,' the
text goes on, 'and eyes that cannot see.' By contrast, Yahweh the
sky-god was, in the very nature of things, present everywhere —
and everywhere at once, at that — which in turn suggested that he
was all-seeing, and possibly all-powerful too.

Clearly there was no overtopping the very sky itself.

But if Yahweh was 'top god', it had to follow that his chosen
people, once it had truly become his representative and counterpart on earth, was likewise destined to be the world's 'top nation'.
There was no escaping the fact. It was to Jerusalem that all the
world's kingdoms would eventually have to pay tribute in the
name of the god whose own capital city it was bound to become.

To an often wretched and oppressed people who were constantly being chased from pillar to post by aggressive and warlike
neighbours, this thought, when first elaborated, must have come
as the most extraordinary and incredible of suggestions. And yet
Yahweh had already shown his power. Had not the twelve tribes
succeeded in surviving despite all the odds? Had they not succeeded in escaping the clutches of the Egyptians through what
seemed to be the most miraculous of means?[44] (The example of the
Dunkirk evacuation of World War II should serve as a salutary
reminder of the way in which a well-conducted operation, given
only a little luck in the matter of weather and opposition
bungling, can be turned by folklore into a case of divine intervention.) Surely, then, the hand of Yahweh must be trusted. He meant
what he said. And that was now spelt out quite unambiguously in
the mountain-covenant with Moses.

Yet there was a snag.

For the covenant made it quite clear that there were conditions
attached. What else, after all, was to be expected of an agreement,
or deal, between two parties? There was a whole battery of provisions which the tribes had to satisfy if they were truly to merit the
title of Yahweh's collective earthly son. Not merely the celebrated
Ten Commandments, but (if the texts are to be believed) a further
603 positive and negative provisions, all of which had to be
scrupulously observed if the nation were to be accounted righteous and pure in the sight of Yahweh. And only then could that
final Golden Age dawn when the Jewish people could fully merit
the name *Israel* — 'ruling with God' — which they had long since
adopted in anticipation of the event. Only then would Yahweh, in
effect, be incarnate on earth, with all the unimaginable blessings

which that would bring, both for the nation itself and, through it, for the world as a whole.

* * *

So, at least, the underlying argument seems to have gone, however submerged its logic has subsequently become by textual verbiage and theological obfuscation. Fundamental to it, clearly, was a view of history which, at least from the Israelite point of view, consisted of a straight-line graph destined to lead — if only the nation played its cards right — directly to heaven on earth. The Kingdom of God, in other words, was there for the grasping, if only Israel chose wholeheartedly to carry out the will of Yahweh as recorded in the words of the Mosaic covenant. Hence, of course, the later, though still essentially Jewish, Lord's Prayer's explicit linking of the two ideas:

Thy kingdom come,
thy will be done
on earth as in heaven

Even during the Jews' captivity in Babylon and the subsequent periods of Persian and Greek domination this linear view of human destiny managed to survive, despite the seductions of the alternative, cyclic view which both Babylonian and Greek traditions offered. True, some elements of the cyclic view were taken on board as minor adjuncts. The adoption of the Babylonian flood-legend of Gilgamesh in the form of 'Noah's flood', for example, witnesses to the official acceptance of the idea that there had been at least one former age on earth which had come to a watery end. The familiar six-day Creation-account, which may equally be of Babylonian origin, may be interpreted in terms of a whole cycle of former earthly ages. Indeed, it was regarded as important enough to be adopted, together with its culminating seventh day — the 'day of rest', or *Shabbath* (from Babylonian *sappattu*: 'new-moon festival') — as the basis of the Hebrew seven-day week on the return of the weary Jewish exiles to the ruined Jerusalem from 534 BC onwards.

A week which has since been adopted by virtually the entire world as the basis of its social calendar.

Yet the cyclic idea of history never caught on as a general principle. The Jewish teaching continued to be that Yahweh had created Israel as his own son, and had predestined it for a role as the ruler of a final Golden Age when heaven and earth would at last be brought into total and everlasting harmony. The concept of cyclism (or at least of recurrent cyclism) just never entered the argument — except, that is, in the case of the extraordinary assertion attributed to King Solomon which stands at the head of Chapter Two above.

What apparently did impinge on the Jews' consciousness, however, was the Zoroastrianism of their later, Persian overlords. This, like Judaism, had developed an essentially linear view of world history under the influence of the prophet Zarathustra (or Zoroaster), who seems to have been alive in Persia (in one of his incarnations at least) at about the time of the Babylonian captivity. Indeed, the Zoroastrian texts known as the *Dinkart* ('Acts of Religion') — a collection of late Pehlevi summaries of the original *Nasks* allegedly dictated by Zarathustra in person — even claim that he visited Babylon itself during that period and 'converted the city from sorcery'.[22] Certainly his teachings were well-known there at the time. Their influence must therefore have been widespread by the time the Hebrew teachings were themselves being finalised with the Jewish return to a now Persian-dominated homeland.

The precise sources of Zarathustra's ideas are, for the most part, unknown. Certainly the influence of some early Aryan notions can be detected in them — as in the case of the *daevas* or evil spirits, which likewise turn up in India, though by this time transformed by reverent Hindu tradition into shining, angelic entities. Possibly, then, Zarathustra's teachings represent an elaboration of an earlier tradition going right back to prehistoric times — for it is of course quite unknown for a prophet to have no antecedents at all and to appear, as it were, out of a total conceptual void.

At all events, Zoroastrianism contained a number of elements which rang definite bells of recognition among the Jews and so were to be eagerly assimilated by the founding theologians of the newly-reconstituted Jewish state. At a time of renewal, after all, minds tend to be unusually open and receptive to any ideas which might help to build up and cement together the prospective new orthodoxy, in a way which they are never likely to be again.

There were, of course, good and cogent reasons for establishing such a Jewish orthodoxy. It represented a desperate — and hopefully final — national attempt to fulfil the long-neglected will of Yahweh, so avoiding any further repetition of the dire calamities which had lately befallen the nation, and — more to the point — bringing into long-overdue manifestation the promised Kingdom of Heaven on earth. Since it is now generally accepted that the first five books of our familiar Bible were drawn up in their present form at this time, and thus under the direct influence of the new orthodoxy, we should therefore not expect them to give us a strictly historical account of what had gone before. And, in particular, we should not assume that the values and precepts of that orthodoxy were as strictly or as widely observed before that time — or even at the time of the exodus itself — as the texts themselves suggest.

Indeed, if they had been, the Zoroastrian cross-fertilisation could never have taken place.

Manifestly, however, it did.

* * *

One of the ideas which had long been prevalent among the Jewish exiles, for example, was a violent nostalgia for the glorious pioneering days of King David's growing empire of around 1000 BC, before the ostentatious opulence of Solomon's reign gave way to a disintegration of the nation and a descent into the ungodliness and depravity to which they and their priests and prophets now attributed all their present ills. Very naturally, therefore, this nostalgia was accompanied by a passionate belief, founded largely in wishful thinking, that a successor of King David would one day re-ascend the throne and put everything to rights. Various of the prophets, indeed — Isaiah, Jeremiah, Ezekiel and (by implication) Micah among them — had directly given voice to the conviction, even going so far as to suggest that the new David would in some sense be a *reincarnation* of his illustrious predecessor, and that his glorious reign of justice, peace and plenty would last literally for ever.[41]

The reign of the historical David, in other words, was already being looked back to as a kind of Golden Age in its own right. And the Kingdom of Heaven, for its part, was being looked forward to as a repetition of it, but magnified to the nth degree.

Quite how this vision of a kind of Davidic world-tyranny, with all its potential for naked power-seeking and international divisiveness, could possibly be reconciled with the gentle 'Garden of Eden' vision of total harmony between heaven and earth, humans and nature, is difficult to see. True, the general idea seemed to be to avoid the risk of divisiveness by the simple expedient of utterly destroying all opposition.

Which, if it worked, would admittedly be one way of achieving world unity, as even Hitler seems to have realised in his day.

Perhaps the answer is that the Jews first associated the 'Garden of Eden' concept with that of the future Golden Age only after their arrival in Babylon. Originally, in other words, there was no paradox to solve. Yet the fact remains that they managed to persist for many centuries after the exile with the apparent contradiction, which even survives among their more orthodox successors to this day.

What they also discovered in Babylon, however — and especially so after the Persian take-over — was a whole series of theological and prophetic propositions which promised to flesh out their existing apocalyptic framework in the most dramatic and fulfilling way.

For the Zoroastrians, too, had views on the shape and purpose of world history. Their vision covered a broad sweep of some nine thousand years. And it began with the prophet Zarathustra.

* * *

Already pre-existent in heaven for thousands of years before his birth, Zarathustra was reportedly incarnated in order to inaugurate a plan for the world's salvation from evil at the behest of the heavenly Ahura Mazda ('Wise Lord'), the god of the entire universe and source of all light who defined himself as 'I WHO AM'. Invisible, eternal and all-good, this divinity had created all things out of nothing and then subjected his creation to a war of opposites in which he himself, so to speak, appeared on both sides. On the one hand was his own holy spirit of truth and light, and on the other Ahriman or Angra Mainyu, the spirit of darkness and Lord of the Lie. (The dichotomy is an interesting one, reflecting as it does the familiar internal civil war between the human unconscious and conscious, between direct perception and conditioned prejudice, between — in brief — enlightenment and illusion, which is very much at the heart of the ancient quest for the Golden Age, but which has long since been degraded by institutional Zoroastrianism, Judaism, Christianity and Islam alike into a mere brute struggle between inherited social and religious dogmas and their opposites.)

From this primal struggle light and truth would, of course, eventually emerge triumphant, but not without grave setbacks.

And it was Zarathustra who was destined to set this victory in motion.

As is ever the case with the search for religious origins, reliable documentation of Zarathustra's life and teachings is hard to come by. Of the two original copies of his teachings allegedly dictated in his own lifetime, one was last heard of in ancient Samarkand and the other, installed in the royal library at Persepolis, went up in flames when Alexander's over-exuberant troops put the city to the torch in 331 BC in the drunken frenzy of victory over the Persians.

Much of what survives is thus based on oral tradition, backed up by second- and third-hand written summaries and reports. But there would have been no risk of Zoroastrianism's disappearance even had these been totally lacking.

For, in the event, its basic principles were to be taken over by Judaism — and later by Christianity and to some extent Islam — almost lock, stock and barrel.

* * *

Zarathustra, it seems, was born in Azerbaijan, then part of the Assyrian empire, in around 660 BC amid all sorts of mysterious omens.[22] Surviving several attempts at murder by a jealous sorcerer, he committed himself at the age of fifteen (the official age of physical maturity) to a religious life. Rejecting the advice of his elders to worship the daevas, or nature-spirits, he subsequently spent many years meditating in silence in a cave on Mount Ushidarena, anxious above all to discover the purpose of life and the nature of righteousness. Only at the age of thirty (the official age of spiritual maturity) did he at last emerge to begin his mission.

On a long journey to celebrate the spring equinox, he first had a vision that he must teach multitudes of people who would be brought to him initially by his cousin Maidhyomaonha. Then, having waded up to his neck through the river Daitya to offer sacrifice to the holy waters, he emerged on the far bank to be overwhelmed by a vision of Vohumanah, the archangel of love, by whose agency he was granted sight of the heavenly court itself, and promptly accepted the task of becoming God's prophet to Iran.

There followed ten years of wandering and rejection, during which he was granted a succession of revelations and visions, as well as undergoing and rejecting a series of temptations — among them the urge to throw in his lot with the prevailing powers and to worship the daevas.

At last, at the age of forty, he scored his first real success. In the north of Afghanistan he succeeded in converting the emperor Vishtaspa to his teachings, receiving the title of 'Prophet of the

King', and forthwith began to demonstrate remarkable powers of thought-reading and inspired utterance.

From then on his position was secure, and the new faith spread far and wide under royal patronage. Among its precepts was that temples should be built for the worship of Ahura Mazda, each enshrining in its inner sanctum a simple fire standing for the ever-living, ever-moving, always untouchable Divinity itself. Once lit, this fire must always be maintained, and if, by chance, it should be extinguished, then it must be relit from the fire of one of the other temples.

The symbolism was, of course, magnificently appropriate. For fire was, patently, not so much a thing as a process — and a powerful, all-consuming, purifying process at that. Moreover, it had no obvious beginning or end. It could go on from generation to generation, ever self-renewing. And it symbolised with great aptness Ahura Mazda, who was the lord not only of heavenly light, but also of the inner light, that illumination which burns in the secret places of the heart.

But the sacred fire was the centre merely of the new religion's *ritual*, which naturally included the universally obligatory animal sacrifices. Its actual *teachings*, on the other hand, were decidedly practical in orientation. Humanity, they revealed, was born to choose between good and evil. To fight for good is to choose the side of God and to observe his precepts. Each human being has an immortal soul which has existed from long before birth. While incarnate, its duty is to love, serve and worship God and his heavenly court, to help, share and encourage, to be kind to all living things and to fight and destroy evil wherever it arises. The golden rule is the familiar one of 'Do as you would be done by'.

In all this the individual is assisted by Ahura Mazda's seven 'divine qualities' or archangelic manifestations. (In point of fact, just as Ahura Mazda was himself originally the local Assyrian god Assara-Mazah, so the seven archangels were likewise based on former gods whom Zarathustra, unable to banish because of popular resistance, seems to have been forced to incorporate into his own scheme of things by way of rendering them harmless.)

These six supplementary 'persons of the godhead' are Asha Vahishta ('Highest Righteousness'), Vohumanah ('Love' or 'Good Mind'), Khshathra Vairya ('Desired Kingdom'), Spenta Armaiti ('Holy Devotion'), Haurvatat ('Wholeness') and Ameretat ('Immortality'). These in turn revolve around Spenta Mainyu ('Holy Twin' or 'Holy Spirit'), equivalent to Ahura Mazda's 'number-one personality', which spearheads the sevenfold Divinity in the great battle that is both personal and cosmic in scale. And on its outcome, influenced in turn by a host of minor angelic entities and long-departed saints and heroes, the fate of each person's soul depends. Those who have chosen good are brought, at death, directly into the divine presence, there to live for ever in bliss. Those who have chosen evil are consigned to a period in hell until such time as their sins have finally been purged away.

As for the world in general, this is visited periodically by charismatic saviour-figures — great prophets such as Zarathustra himself, whose task it is to reveal the divine will to humanity and initiate new stages in the world's evolution towards righteousness and truth, much after the style of the Hindu avatars and Buddhist bodhisattvas.

The various surviving texts proceed to delineate the stages of the nine-thousand-year-long struggle, which is set to follow immediately on the heels of an initial three thousand years of purely spiritual existence for the universe as a whole. First, it seems, there is a three-thousand-year period of heaven-on-earth, with the Evil Spirit banished to outer darkness. Then follows a second three-thousand-year period during which good and evil exist in precarious balance. And finally comes the last age of three thousand years, when 'the Evil Spirit is disabled', and at the conclusion of which those who have merited the title of 'God's creatures' inherit immortality, while 'the creatures of the Evil Spirit' are destroyed for ever.[22]

The later texts (mostly translated and compiled a good thousand years after Zarathustra's time) then go on to offer more detailed dates and information within this overall framework — though the various correlations are not always easy to establish with any precision. Certainly the general scheme revolves around the birth of Zarathustra himself, which seems to mark either the onset of the second earthly period of three thousand years or a point very near it. This would suggest that the original Golden Age was thought of as lying not so very far back in the past by whoever drew up the scheme in the first place. It would also, however, place both Zarathustra himself and our own era firmly within the period of balance between good and evil. The Zoroastrian religious and moral teachings thus constitute a body of advice for dealing with this tightrope situation. There is much stress on good works, on atonement for wrong-doing and on confession of sins. It is not ritual that delivers the individual soul from hell, but its record of daily acts. It is sufficient for ultimate salvation that one's good deeds should outweigh the bad.

Nevertheless the struggle is a hard one. And so the first of the great prophets — posthumously begotten by Zarathustra by semi-miraculous means when his seed, preserved in the waters of lake Frazdan (or Kansava) in Afghanistan, enters the body of a pure virgin of Zarathustra's line while she is bathing there — incarnates to bring about a revival of true religion. The text of the *Bahman Yasht* dates this event to 1600 years after Zarathustra, i.e. some time between AD 1193 and 1235 — datings which, coincidentally or otherwise, correspond almost exactly to those of St. Francis of Assisi.

But evil returns, and so a further prophet arises in similar manner to bring about a further reform in around AD 1341. Yet this initiative, too, gives way to a falling away from true religion. Admittedly, medicine makes great strides and diet improves during the thousand years which follow, but spiritual values are neglected, charity falls by the wayside and morality is widely flouted.

At this point the ancient tyrant Azhi Dahak arises from his ancient sleep, and gobbles up one third not only of humanity, but of all cattle, sheep and other creatures too. At the same time deceit and hypocrisy become ever more rife, and there is a widespread delight in the works of darkness.

The familiar story, in other words, of universal decline and decay.

And so it is time for the final prophet known as Saoshyans, or Astvat-ereta, to be born.

His birth duly takes place in AD 2341 (according to the *Bundahishn* chronology), and by the end of his fifty-seven-year mission he succeeds in purging all evil from human nature and in conquering disease, old age and even death itself. The earth's vegetation blooms anew, and all the dead are brought back to life, with each soul being rejoined to its newly-resurrected body. There follows a great Final Judgement and separation. A giant meteor falls upon the earth, turning metals into a vast river of molten liquid through which the righteous pass unscathed, while evil-doers are purged and purified, albeit at the cost of great agony. Even hell itself is redeemed by the process and reabsorbed into the wholeness of the cosmos.

And so the Universal Renewal occurs, and the world becomes immortal for all eternity. Thanks to the rivers of molten metal, the mountains are levelled, the valleys filled. As for humanity, those who died as adults assume a perpetual age of forty, while those who died as infants are for ever fifteen years of age — the traditional age of perfect physical maturity. There being no more death, there is no cause for procreation either, and so no further marriage or sexual activity. This apparent drawback notwithstanding, the never-ending age which begins with the year AD 2398 is truly the long-awaited Golden Age, in which all humanity becomes of one will and one voice, and is united in God's own religion, in accordance with the will of the Creator.

And this, it should be recalled, is precisely what the *Jewish* theologians had always said that the promised Kingdom of God would be like, too.

But then this was not the only point of contact between the two religions. In a number of ways their respective thinkers had come up with ideas and conclusions which were either identical or potentially complementary. Small wonder, then, if the Jews whom the tolerant Persian invaders sent back home from Babylon from 534 BC onwards — and who were to remain under strong Persian influence for the next two hundred years — were prone to confuse the two sets of teachings. Or that later Christians and Muslims should continue to do so to this day, so providing — however unintentionally — the conceptual groundwork for a whole variety of basic New Age assumptions.

6
As It is Written

Adam lay ybounden,
Bounden in a bond;
Four thousand winter
Thought he not too long.
And all was for an apple,
An apple that he took,
As clerkes finden
Written in their book.

Fifteenth-century carol

At the time of the great return from Babylon, it was reportedly to the priest Ezra and his company of scribes that the task fell of piecing together and setting down what was still known of the circumstances surrounding the Jewish exodus from Egypt of some nine hundred years earlier — and in particular the precise teachings of Moses. For the surviving Jews were determined this time to 'get it right' and ensure, through the strict observance of their new orthodoxy, that Yahweh their God would be held to their ancient bargain with him and so be persuaded at last to come up with the millenarian goods.

Significantly enough, the massive task was apparently undertaken not in Jerusalem, but in Babylon itself. The ancient book of the Jewish Law, or *Torah*, had been destroyed during the original Babylonian sack of Jerusalem. Its detailed teachings had long since been forgotten and their application abandoned. So, at least, the apocryphal second book of Esdras (the Greek form of 'Ezra') states, almost as though it were common knowledge. Yet now it was essential as never before to know what those teachings had been. And, of all people, Ezra was perhaps best placed to undertake the job of finding out.

For Ezra was not only a priest in his own right, but a professional scholar with direct access to the imperial archives. That much is quite clear from the texts themselves, since he repeatedly quotes imperial documents verbatim. Moreover, the contents of those documents in turn suggest that he held a position in the imperial court which involved special responsibility for Jewish affairs. Lest this should sound improbable, it should be remembered that the new Persian rulers were sensitive to the power vacuum which the relatively deserted Jewish homeland left on their south-western frontier, and therefore had good reason for seeing that it was both repopulated and strong. And since they valued the social cohesiveness which tends to result from a shared religious orthodoxy — *any* religious orthodoxy, for they were not particular — they were keen to see the re-establishment in that homeland of the native Jewish religion.

Which, of course, is where Ezra came in.

The task may have taken many years. Quite possibly working amid the imperial archives themselves, Ezra and his scribes assembled all the information they could find on the ancient Israelite dispensation. Since this was necessarily scanty, and based entirely on second-hand reports, they also had to rope in whatever word-of-mouth traditions were still preserved among their compatriots, none of whom was of course old enough actually to remember at first hand what life in Palestine had been like all those decades before. As is usually the way with oral traditions, what had been passed down no doubt took the form mainly of snippets of verse or semi-verse — always much more easily memorised than mere prose — and these were duly quoted verbatim in the eventual text, on the assumption (right or wrong) that they represented actual words from the former Torah. (Compare, for example, the traditional Jewish blessing quoted at Numbers 6:24-26, which the recent discovery of an inscribed amulet in an ancient Jerusalem cemetery has indeed shown to date from before the Babylonian exile.) This somewhat unpromising mixture of recorded hearsay and oral folklore Ezra and his collaborators then had to cement together in the light of their own priestly traditions, while elaborating them with whatever personal insights they themselves could bring to bear on the task.

Now it seems likely that Ezra and his colleagues were students of much more than just the Jewish teachings. King Ataxerxes I, in his original commission to Ezra of 458 BC to visit the now-repopulated Jerusalem and report back on what was going on there, addresses him as 'Ezra the priest and scribe learned in the law of the God of heaven'. This expression suggests that Ezra was also thoroughly versed in the teachings of Ataxerxes' own religion — for Ataxerxes is known to have been a keen Zoroastrian,[22] and by 'the God of heaven' almost certainly means the great Ahura Mazda himself. Indeed, the document quoted in chapter seven of Ezra's account actually seems to distinguish specifically between this 'God of heaven' and 'your God . . . the God of Israel'. At the same time it has to be said that Ataxerxes seems to refer to the Jewish God as though he were a particular *manifestation* of Ahura Mazda — rather as though he were one of the seven main 'divine principles' already referred to above — no less than Mithras and the other former gods who, as 'angels', came to receive the same divine accolade, as Zoroastrianism adjusted to the general religious climate of contemporary Persia.

From all of which it would tend to follow that even the supplementary insights of Ezra and his helpers were liable to be coloured by the Zoroastrian teachings.

The result was almost inevitable. When Ezra and his party eventually turned up in Jerusalem bearing official gifts of gold and silver for the newly-rebuilt Temple, they found a populace who had already devoted over seventy-five years of poverty and sheer hard grind to the business of survival and reconstruction — and who had had little if any time in the course of it for religious thought or practice. Summoned to hear Ezra read out the Law of Moses from the now-completed documents which he had also brought along (a recital which apparently took all of seven days), they were continually both moved and amazed at what they heard. Not merely because three more generations had had ample chance to forget anything they had ever known about the original Torah, but presumably also because much of the material had never been part of the historical Mosaic dispensation in the first place. Indeed, to the hardy pioneers even much of the new, Zoroastrian-influenced lore must have been equally unfamiliar, since they — or rather their parents and grandparents — had spent, at most, a couple of years or so under the new Persian regime in Babylon before beginning their long homeward trek to Jerusalem. Again and again, consequently, the text of the book of Nehemiah records that 'they found written in the law that Yahweh had given commandment through Moses that . . .' or that 'it was found to be laid down that . . .', and that the settlers promptly set about fulfilling whatever ritual demand was involved with all the enthusiasm reserved for some new revelation.

Which indeed, for the most part, it was.

Small wonder, then, that Ezra should subsequently have been credited (a tradition reflected in the second book of Esdras) with having recomposed the entire Torah (and much else besides) under divine inspiration, very much after the manner of Moses himself.

The implied comparison was not an idle one. Ezra, like his illus-

trious predecessor, was dedicated above all to founding a resplendent new dispensation for his people and, through them, for the
world as a whole. His mission was truly millenarian. His overriding concern was quite literally to help establish the New Jerusalem
on earth.

That image and objective was to be taken up again and again by
later generations of Jewish seers and prophets. And we still use it
to this day as a prime code for the great New Age initiative.

* * *

Looking back at the principal Zoroastrian teachings, it is now relatively easy, with hindsight, to trace their transition into Judaism
and their superimposition upon the former traditions which are
reflected in the writings of the early biblical prophets. The notion
of sacred fire, for example, had long been present in those traditions. Not only did Yahweh send fire down from heaven upon
those who disobeyed his will — notably in the case of the execrat-
ed Sodom and Gomorrah — but he had also led the tribes during
their long exodus by means of a pillar of cloud by day and a pillar
of fire by night. On Horeb, indeed, he had actually spoken to
Moses out of the mountain's fire and smoke, as the texts endlessly
recall. Sacrificial fire and the holocaust, or burnt offering, had also
long been a part of tribal tradition, as it still is to this day among
primitive societies the world over.

But now a whole new emphasis seems to have been placed on
the concept of fire. At Leviticus 6:13 Yahweh instructs Moses that
'Fire shall always be kept burning on the altar; it shall not go out'
— a direct reflection, it seems, of the Zoroastrian tradition, and
one which can hardly have applied during the wanderings of the
original exodus, since there was then, of course, no permanent
altar for the eternal fire to burn on.

Indeed, with the book of Deuteronomy such startling statements begin to appear as 'Yahweh your God is a devouring fire'
— a concept so inherently Zoroastrian as to confirm the now
widely-held view that this last book of the Mosaic canon is almost
entirely Ezra's own copyright. (Certainly it can hardly be that of
Moses, since at the end the text actually describes the latter's
death and records that 'to this day nobody knows his burial-
place'.)

A further requirement laid down in Exodus 25 is that Moses
shall construct a *menorah*, or seven-branched candlestick, for use
in the sacred ritual. It is quite clear from the text that this is to be

seen as a single, central candlestick with six subsidiary branches
— since specific directions are given for the central member to be
decorated with *four* 'cups shaped like almond blossoms', whereas
the other six merit only three apiece. If the Divinity itself, in true
Zoroastrian fashion, is henceforth to be associated with fire, then,
the *menorah* inevitably begs to be associated with Zarathustra's
seven archangels, the central one of which — i.e. the holy spirit,
Spenta Mainyu — has special prominence as the divine *alter ego*
itself. And certainly we know that the doctrine of the seven
archangels survived in Hebrew tradition, since it was to resurface
in the secret teachings of the Essenes of some four centuries later,
as reflected in the fragment of the *Angelic Liturgy* discovered
among the Dead Sea scrolls.[81]

Yet what of the Divinity itself? If there are suggestions in the
texts edited or composed by Ezra that Zoroastrian thought was
now exerting considerable influence upon contemporary Jewish
conceptions of Yahweh, notably in a pronounced tendency to symbolise the godhead by means of fire, just how far did that influence go?

We have already noted, for example, the well-known Hebrew
taboo on speaking the name of Yahweh aloud. Yet we have no
clear idea of how far back this custom goes. It seems distinctly
possible, however, that it actually dates from the time of Ezra's
reforms. Ever since that time, certainly, reverent Jewish tradition
has insisted, even where the divine tetragrammaton YHWH
appears in the biblical text, on reading it as <u>Adonai</u>, 'Lord'. Yet this
is precisely the meaning of the Persian word *Ahura*, too. Could it
be, then, that the stern taboo reflects not so much a sense of awe at
naming the divinity, as a determination on the part of Ezra and his
scribes to amalgamate the Hebrew and Persian godheads, much as
his own reports of Ataxerxes' decrees appear to do? Sacrilegious
the idea may seem in the light of later Hebrew religious purism,
yet it now appears that many of the ideas of which later Jewish
fundamentalists (and notably the Essenes themselves) were to be
so jealous were in fact of distinctly hybrid origin. Among them, as
we shall see, were not only the familiar Zoroastrian fire-symbolism, but the notion of the eternal war between Light and Darkness
and much of the expectation surrounding the messianic initiative
— not to mention the quintessentially 'Jewish' idea of the sabbath
itself, already referred to above.

In Ezra's day, however, it was not so much purism that was
lacking as a sense of, or commitment to, any recognisable form of
Jewish religion whatsoever. Thus, it was by no means too far

beyond the contemporary pale to suggest that, if Ahura Mazda was the lord of the universe, and Yahweh the god of creation — and if, for that matter, both could be referred to by any number of different names, as both sets of scriptures confirmed — then both were in reality one and the same, especially since they clearly had so many attributes in common.

And if that were the case, then there was no reason why the Persian tradition should not be allowed to amplify and generally shed light on the traditional Hebrew teachings — especially since, for good or ill, much of it had already become a well-loved part of Jewish folklore, at least among those exiles who had yet to return from Babylon.

Such, then, might have been the conscious argument. Consciously or unconsciously, however, it is quite clear that a considerable cross-fertilisation did take place. And not merely in the matter of fire-symbolism and archangelic speculation.

* * *

The Zoroastrian view of the human condition, as we have seen, was that humanity was in the midst of a cosmic struggle between the forces of Light and Darkness. That struggle had been going on for hundreds, if not thousands, of years, and its outcome was destined to be decided by the actions of the various predicted saviours — manifestations of an elevated, quasi-messianic soul which itself had been in existence almost since the very beginning of time. Humanity's role was thus to cooperate in this mighty venture. Each human soul, indeed, was intimately wrapped up in the whole enterprise, having itself existed from long before birth. While incarnate, its task was to cooperate with the divine powers and to resist the efforts of the Evil One. Upon its success or otherwise in this venture its fate at death would then depend. A life devoted primarily to evil would inevitably lead to a season of agony in hell, but a life of righteousness would be rewarded with eternal bliss in the light of the divine presence. As for the world as a whole, this would remain in precarious moral and ethical balance until the advent of the expected Saoshyans and the final transformation of the universe, when a new Kingdom on earth would begin, inhabited by all the righteous dead for ever and ever.

Nearly all these ideas are, of course, almost startlingly familiar to modern Jews, Christians and Muslims alike. A good many of them — with the virtually sole exception of the notion of *post mortem* punishment or reward — even figure largely in the typical 'New Age' outlook, no doubt because so many New Agers are themselves lapsed members of one or the other of the three traditional religions in question.

Meanwhile, the very similarity of ideas involved is more than sufficient evidence to suggest what actually occurred back in Babylonian times.

To the Jews of the exile, after all, the transcendent Persian vision of human destiny must have presented almost irresistible attractions. Not only did the notion of the expected Saoshyans fit in with the existing Jewish tradition of the returning Davidic king, or Messiah, but the promise of a final Millennium of everlasting bliss likewise married in with traditional expectation, save only in the respect that the Jewish version of the idea had strong nationalistic overtones that were apparently lacking in the Zoroastrian model.

But this left a good many ideas that were foreign to Israelite tradition. Thus far, at least, there had been little or no suggestion in the Hebrew scriptures that the universe was engaged in a life-or-death struggle between the forces of Light and Darkness, let alone poised in a state of precarious balance between the two. And yet the idea could still be squared with the scriptures as they stood. The very first act of God in Genesis (even if in this case attributed to him in his persona of *Elohim* rather than of Yahweh) had, after all, been to create light out of darkness, and it was therefore not unreasonable to suppose that he was on the side of the former and opposed to the latter. Possibly it was in response to this conclusion that the idea of a kind of 'Cosmic Adversary' was soon to appear in Judaism — an Adversary who duly progressed, much as in Zoroastrianism, from a kind of 'Devil's advocate' or examiner merely serving the divine educational plan (as, for example, in the book of Job) to Yahweh's mortal enemy, the Lord of Darkness himself. From which viewpoint, of course, it was but a short step to seeing the universe as fundamentally divided down the middle — a state of dynamic, if finely balanced, civil war very much after the Zoroastrian model. This, it has to be said, fitted in quite satisfactorily with the observation (already referred to above) that the nation seemed to be continually subject to an extraordinary mixture of good and bad events which were difficult to explain other than in terms of Yahweh's exercise of a particularly stern form of 'parental' training.

The matter of the pre-existing soul, however, was potentially a more difficult nut to crack, as was the concomitant idea of its immortality in the divine presence. That each human being *had* a soul had never been in dispute, but this entity was more in the nature of an animating spirit (*nephesh*) than of an immortal double after the manner of the Egyptian *ka*. When the body died, in other words, the soul died also — or, rather, it was the demise of the soul that inevitably produced the death of the body.

To put it another way, death was simply the result of the withdrawal of life.

As a result, all that could be looked forward to was the subterranean mouldering and corruption which is the eventual lot of all flesh — an existence, if existence it is, that could only be described by the Hebrew word *sheol*, just as it also was by the Greek word *Hades*, whose English equivalent is, of course, the uncompromising term 'Hell'.

The Zoroastrian idea that an alternative and glorious afterlife was the inalienable right of those who had, on balance, done the divine will during life was a considerable revelation, but a very welcome one for all that. For now there was cause for individual hope, where previously there had been next to none. And this hope was immeasurably increased by the new prospect that Zoroastrianism also offered — namely the assurance that even the righteous *dead* would somehow be magically restored to life to enjoy the promised ultimate era of divine bliss when it finally dawned on earth. All of a sudden a new spirit of optimism was possible, and one which was above all needed at a time when the nation's whole life and culture were going to have to be laboriously rebuilt. Not only was the rather pious hope of a final Millennium transformed into a glorious and inevitable certainty, but the whole idea now acquired a relevance that was not merely collective and national but truly personal in character.

And, as even the most collectivist of modern socialist leaderships eventually discover, it is often the introduction of such purely private and personal incentive schemes that alone seems capable of securing maximum effort from the populace at large.

Possibly Ezra and his scribes were canny enough to realise this. Either way, there can be no doubt that this whole complex of ideas now started to play an increasingly important role in the life of the Jewish nation. The writings of the later prophets were to give voice to them again and again, duly amplified and elaborated with the aid of the various subsidiary ideas with which they were further linked by the Zoroastrians.

Thus, real atonement started to receive a new stress; the importance of actual deeds started to be emphasised at the expense of mere ritual; and, perhaps above all, the details of the expected messianic initiative and its millennial aftermath started to be fleshed out in ways largely in accord with the Zoroastrian view.

Already an early text in the book of Isaiah (7:14) begged to be interpreted in terms of the birth of the coming saviour from the womb of a young girl who had previously been a pure virgin. The original Hebrew, though, is entirely innocent of the Zoroastrian idea that she would be magically inseminated with the Prophet's seed while bathing in a mountain-lake, and even more innocent of the extraordinary suggestion — retrospectively adduced, even today, by a surprising number of otherwise perfectly level-headed Christians — that she would remain a pure virgin in the process.

The newly-revealed text of Deuteronomy itself, meanwhile, reported Moses as promising that Yahweh would send his people 'a prophet like myself'. In the light of our exegesis thus far, this text is particularly revealing. For Moses, like Zarathustra, had reportedly been threatened at birth by murderous enemies, and had similarly received his divine insights during a spell on a sacred mountain. Consequently a measure of popular confusion between the two was almost inevitable, to the point where it became difficult to dispute the assumption that the two must have been one and the same. And certainly, if Zarathustra had indeed been a true prophet of God, then there was no way which the Jews' own Moses could be credited with any less power of foresight. If, then, Zarathustra was destined to reappear as the future Saoshyans, it was inevitable that either Moses, or one uncommonly like him, must similarly reappear to fulfil the synonymous role of Jewish Saviour.

Whence, presumably, the relevant verse in Deuteronomy.

Yet there was also the ancient Israelite expectation of the Davidic succession to satisfy. Somehow the two traditions had to be persuaded to coalesce. The future Messiah had to be both a prophet of the stamp of Moses and another King David. Accordingly the post-exilic prophets — notably Zechariah, Malachi, Joel and the later prophets of the Isaiah school — set to work to fill in the details of this general expectation.

The groundwork had, of course, already been done by earlier figures such as Jeremiah and the original Isaiah in pre-exilic times. Ezekiel and Micah, too, had done much to flesh out the millenarian vision. Micah, in particular, had specified that the Messiah's birth must take place in David's own city of Bethlehem. But then it needed remarkably little prophetic insight to make such deductions. Thus, the very details of David's own life led to the further conclusion (though one not specifically expressed in the scriptures themselves) that the Messiah, like both David and — for that matter — Zarathustra before him, must come into his own at the almost ritual age of thirty.[41] Then would follow a glorious Golden Age whose nature all the later prophets were to celebrate with great gusto, much as their predecessors had done.

Yet not before the dire warnings newly introduced from the Zarathustrian canon, with its by-now familiar story of universal decline and renewal, had been fulfilled. Religion would be neglected, morals fall into decay. A time of great distress would follow. The stars would fall from heaven, the earth be rent by earthquakes and laid waste by pestilence and famine. Only then would the promised Saviour, finally victorious over his deadly enemies, and having at last reduced the whole of the world to submission in the name of Yahweh, appear on the sacred Mount Zion in Jerusalem to set up his ultimate and everlasting Kingdom. During it disease, hunger and death would finally be abolished, the deserts would bloom, the mountains be levelled, the valleys filled, and the nation's dead would be physically resurrected — the righteous to inherit the new and blissful (if sexless) Kingdom of peace, justice and plenty, and the evil-doers to be consigned unceremoniously to the fires and torments of hell. Even the long-lost Jewish exiles would be re-assembled from the world's four corners to be restored to their rightful inheritance. And thereafter the will of Yahweh would be done on earth for ever and ever, thanks to the priestly agency of the Jewish nation itself.[41]

The New Age, in other words, would be both a new beginning and an ultimate end, totally immune to the ever-recurring cycles of decay and corruption predicated by other religions such as Hinduism and Buddhism.

(Much of the flavour of this expectation still remains even in today's New Age conception of things to come. The imminent time of degeneration and distress is half-expected, though generally played down in the name of 'positive thinking', or simply identified with the current world crisis. The subsequent inception of the age of peace, justice and plenty is a basic article of faith, though unaccompanied these days by any overtones of military violence or coercion, let alone ideas of retribution for evil-doers. And even the idea of the redemptive elite has its modern counterpart in the the typically New Age concept of groups of enlightened 'world servers' either led or inspired by claimed initiates.)

In all this the resemblance between the newly-developed body of Jewish doctrine and the Zoroastrian scheme of things was, of course, almost total, except in respect of the Jewish version's nationalistic overtones — understandable though these are in view of the native Davidic tradition. And the fact that all the various ideas involved duly appeared in the writings of the later Jewish prophets, for the most part *without* being recorded in Ezra's canon of five official sacred books, makes it clear that the Zoroastrian teachings were so firmly embedded in the Jewish psyche by the time the final exiles returned from Babylon as to be capable of surviving via oral transmission for several centuries to come. Hence, no doubt, the tradition recorded in the second book of Esdras that Ezra, under divine inspiration, composed — or rather re-composed — not merely the familiar five-book Law, or Torah, but a further eighty-nine books, *seventy of which Yahweh ordered him to keep secret, being designed for the eyes of the wise only*. Hence, too, the parallel tradition that Moses, on Sinai, had been given a whole body of teachings, of which the Torah was merely, so to speak, the outer husk, while its real doctrinal core was reserved strictly for secret oral transmission to those who needed to know. (It is this tradition that lies at the basis of what today is known as Kabbalism or Qabalism — the study of the hidden, underlying meaning of the Old Testament — which has been popular among Western esotericists ever since the Middle Ages, and continues to exert its intriguing appeal within certain sections of the modern New Age movement.)

No doubt both reports are attempted explanations of the same fact — namely that there remained in oral circulation after the return from exile a great deal of post-Zarathustrian teaching which found no place in the original Torah as recomposed by Ezra, but which continued to provide grist to the prophets' mill for centuries to come.

Indeed, as we shall see, that tradition continued to survive undiminished into even later times, when the Jewish teachings themselves were to be turned topsy-turvy by a new religious movement which, thanks partly to intention and partly to mischance, was actually the direct result of the combined Golden Age expectations of Zoroastrianism and Judaism.

Or rather, of the by-now hardly unexpected fact that the whole thrust of that expectation was, in the event, to be most cruelly dashed.

7
As Soon As May Be

Nearer and nearer draws the time, the time that shall surely be,
When the earth shall be filled with the glory of God as the waters
cover the sea.
A.C. Ainger: Hymn

The death of Alexander the Great in 323 BC finally brought to an end the period of benign domination of Palestine inaugurated by the Persian Empire — a paternalistic regime which he himself had been only too happy to continue. During this time, the returned Jewish settlers had, by and large, been far too busy eking out a precarious physical existence to devote over-much attention to the somewhat rarefied ritual demands of their newly-reconstituted religion. Not only did the poor soil of their long-neglected hill-country demand almost unremitting toil from morning until night, but this work had to be carried out under constant threat from jealous interlopers from other tribes who had long since come to consider the vacated area as their own domain.

True, hopes had sometimes arisen — especially during the heady pioneering days — that the promised saviour might either already have arrived or be in the immediate offing. The prophets Haggai and Zechariah both seem to have been convinced, for example, that Zerubbabel, their first provincial governor, might fulfil this role, assisted by Joshua, his High Priest. But it was not to be. Life remained hard and unforgiving, and it was quite clear to everybody that the promised Millennium was likely to be a long time coming.

Very naturally, then, the whole idea started to fade into the background. The expectation of the Messiah increasingly took on the quality of a piece of wishful thinking, the notion of the Golden Age that of a priestly mirage. And with the consequent virtual disappearance of its chief incentive-scheme, the Hebrew religion itself started to sink into relative decay and disregard, except — naturally enough — among the privileged circles of the ruling priesthood, their ritual attendants and the inevitable official bureaucracy.

With Alexander's unexpectedly early death, however, the

whole religious and cultural climate started, imperceptibly at first, to change. Since he had made no clear provision for a successor, his leading generals each grabbed whatever slice of his vast empire they could most easily lay hands on. Egypt was fortunate enough to acquire the enlightened Ptolemy as its overlord, and for over a century his writ and that of his successors prevailed over Palestine as well. During this period the Jewish religion continued to be encouraged, especially among the by-now exclusively Greek-speaking Jews of Alexandria, for whom a Greek version of their native Torah was even prepared by royal command. Indeed, it was this celebrated document, known as the *Septuagint* after the seventy scholars who are supposed to have prepared it, which was at last to make known the Jewish scriptures and the teachings they enshrined throughout the then civilised world, however little popular respect they were currently being accorded in their native land.

In 195 BC, however, Ptolemy V was defeated at the sources of the Jordan by a descendant of the Greek general Seleucus (the commander of Alexander's Elephant Corps) to whose lot Syria had originally fallen. Syria, in consequence, now took over the running of Palestine. And from this point onwards the Greek influence, which had so far presented itself as an invaluable friend of Judaism, started to change into an intolerable imposition.

Soon even the ruling Jewish priesthood in Jerusalem was falling prey to the seductive lures of Greek culture. Not only did the High Priests themselves start to take Greek names, but one of them went so far as to order the construction of a Greek sports-stadium — with all the compulsory athletic nudity which that involved — in full view of the sacred Temple. As a result, embarrassed would-be Jewish participants started to undergo operations to reverse the ritual circumcision which had long since become the mark of their identity as Jews subject to the terms of the ancient Mosaic Covenant. Yet on that Covenant the very destiny of the nation was held to depend. The *Hasidim*, or Pious — for there were, as ever, a few devoted souls who still remained true to their religion — were consequently enraged almost beyond measure.

As if that were not enough, the general unrest and even civil disorder resulting from the power-struggles of the increasingly corrupt ruling priesthood soon led to a major social disaster. For the notorious Seleucid king Antiochus IV (surnamed Epiphanes), on his way back from a marauding expedition against Ptolemaic Egypt in 167 BC, somehow got the impression that a widespread revolt was in progress and, following a general bloodbath, issued a decree finally abolishing the Jewish religion for good. At the same time he ordered that the Temple (whose treasures the current High Priest had already ransacked for his own personal gain) was to be turned over to the worship of Olympian Zeus.

To the Pious, this was of course the last straw. For a start it represented the most blatant form of sacrilege. True, Zeus, like both Yahweh and Ahura Mazda, was essentially a sky-god, but the brutal manner of the imposition of his cult and the abolition of the native religion meant that no kind of assimilation was possible, as it had once been under the more tolerant Persian dispensation. The Greek determination to have Zeus worshipped in the form of a man-made statue made such an assimilation even less likely.

But a more important barrier to any possible reconciliation was the fact that, by now, the Jews had a firmly-established body of scriptures which, for all they knew, went back all the way to Moses and so represented the inviolable and eternal decrees of Yahweh himself.

There was thus only one possible outcome. While some devout souls sensed in current events the shadow of the threatened Last Times and, obedient to what the scriptures laid down, duly fled to the desert — where they were promptly massacred because, still obedient to the scriptures, they refused to fight on the Sabbath — others took matters firmly into their own hands and, under the magnificent guerrilla-leadership of Judas Maccabeus, staged a bloody and remarkably successful national revolt against the whole Seleucid regime. By 164 BC the Temple had been cleansed and rededicated. By 142 BC, despite violent encounters involving the Seleucids' use of their celebrated elephants, Israel was free and independent, and in control of an area almost as large as before the Babylonian exile.

Perhaps inevitably, however, the intervening years had seen success go to the heads of the Maccabean leadership. In 152 BC, for example, the Seleucid usurper Alexander Balas had offered the High Priesthood to Jonathan Maccabeus, brother and successor of Judas. The latter had accepted, even though he knew perfectly well that the office properly belonged only to a direct descendant of Zadok, High Priest in Solomon's time — which he manifestly was not.

To the Pious it was clear as a result that things were once more starting to go wrong. Once again fundamental aspects of their religion were being flouted — even though this time at the behest not so much of Greek culture and idolatry as of sheer greed and power-seeking. And as a result the nation's future was once more in peril, the messianic dream and the ancient promise of a once and future Golden Age fatally betrayed.

Once again, therefore, there was a strong reaction among the Devout — and one which was, if possible, even more puritan in nature than before. Moreover, it was given considerable extra impetus by a remarkable document which — as it now seems — had first come to light only a few years before.

This document was the book of Daniel.

* * *

Though it purports to date from the time of the Babylonian captivity, modern scholarship has been largely forced to the conclusion that the book of Daniel was in fact written in about 165 BC, only a couple of years after Antiochus IV's sacrilegious atrocities.[41] About the real Daniel's power of prophecy at the time of the exile, consequently, it says next to nothing. But about the temper of the later times and the contemporary state of messianic and millenarian expectation it says a great deal.

For, if nothing else, it tells us that Antiochus's act, and the ensuing state of virtual national emergency, had the effect of revivifying and galvanising into renewed action the whole Jewish religious tradition. As the text of Daniel makes quite clear, the desecration of the Temple was to be seen as the final 'abomination of desol-ation' signalling the onset of the long-expected Last Times — the period of cataclysmic upheaval immediately preceding the appearance of the messianic Saviour and the inauguration of the final Golden Age. The Seleucid oppressors, in other words, were to be seen as the personal representatives of the Powers of Darkness, and must be resisted with all the fury and determination appropriate to the enormous and ultimate task of saving the universe itself.

Much the same way of interpreting events can be observed among today's New Age groups, many of whom are similarly convinced that the dire circumstances of the modern world — with its nuclear threat, its famines, its resource shortages, its pollution problems and population pressures — are merely the darkest night immediately preceding the dawn of the long-awaited Millennium.

Naturally enough, in ancient Palestine the message fell on ears just as receptive as those of our own time. Like the modern New Age initiative, it had the effect of drawing together a great many different strands of thought and expectation. At the same time, thanks to its starkly political context, it helped to transform what had previously been little more than a pious religious hope into a national crusade backed by a conviction of absolute rightness — always a sure winner where public support is concerned, as regimes as diverse as the Nazi and the Islamic fundamentalist have more than adequately demonstrated in our own century.

And, like all such crusades, it produced its own brand of fanatic prepared to make almost any sacrifice in the service of the sacred cause.

On the purely physical side, as we have already seen, that fanaticism proved itself capable of almost incredible military achievements under the leadership of Judas Maccabeus. And when the fruits of those achievements started to turn sour under his brother and successor, it began to produce other achievements of a very different kind.

For when Jonathan was unwise enough to accept the High Priesthood to which he was not entitled, the reaction of the *Hasidim* was to regard as finally confirmed the conclusion to which they had already been inclined for some time — namely that military force alone was not the answer, unless and until it was exercised in the support of a truly enlightened religious dispensation. In support of this view they could quote the text at Zechariah 4:6 which read: 'Neither by force of arms nor by brute strength, but by my spirit! says the LORD of Hosts.' There had, in other words, to be a period of rethinking, of careful consultation of the scriptures, of meditation on the true will of Yahweh, of a total national rededication to the Mosaic Covenant.

And it was out of this conviction that a powerful religious revival now set in, spearheaded by three relatively small groups of exceptionally motivated Jews, ranging from mere upholders of religious convention to what we should no doubt regard today as out-and-out bigots.

The first of these groups, described in contemporary documents as the Sadducees, represented what might be termed the religious and priestly faction of the Maccabean establishment. Linked as they were to the party of power and the ruling High Priesthood, they tended to be decidedly conservative and right-wing, and so did not long preserve the revolutionary ardour of their early days. As a result, they soon came to adopt a fairly rigid and unadventurous stance, preferring the social and ritual certainties of the original Law, or Torah, to the much more challenging insights of the later collection of books known as the Prophets, let alone the third group of scrolls (including that of Daniel) which were only much later to be accepted into the official canon under the title of the Writings.

The Sadducees, consequently, quickly ruled themselves out as true religious revolutionaries in the eyes of the two other groups who appeared at about the same time — i.e. during the years leading up to 150 BC. Of these, the best known are the Pharisees, whose direct doctrinal descendants most Western adherents of Judaism still are to this day. Unlike the Sadducees, the Pharisees were a lay group who presented themselves as the party of the people. They were well known for their devotion to charity and good works, and were particularly skilled in interpreting all sections of the scriptures in the light of contemporary circumstances. The celebrated gospel caricatures of them notwithstanding, they were widely respected in contemporary Palestine, and to the extent that they participated in such national institutions as the Sanhedrin, or Jewish Council, they came to be regarded as pillars of Jewish society.

But this fact alone was quite sufficient to damn them in the eyes of the third main group of religious revolutionaries who are loosely referred to today as the Essenes ('Holy Ones' or 'Saints').

For the Essenes, led by a particularly purist cell of priests, quickly came to the conclusion that contemporary society was altogether too corrupt to permit of any association with it at all. Consequently most of them withdrew to tented camps which originally lay in the desert, well outside the towns and cities, while the most fanatical of them went so far as to condemn themselves to voluntary exile abroad — somewhere in the north, in what they termed 'the Land of Damascus'. Here they submitted themselves to a spartan and severely penitential way of life by way of making communal atonement for their nation's sin and corruption, and devoted themselves to prayer and meditation on the scriptures in order to discover, if possible, the will of Yahweh for the current times. Thus, not only did they feel able to see themselves as a 'faithful remnant' of Israel, alone in preserving the terms of the original Mosaic Covenant and so, at the same time, both the messianic hope and the promise of national and cosmic salvation. They also saw themselves, by the same token, as the potential inaugurators of the *New* Covenant promised by the prophet Jeremiah at 31:31-4, under the terms of which humanity would be inspired to carry out the will of Yahweh as it were instinctively, rather than merely on command.

Which, by definition, would mean that the Kingdom of Heaven would once again be spread abroad upon the earth.

True, the library of documents that they left behind them — the so-called Dead Sea Scrolls[58,81] — reveal the Essenes of Qumran, at very least, to have been almost obsessively spartan and secretive, and quite extraordinarily prone to doctrinal and hierarchical rigidity — not to say sheer narrow-mindedness and religious bigotry. In this they may or may not have been typical of the movement as a whole. But contemporary historians recount that its members generally were also widely respected in their day for their personal sanctity, their religious devotion, their fortitude in adversity and their unfailing kindness to those in trouble.[58] With their total devotion to the cause of the coming Kingdom, they could thus in some ways be seen as the contemporary equivalent of the more committed of today's New Agers.

For the Essenes, certainly, there was to be no beating about the bush. Having voluntarily dedicated themselves to the New Covenant by adopting a severe and special code of moral and religious observance drawn up by their leader — the revered and anonymous 'Teacher of Righteousness'[41,71,80,81] — the exiled Essenes now regarded themselves, *ipso facto*, as a community of that same New Covenant.

Now the term 'New Covenant', it is well known, can be equally well translated by the term 'New Testament'. Yet it was as 'Communities of the New Testament' that the earliest groups of *Christians* similarly regarded themselves. Whence, of course, the application of the term to Part Two of the familiar Christian Bible.

Mere similarity of terminology is, of course, no proof of actual relationship, let alone of identity. Yet the evidence suggests very strongly that, in this case, the similarity was no accident. The Essenes, in fact, seem to have been intimately involved in the very events surrounding the subsequent Jesus-initiative and the founding of Christianity.[41] And that involvement sprang directly out of an extraordinary approach to the biblical prophecies and their fulfilment, strongly informed by a profound familiarity with the still-surviving Zoroastrian traditions.

* * *

The Essenes, it is perfectly clear from the evidence of the Dead Sea Scrolls,[81] were totally convinced that, by virtue of their piety and intense meditational practices, they held the key to interpreting for their own age the true meaning of the biblical prophecies relating to the Last Times, the coming of the Messiah and the advent of the millennial age. Indeed, they were as famed throughout contemporary Palestine for their predictive skills as they were for their parallel skills as herbalists and healers.

In an earlier book entitled *The Armageddon Script*[41] I set out the almost inescapable evidence for the view that the sect's attitude to prophecy was not merely predictive, but positively creative in character. Bible-based prophecy, in other words, was to them a perfectly legitimate tool for deliberately shaping the future by act of human will, provided only that that will was — as they were convinced it was — truly aligned to the will of Yahweh.

And so it was possible for them (so, at least, they believed) to draw up a definitive prophetic blueprint for their times, under the terms of which the contemporary faithful (and the Essenes were, of course, alone — in their own eyes, at least — in being truly faithful to the Yahwic Covenant) would take it upon themselves to act as Yahweh's physical agents, deliberately bringing to pass those prophecies upon whose fulfilment the inauguration of the promised Kingdom was shown by scripture to depend. Clearly such an initiative was in accordance with the divine will, since the doing of that will was the very state of affairs which *defined* the promised Kingdom.

Accordingly, they boldly embarked upon their extraordinary prophetic initiative. Having ransacked the scriptures for possible references to what had to befall, their founding leader — the 'True Teacher' or 'Teacher of Righteousness' — evidently laid down in writing precisely what had to be done by the sect in the form of a sequence of actions geared to such portentous, if random, external events as earthquakes, acts of official sacrilege and political persecutions. The result was the Essene *Hagu*, or Book of Meditation.

Among those actions — so, at least, the evidence now makes it difficult to avoid concluding — was *the deliberate breeding and preparation of the future Messiah himself*. And not merely that, but the elaboration for him of a kind of life-script laying down exactly what actions he must perform in order to carry out the messianic function as defined by scripture, and so to bring about a state of affairs whereby — all the relevant prophecies having been duly fulfilled — Yahweh would have no option but to inaugurate his own promised Kingdom on earth.

To Christians who may find such ideas offensive or even blasphemous I can but recommend that they examine for themselves the available evidence[41,81] — and by this I mean *all* the evidence, and not merely the highly selective evidence presented, very understandably, by exclusively Christian early writers who, as we shall see, had their own reasons for wishing to put a particular gloss on the events surrounding the life and death of Jesus the Nazarene.

For the fact is that the Jewish expectation was never other than that the Messiah would be born an ordinary mortal — and what more natural than for the Essenes to assume that he must be born from among their own sect, which alone, in their own eyes, stood righteous in the sight of God? The idea of twisting the divine arm, similarly, is a perfectly familiar feature of Judaism — and quite understandably so, since it was clearly understood all along that Israel had entered into a binding Covenant, or bargain, with Yahweh on Mount Horeb. Every bargain, it goes without saying, has two sides. If, therefore, Israel (as represented by the Essenic 'faithful remnant') now managed to fulfil its side of the bargain, then surely it had every right to expect and demand that Yahweh should do the same?

There seems to be little alternative, in fact, but to conclude (however reluctantly) that Jesus, far from being the well-meaning victim of fate which he is so often depicted as having been, actually planned the events of his ministry — *including his own subsequent execution* — with great care and skill, according to the Essenes' comprehensive blueprint. Again and again the gospel-accounts have him explaining the necessity for his acts in terms of what *must* be done in order that what was written of the Messiah might be fulfilled — and never more insistently than in connection with his clearly suicidal Passover-mission to Jerusalem. And in doing so he took full account of the concepts and beliefs which the Essenes had derived not merely from the scriptural texts, but also — however unbeknown to themselves — from contemporary Judaism's Zoroastrian antecedents.

Thus, the Essenes were passionately wedded to the ancient Zoroastrian concept of the cosmic war between Light and Darkness. Their texts refer to the idea repeatedly.[81] Not merely did they refer to themselves as 'Sons of Light', and to their enemies as 'Sons of Darkness', but they also understood these ideas in precisely the same terms as the Zoroastrians. In the words of their *Community Rule*, referring to Yahweh,

He has created man to govern the world, and has appointed for him two spirits in which to walk until the time of His visitation: the spirits of truth and falsehood . . . The nature of all the children of men is ruled by these (two spirits), and during their life all the hosts of men have a portion in their divisions and walk in (both) their ways. And the whole reward for their deeds shall be, for everlasting ages, according to whether each man's portion in their two divisions is great or small. For God has established the spirits in equal measure until the final age . . . But in the mysteries of His understanding, and in His glorious wisdom, God has ordained an end for falsehood, and at the time of the visitation He will destroy it for ever.[81]

The 'visitation' in question refers, of course, to the final, divine intervention at the end of the age, and the inauguration of the long-awaited Kingdom of God.

The Essenes' use of the term 'light' itself, meanwhile, shows further similarities to Zoroastrian practice. The very fact that they referred to themselves as 'Sons of Light' naturally suggests that they saw themselves as in some sense having that Light for a father — which might suggest either that they saw Yahweh himself as consisting of pure Light, or that they saw Light as his chief symbol and manifestation on earth. This would accord almost totally with the Zoroastrian understanding of their own Lord of Light, Ahura Mazda. It seems, indeed, to have been part of the Essene doctrine that the primeval *Adam Kadmon*, or Man-Thought-in-the-Mind-of-God, was a being of cosmic proportions composed entirely of invisible Light — a Light out of which the whole of the physical universe was subsequently created. Both the later Philo of Alexandria and the author of St. John's gospel are clearly deeply indebted to this idea, the latter in respect of his now-celebrated opening hymn to the *Logos* or Word.[70] (No less so, did they but know it, are many of today's New Agers, who constantly invoke, and see themselves as irradiated by, that same Light.) And the coming Messiah was of course himself expected to be an incarnation of the identical heavenly Light, Logos or Word.

Meanwhile the Zoroastrians had long ago come to see their co-opted sun-god Mithras as the visible manifestation of the divine Ahura Mazda — an entirely understandable attitude in view of the fact that the sun was patently the most resplendent of all sources of terrestrial light. It comes as little surprise, therefore, to discover that the Essenes attached a strong messianic symbolism to the sun, and particularly to its rising. In a well-known passage from his *Jewish War* the Jewish general and historian Josephus, who had himself studied under the Essenes, writes:

> *Before the sun rises they speak not a word about everyday matters, but offer up certain prayers received from their forefathers as though in supplication for its rising.*

That this symbolism was nothing new is evidenced by the Jewish prophet Malachi, who had written not long after the return from Babylon itself:

But for you who fear my name, the sun of righteousness shall rise with healing in his wings, and you shall break loose like calves from the stall.

Moreover, this symbolism was to continue into Christian times, as the author of St. Luke's gospel reveals in his report of the aged priest Zechariah's ecstatic prophecy concerning his son John, the Messiah's expected forerunner:

For in the tender compassion of our God the morning sun from heaven will rise upon us, to shine on those who live in darkness, under the cloud of death, and to guide our feet into the way of peace.

Perhaps it was inevitable, then, that the Zoroastrians' Mithraic, solar symbolism should find its way via the Essenes into Christian tradition, which duly adopted Mithras's holy-day (Sunday), his birthday (December 25th), and the Mithraic rituals surrounding both the eucharist and the spring rebirth of nature (Easter).

* * *

Nor were these the only similarities between Essene teaching and Zoroastrian lore. The seven Mazdean archangels, too, duly surfaced in the Essenes' *Angelic Liturgy*.[81] This particular text, indeed, has latterly become the basis of much New Age speculation on the subject of Essenes and angels, much of it fuelled by would-be 'Essene' documents such as Edmond Bordeaux Szekely's popular cult-classics *The Gospel of Peace of Jesus Christ* (1937) and *The Gospel of the Essenes* (1974).

With their tolerant, easy-going, nature-oriented philosophy and approach to healing, their ecstatic angelic utterances and their strangely un-Judaic celebration of the Earthly Mother as well as of the Heavenly Father, these supposed Essene 'lost gospels' are admittedly appealing, even inspiring at times — indeed, they are curiously reminiscent of other well-known inspir-ational books such as Kahlil Gibran's *The Prophet* (1926). Unlike the latter, though, they also claim to have been translated from unknown Essene manuscripts hidden in the Vatican and elsewhere, while the second book includes not only several pages of printed

Hebrew script, but a selection of passages virtually identical to the Dead Sea Scrolls (first discovered in 1947) by way of apparent validation. In consequence, they are widely regarded by New Agers as authoritative reference-texts and thus as a basis for a good many of their own views and actions. Unfortunately, however, the two 'gospels' in fact have next to nothing to tell us about the doctrines and attitudes of the real Essenes, since there is a good deal of cogent evidence, both internal and external, to suggest that the remainder of the text (apart from odd phrases borrowed from the Bible and the Hindu scriptures) is of purely modern origin, and has no more to do with ancient texts, either known or unknown, than with the teachings of any Judaic sect past or present, least of all Jesus or the historical Essenes — as even the most cursory comparison with the Biblical Torah or the Dead Sea Scrolls[81] will confirm. Moreover, the subsequent spin-off industry of 'Essene' lifestyles, 'Essene' therapies, 'Essene' diets, 'Essene' cookbooks and yet further 'Essene' tracts by eager imitators (however potentially valid in themselves) does nothing to bolster confidence in Szekely's original claims.

But then it is not as if such claims were ever necessary in the first place. The beliefs and activities of the historical Essenes were quite remarkable enough in themselves — especially for a group that regarded itself as purely and quintessentially Jewish in character — to make unnecessary any embellishment or exaggeration by modern hands. For not only did such colourful occupations as healing, herbalism, astrology and prediction all figure among their recorded activities, but the exotic, Zoroastrian elements in their teachings were by no means limited to mere beliefs about angels. Other Mazdean doctrines that surface in their writings include the pre-existence of the soul and the corresponding conviction that the souls of the righteous would be translated, at death, directly into the divine presence. As Josephus points out,[58] this untypically Jewish belief was largely responsible for the Essenes' almost legendary courage in the face of suffering and death, just as its direct counterpart and successor still is today in parts of the Islamic world. As we shall see, it was also to have an important part to play in their handling of the subsequent messianic initiative.

Again, the Essenes' whole eschatology reflected almost exactly — whether directly or via the mirror of the Jewish post-exilic prophetic writings — the familiar Zoroastrian scheme of decaying morals and piety leading to the ultimate war between the forces of Light and Darkness, which would be accompanied by world-wide famine, pestilence and natural cataclysms. The Qumran *War Rule* even spells out in ritualised form the successive phases of the great conflict.[81] Then would come the predicted great renewal, with the levelling of mountains and valleys, and the deserts blooming anew amid a new era of peace, justice, plenty and immortality for the nation's resurrected dead. True, the Essenes saw this new era in terms of a subtly-transformed, spiritualised universe — which we could possibly understand as a return to the supposed former dispensation of pure Light itself — but there can be no doubt that theirs was still a vision of a future kingdom of heaven *on earth*, even if a *new* heaven and a *new* earth.

Quite how the pious, nationalistic sectaries would have reacted had they realised that all these beliefs were of largely foreign origin almost beggars the imagination. But the fact was that they were so wedded to the notion that the nation's destiny depended on strict devotion to the scriptures and the associated oral traditions that it clearly never occurred to them to question the historical origins of either. It was by now axiomatic, after all, that both had been delivered directly to Moses by Yahweh himself; it was Israel's subsequent neglect of them that had led to the whole sorry state of present affairs which the Essenic movement had been designed to redress. Thus, even to harbour such doubts would have seemed the worst form of blasphemy.

So it was, then, that the hidden influence of Zoroastrianism continued unabated.

And notably in connection with the expected messianic initiative itself, which was of course the very linchpin of this whole complex of Jewish apocalyptic expectation.

8

Another Time, Another Place

Ah, but a man's reach should exceed his grasp,
Or what's a heaven for?
Robert Browning: 'Andrea del Sarto'

The term 'the Christ' has very different meanings to different people. Thanks largely to the writings of the post-Theosophist leader
Alice Bailey and others,[42] New Agers traditionally use the term to
refer not so much to the historical Jesus as to a semi-arcane, even
superhuman entity, the supposed head of a remote hierarchy of
elevated, if not actually ascended 'Masters' who are said by some
to dwell in the Himalayas and to be responsible for overseeing
and directing the destiny of humanity. More recently, under the
general influence of the equally post-Theosophical Rudolf Steiner,
New Age philosophers such as David Spangler[42,75] have shifted the
emphasis somewhat, stressing instead the deeper reality said to
underlie that figure and possibly other 'Christed' beings too —
namely a kind of universal evolutionary energy or intelligence
which, by incarnating in a human body in Palestine some two
thousand years ago, took on the responsibility for 'raising the
vibrations' of Planet Earth to a supposedly superior cosmic level,
thus eventually re-establishing the long-lost link between the two.

This latter concept clearly has a good deal in common with the
orthodox Christian doctrine from which it manifestly derives,
though conventional Christians may still find its assumptions
dubious, its details incomplete and its vocabulary distinctly worrying. The usual Christian practice, after all, is to strip the term
'Christ' of its definite article and turn it into the virtual surname of
a historical man who, it is alleged, was (either from birth or from
his baptism) no less than God in human form. As such he was
involved in an extraordinary cosmic atonement scheme devised
by an angry Yahweh in order to reconcile himself to sinful humanity by sacrificing himself to himself, so placating his own righteous indignation and saving humanity from a fate that was literally
worse than death. Christ himself, having been duly crucified
under the terms of this macabre rescue-effort, now reigns in heav-
en where, thanks to his suffering and sacrifice, the faithful can

hope to join him at death for an eternity of unalloyed bliss. The associated belief that he will at some unspecified date return to earth to judge all humanity — whether alive or dead — and to inaugurate the earthly Millennium has tended of recent years to fade somewhat into the background (for reasons that will emerge later), though it still remains a nominal part of the official creeds.

Christian millenarianism, in other words, has tended to 'spiritualise' the expected Golden Age on earth, if not actually to banish it entirely to outer space.

Yet even this general understanding of the term 'Christ' owes far more to the belated influence of ancient Greek mythology and its middle-eastern counterparts than to the Jews who, after all, were the ones who actually invented the characteristic Hebrew term *mashiach* ('anointed one'), of which *christos* ('Christ') is merely the Greek translation.[41] To them the word simply referred to any anointed King and/or High Priest of Israel, and specifically to the one who was expected to arise during the terrible Last Days at the end of the age to save the Jewish nation from its enemies and restore the world to the rule of Yahweh through their own collective agency, thus finally inaugurating the everlasting Kingdom of Righteousness *on earth*. Estericists among the Pharisees additionally saw the future *mashiach*, or 'Messiah', in something of a collective light, as the final and perfect embodiment of the *Adam Kadmon* or Man-Thought-in-the-Mind-of-God — the celebrated *logos* of St John's gospel.

To the Jews of the first century BC, then, the eventual advent of the Kingdom clearly depended to an overwhelming degree on the correct interpretation and fulfilment of the messianic office. Yet this was by no means a simple or straightforward matter. Basic to the contemporary Jewish understanding of the messianic role was the idea that the Messiah, or saviour, would in some sense play a multiple role. He would be a king after the style of David and a lawgiver after the style of Moses. Yet he would also fulfil a priestly function, if not also a prophetic one.

Quite how these various expectations were to be fulfilled and reconciled was a matter of frenzied debate among the three main religious factions. The Sadducees tended to stress the kingly function, while the Pharisees insisted that, since the scriptures clearly portrayed the messianic role as both kingly and priestly in character, there would have to be *two separate* Messiahs — an anointed king on the one hand, and an anointed High Priest on the other — as had already been foreshadowed by Zerubbabel and Joshua respectively as long ago as the nation's re-establishment after the

Babylonian exile. The Dead Sea scrolls suggest that the Essenes, too, eventually fell in with this view, though it is clear from their founding *Damascus Rule*[81] that originally they expected a single person to fulfil both functions.

As for the prophet, he was widely expected — thanks to Malachi's promise in the very last two verses of the contemporary scriptural canon — to be a reincarnation of the ancient priest-seer Elijah. But whether he was merely to act as a precursor of the Messiah himself, or actually to fulfil the role of Priest-Messiah in his own right, was never settled with any measure of common agreement.

For all of which, of course, ample scriptural precedent could be found. Had not Moses acted both as lawgiver and (by virtue of his personal intercession with Yahweh) as priest? At the same time, had not his brother Aaron been specifically consecrated as a priest by Moses himself, so foreshadowing a dual messianic team? And yet Moses himself had seemingly promised to send a prophet 'like myself', so apparently identifying himself as a prophet as well . . . .

All was clearly ripe for a major bout of doctrinal confusion, especially when the expectation of a returned King David was thrown into the melting-pot. Added to this confusion, moreover, there was the continuing influence of Zoroastrian ideas — which may, indeed, already have contributed *incognito* to the argument via their direct effect on the spiritual records at the time of Ezra. For somewhere deep in the communal unconscious, continually fostered and revivified by the oral traditions, there seems still to have lurked the memory not only of Moses the great prophet and lawgiver, but also of Zarathustra the equally great prophet and priest, who had been presented to the people by his cousin on the occasion of his fording a great river and experiencing a vision of the heavenly court — a vision which had led directly to his acceptance of his vital prophetic mission . . . .

* * *

It was out of this chaotic scribbling-pad of messianic expectations that the Essenes' Teacher of Righteousness and his successors had somehow to fashion their prophetic blueprint for action. Confident in their ability to interpret the will of Yahweh through meditation on the scriptures, they nevertheless seem to have come up with a remarkably clear and unambiguous plan not only for producing the Messiah, but also for training him in the steps which would be necessary to bring to fruition its final and most crucial stages.

It is this plan whose outlines I have tentatively sketched in my book *The Armageddon Script*.[41]

Having produced from within their own ranks both the expected prophet (whom we now know as John the Baptist) and the Messiah himself (one Joshua, or Jehoshua, now known to us as Jesus, after the Greek form of his name), the Essene leadership, it seems, arranged for the former, duly dressed as the prophet Elijah, to present to the people his messianic cousin (for such, apparently, he was) while performing the purificatory ritual of immersing him in the waters of the river Jordan. The similarity to the legend of Zarathustra is, of course, hardly likely to have been accidental. The biblical accounts even suggest that Jesus, again like Zarathustra, went on to experience the appropriate heavenly vision. And with that event, similarly, his great mission on earth is said to have begun.

In this case, however, the mission in question was to be part of a carefully laid down Essene plan whereby he would first of all fulfil the role of redeeming Priest-Messiah and then go on to assume the glorious royal mantle of King David. So, at least, the biblical records would suggest — in which case the plan must have been drawn up before the Essenes' well-documented change to the idea of a two-man messianic team.[81]

The Essenes' understanding of the priestly role, though, was dramatic in the extreme. For, instead of offering the customary ritual animal as atonement for the past sins and shortcomings of Israel, they had deduced that the Messiah must himself act as both priest and offering. Only by such an extreme act of self-sacrifice, they had concluded — an act of expiation which they themselves were already foreshadowing as a group through their life of penance and self-denial — could the extreme nature of the nation's sin and apostasy possibly be atoned for with any assurance that Yahweh would thereby be goaded into ultimate action on the nation's behalf.

The Messiah, then, *must arrange for himself to be put to death as a sacrifice for his people,* in a manner that could itself be deduced from such scriptures as Psalm 22 — a text which could be regarded as relevant to the issue for the very good reason that it had supposedly been composed by the original David in person.* Yet

---

* Since, after all, the coming Messiah was to be the former King David in the flesh, it followed that every first-person statement in the Davidic psalms could be applied directly to the anointed saviour, and that the book of Psalms could thus be regarded as a coded prophetic text relating to the End Times.

scripture also repeatedly made clear that he was to be rescued from the very jaws of death in the nick of time. It even seemed to specify the manner in which that deliverance was to be achieved. 'They put poison (*rosh*: 'toxic herb') in my food and gave me vinegar when I was thirsty,' ran the words of the equally Davidic Psalm 69, thus apparently indicating that the Messiah must be drugged to give the *appearance* of death before life actually left him. As skilled herbalists, the Essenes were in an excellent position deliberately to bring to pass this aspect of what had seemingly been prophesied. By the same token, they were equally well equipped to apply the appropriate antidote, heal his wounds, and nurse him back to health to such good effect as to enable him to fulfil the next part of the plan.

For within three days (so the scripturally-based prophetic blueprint laid down) he must be fit enough to ride in triumphant procession into Jerusalem, there to be crowned and anointed as King-Messiah in full view of all the people. Hence, of course, the numerous gospel-references to a three-day interim period. Visibly sanctified and overshadowed by the divine presence, he must then set in motion the forty years of world-wide conflict which would eventually result in Israel's victory over all its enemies and the bringing of the whole world under the direct sway of Yahweh. Cataclysms and holocausts there must be, but at the end of it all the long-promised Kingdom of peace, justice and plenty would at last dawn for the whole of humanity — or at least for that part of it which had managed, by dint of courage and dogged faithfulness to Yahweh through thick and thin, to survive the horrors and ordeals of the period of transition.

* * *

Such, then, it seems, was the daring plan upon which Joshua the Nazarene duly embarked on behalf of his sect, for the ultimate salvation not only of his people but also — as he believed — of the world as a whole. The sheer idealism and single-handed heroism of the enterprise can only excite in us the utmost admiration and respect, however much we may now choose to regard the whole thing as a piece of wishful thinking founded ultimately in communal delusion.

And indeed, the first part of the plan seems to have been carried out with consummate skill by all concerned. The advent of the Messiah was duly proclaimed by John, dressed up as Elijah. The imminence of the Kingdom and the consequent urgent need for national repentance and renewed observance of the strict terms of the divine Covenant were emphasised by both John and Jesus. That there were various hitches along the way seems evident from the gospel accounts.[41] That Jesus himself had a will of his own, and magnificently transcended the Essenes' typical, blinkered views, is also clear for all to see. And this because, much to the Essenes' apparent surprise, he actually turned out to be the Messiah whom they had been at such pains to produce, and not a mere political pawn in their own hands. Yet the original Teacher's master-plan was still adhered to, and the operation duly reached its initial climax with the self-engineered condemnation to death of Jesus at a place and time of his own choosing. Even the administration of the life-saving drug at the last moment went — it would appear from Matthew's gospel — exactly according to plan. And if matters had rested there the ritual necessity for the body to be removed from the cross before the impending Sabbath might well have enabled the Messiah to be taken down, still alive, from the cross and removed to the cool of the nearby converted rock-tomb that had been reserved to receive him, where waiting Essene physicians could immediately begin their healing work.

But matters did not rest there.

Out of the blue came the unforeseen, chance event that was to shatter the whole immense initiative. Before the drugged Messiah could be removed from the cross, an over-zealous — or possibly over-vindictive — Roman soldier chose to plunge his spear into the crucified Messiah's side. Whether the blow killed him at once we cannot be sure. Possibly he survived for a while. But even the skills of the Essene physicians were not equal to the challenge of a punctured lung in an already-weakened man. Whether in the makeshift 'tomb' or while under intensive care in the Essene monastery at Qumran by the Dead Sea, the would-be Messiah eventually succumbed to his wounds.[41]

And there, but for the Essenes' addiction to scriptural interpretation, the initiative might have ended.

Yet out of their renewed examination of the scriptures, combined with the continuing influence of Zoroastrian doctrine, a new possibility suddenly occurred to them. The Messiah's soul, it went almost without saying, had been translated at death directly into the divine presence. Perhaps, then, it was not, after all, part of his role personally to lead and supervise the impending world-wide conflict on Yahweh's behalf? Perhaps it was instead intended that the Essenes, together with their militant Zealot associates, should themselves collectively fulfil this role, and that only at the end of the time of ordeal would the Messiah's soul return from the heavenly court to be rejoined to his former body as the first of the resurrected dead, thereupon to set up Yahweh's everlasting rule on earth? Reference to the scriptures quickly confirmed this possibility.[41] And so the Essenes and those allied to them now set about making preparations to endure and survive the impending Time of Wrath in the absence of the comforting physical leadership of their Messiah.

Perhaps in obedience to what I have elsewhere described as the law of prophetic self-fulfilment,[41] just such a Time of Wrath duly arrived.

* * *

The Romans having, for nearly a century now, taken over the Greeks' former role as regional overlords, a whole succession of particularly obnoxious Roman emperors — obnoxious even by Roman standards — proceeded to preside over a colonial regime of increasing corruption and cruelty. Contrary to the Romans' usual policy of general religious tolerance, ever more flagrant sacrileges started to be committed against the Jews' religion and culture. Even nature seemed to be conniving in the infernal plot, as famine struck the land and reports of earthquakes, comets and volcanic eruptions came in from all over the Empire.

Eventually crisis-point was reached — or possibly it was engineered by the Essenes and their allies. Using a spontaneous tax-revolt as their occasion, the Zealots set in train a full-scale war of liberation against the Romans in the spring of AD 66.

At first the campaign was astonishingly successful. It took the Empire all of four years and sixty thousand troops to re-assert eventual control over Palestine. When it did so, however, it employed its customary iron fist. The Sea of Galilee, it is reported, was at one time red with blood and littered with bloated corpses. During the final siege of Jerusalem, would-be escapers were either crucified or disembowelled for any valuables they might have swallowed for safe transport. Conditions inside the city became indescribably horrific. Even cannibalism was reported.

At last, however, the inevitable happened. The sacred city was sacked and put to the torch, its Temple destroyed, its ancient treasures looted.

The fight was over.

And yet not quite over. Far to the south, in King Herod's massive and virtually impregnable fortress-funkhole of Masada, a determined and expertly-organised band of guerrillas had esconced themselves with ample provisions for a siege as early as the beginning of the war. In fact it was their slaughter of the Roman garrison there that had sparked the conflict in the first place. Left more or less to their own devices during the siege of Jerusalem, they continued to hurl defiance at the Romans for a further two-and-a-half years after the city had finally been sacked.

Rome, however, was not to be thwarted by a mere rabble of Zealots and Essenic hangers-on down by the shores of the Dead Sea. Implacably the sweating legionaries commanded by General Flavius Silva, and augmented by a labour-force of enslaved Jewish dissidents, set about constructing a huge siege-ramp — so massive that it is still to be seen there to this day — to scale Masada's forbidding and almost sheer rock ramparts. Neither heat nor drought nor an intermittent rain of projectiles and ordure from above succeeded in deterring the work's slow progress.

And so it was that, with the spring of AD 73, the ramp was nearing completion. As chance would have it, all was ready for the final assault on the eve of that year's Jewish Passover.

And then the incredible happened.

High in the night-sky flames erupted from the summit of the towering citadel. Soon the entire fortress seemed to be ablaze. What devilish scheme could possibly be afoot?

Dawn soon revealed the answer. As the Roman assault-troops made their massed charge up the slope, they were surprised to encounter a total lack of resistance from the defenders. Then, vaulting over the still-smoking ramparts, they quickly discovered the reason why.

As they broke into room after room of the fortress, they discovered only corpses. Whole families lay huddled together in death, clearly the victims of some kind of communal suicide-pact. In all, there were just under a thousand dead. Out of the entire rebel garrison, only some half-dozen women and children were found still alive, hiding in a cave.

But what did it all mean? What was the reason for this appalling act of self-destruction? Was it sheer bravado — a final gesture of quixotic defiance in the face of impossible odds? Was it terror of the awful brutalities which the guerrillas knew awaited them if they were captured by the Roman occupation-forces? Neither answer seems satisfactory, since the defenders could just as easily have ensured their own death in combat, whatever special additional arrangements might have been necessary to spare their women and children any suffering.

And indeed, there is a much more obvious and relevant answer. For the Passover of AD 73 came — it is now evident[41,44,66] — *exactly forty years after the crucifixion of Joshua the Nazarene.* For obvious reasons, then, it was at the Passover that the Messiah should have returned from the skies to free Israel at last from its mortal enemies and inaugurate the long-awaited Kingdom of Yahweh. (To this day, indeed, it is axiomatic among orthodox Jews that the Messiah will eventually appear at Passover.) Manifestly, however, he had not done so. And so sheer despair seems a much more likely reason for the mass-suicide of Masada, which still ranks today as one of the most dramatic and courageous acts of popular resistance known to history.

And yet there is another possibility.

Buried deep in the texts of scripture, in the eighty-fourth Psalm, lie the enigmatic words which the relatively literal King James Bible translates as 'For a day in thy courts is better than a thousand.' Could it be that the religiously-minded defenders of Masada, and specifically the Essenes who are known (on the basis of on-site discoveries of religious documents from Qumran) to have been among them, had let loose their exegetical skills upon the ambiguities of this well-known text to deduce that the price of the messianic 'day', or Millennium, might be the willing surrender not merely of one life (that of the Messiah himself) but *of a thousand lives at once*? Could their mass-suicide, in other words, have been one last, desperate attempt to 'buy' for their nation the promised Kingdom of God with their own communal blood?

The possibility cannot be excluded. In which case the sheer heroism of their act attains a pitch which can surely never have been excelled by any people at any time.

* * *

Yet, for all that, the Kingdom still failed to dawn. If there was a New Order at all, it was in Vespasian's Rome, not in Palestine. The whole body of Essene expectation had come to nothing. And what applied to the Essenes applied equally to the new sect of pseudo-Nazarenes whom their enemies were soon to dub 'Christiani'. Founded by a Pharisee called Saul of Tarsus — a visionary religious activist nowadays known to us as St Paul (Greek for 'Titch') — this group originally embraced both Jews and non-Jews in a loosely-knit network of cells, or churches, dedicated to a somewhat idiosyncratic version of the Judaeo-Zoroastrian apocalyptic ideas already so familiar to the Essenes. But whatever the differences between the new Christianity and traditional Essenism, one expectation was common to both — and indeed was largely responsible for most of the persecution which the Christians in particular were to suffer at the hands of Rome during their early years.

The expectation of the Messiah's imminent return as Universal King to restore the world to rights.

Spiritualised that new world might be, yet into it all the living faithful would be physically caught up, to be joined by all the faithful dead as well. By the same token, however, the *present* world was doomed to extinction, along with Rome, its hated Empire and the Emperor himself.

No wonder the Christians were so feared and hated by the Roman ruling classes.

The timescale involved, moreover, was entirely consistent with that of the Essenes. Within forty years of the crucifixion the Messiah would have returned, the prophecies would be fulfilled and the run-up to the Golden Age be in full swing. This expectation, or something very like it, clearly informs the early writings of St Paul. His followers were so convinced that deliverance would come in their lifetime that many of them gave up their jobs and donated their money and possessions to 'the Poor' — their cryptic name for their own underground groups and associated dependants.

The brutal anticlimax of AD 73, consequently, struck the Christians with just as much force as it did the now-scattered and decimated Essenes. Perhaps, as the second letter attributed to Peter was to suggest (and as we ourselves saw earlier), the various references by Jesus to 'the third day' meant that deliverance was to be postponed until the *third millennium* after the crucifixion? Alternatively, as the later Revelation of John hinted, possibly it depended upon the number of the Jewish faithful reaching a kind of 'critical mass' — and specifically the magic total of 144,000.

At all events, the whole complex of Golden Age expectation now started to become riddled with doubts, half-expectations and general wishful thinking. In place of the former apparent certainties, it started to become generally accepted that almost anything could happen at almost any time.

The result was fairly predictable.

As year gave way to year, decade to decade, and century to century, a whole succession of would-be Messiahs started to announce themselves, or to be announced by others. There was absolutely nothing new in the phenomenon. Jesus himself, after all, had been a product of precisely this messianic syndrome —

with what degree of ultimate justification readers must decide for themselves. Moreover, he had not been alone in this. Even in his own day the Samaritans had likewise flocked to the banner of their own *Taheb*, who had duly been executed by the Romans before he could perform the highly symbolic act of revealing the sacred vessels of the ancient Tabernacle allegedly buried by Moses on the Samaritans' sacred hill of Mount Gerizim. Within a hundred years of Jesus' death, moreover, the Pharisees, led by the venerable Rabbi Akiba, were to see in Simeon Bar Kokhba, the charismatic leader of the second (and, for a time, equally successful) Jewish revolt against the Romans, their own candidate for the Messiahship.

And the fact that Bar Kokhba was eliminated in his turn, and the nation even more brutally laid waste than before, did nothing whatsoever to discourage further applicants from claiming the title of Messiah, whatever its obvious risks.

Indeed, the advent and spread of Christianity, with its developing message that salvation was not restricted to the Jews, did much to fling open the gates for potential applicants world-wide.

The results were inevitable. From that day to this there has been a steady stream of messianic claimants, all no doubt distinguished in this way or that, but all, in the event, to prove themselves false claimants and fraudulent prophets — except, of course, in the eyes of their devoted followers, who have always been far too attached to the seductive mirages of their leaders' respective 'final answers' to dare to open their eyes to the true state of affairs.

Nor has the phenomenon even been confined to Christianity. Islam, too — whose own founding ideas were clearly informed (as the Koran itself reveals) by a determination to jettison the extravagant ritual dogma of Christianity in favour of messianic ideas that were in fact much closer to the basically Essenic insights of the early Jewish Nazarenes — has had more than its fair share of would-be Messiahs, or *Mahdis*. Perhaps the best-known of these 'Guided Ones' was the comparatively recent Sudanese leader Mohammed Ahmed, the celebrated opponent of General Gordon during the 1880s. Even during the last few years the famous Great Mosque of Mecca was taken over for a few days by a latter-day claimant to the title, before he, like nearly all of his predecessors, was summarily put to death. The event could have been predicted. For the Shi'ite sect of Islam, to which he belonged, insists that the true 'Awaited Saviour' has already been living *incognito* among us for over eleven centuries, only awaiting the right moment to reveal himself and inaugurate the final war against the forces of evil — the war which ever since Zoroastrian times has been confidently expected to lead to the promised Golden Age on earth.[1]

The world-wide spread of both Islam and Christianity has in the meantime created further opportunities for messianic claimants and an even wider context for their various claims. The respected nineteenth-century Persian prophet and divine who was to adopt the name Bahá'u'lláh ('Glory of God') made it perfectly clear through his writings that he represented the fulfilment of Christian and Islamic messianic hopes alike,[16] so giving rise to what is now known as the Bahá'i faith. This movement's well-known universalism and religious tolerance are of course admirable. But the spread of European imperialism over recent centuries has also resulted, among other things, in the grafting of Western messianic ideas onto almost any creed with similar universalistic tendencies.

And so Hinduism, in particular, has of recent years taken to producing acknowledged gurus who, in addition — and despite their own evident ignorance of the true meaning and implications of the Jewish term — have gone on to claim the title of World Messiah, or to allow that title to be foisted upon them by admiring followers. Among them have been the enigmatic Meher Baba, the Theosophists' former protégé Krishnamurti, the young and wealthy Maharaj Ji, the astonishing and apparently magical Sai Baba, and the ever-controversial Bhagwan Shree Rajneesh — all of whom have had the advantage of having their messianic credentials underpinned by the already-existing Hindu tradition of the re-appearing avatar, or human embodiment of the Divine, at times of great stress or moral and religious darkness.

And the increasing tendency, in our own day, for new religions (generally based on an uneasy amalgam of ideas misappropriated from the old ones) to spring up like mushrooms almost overnight has, of course, opened up almost unlimited possibilities for new Messiahs to proclaim themselves.

We can confidently expect, then, an almost unending stream of new messianic pretenders in the years to come. And, in particular, it would seem almost inevitable that a new Jewish Messiah will eventually announce himself. Otherwise — curiously enough — no New Age can ever dawn for orthodox Jews, since it is axiomatic to their faith that any such New Age must, of necessity, be inaugurated by the long-promised Messiah in person . . . .

* * *

Just as the dramatic anticlimax of the year AD 73 created an atmosphere of uncertain anticipation which made it possible for a whole succession of would-be Messiahs to come forward over the centuries, so it also created a situation in which almost any date could be proposed for the dawn of the anticipated Golden Age. In consequence, hopes were repeatedly raised not merely by the appearance of the various messianic claimants, but also by a string of events natural, unnatural and purely calendrical. Earthquakes, plagues, comets, major wars, the turn of centuries and of millennia — all have over the centuries sparked off speculation that the ultimate Millennium might be at hand, just as they continue to do today. And with that Millennium, of course, its necessary precursors — the long-expected final conflict, the time of hell on earth and the dreaded Last Judgement.

The repeated failure of such speculation seems to have done little to dampen it and prevent its repetition. Fear — like hope, it seems — springs eternal in the human breast.

And yet, as century succeeded century, a subtle change of emphasis did set in.

While Islam remained strictly faithful to the idea of an eventual Kingdom of Heaven on a transformed earth — i.e. a restored Garden of Eden — the Christian church, while continuing ritually to recite the words

Thy kingdom come,
thy will be done,
on earth as in heaven

started, almost imperceptibly at first, to do so with less and less conviction.

As it happens, there were perfectly good reasons for this. It had, after all, long been an article of faith that the souls of the righteous were automatically translated, at death, directly into the divine splendours of the heavenly court. The belief, as we have seen, dated from at least Zoroastrian times. And if it were true, then those souls had, in a sense, already made their transition into a 'new world' — a world which, just like the one which millenarian expectation foresaw, was a spiritualised version of the existing one (for the divine court, it hardly needs saying, had long since been faithfully modelled on its traditional earthly counterpart). But, that being so, there was singularly little point for those souls in the coming of the promised Millennium.

They were, in effect, already enjoying it.

As for the souls of the wicked, it was equally an article of faith that they would *not* be admitted, at death, into the divine presence — a presumed fact which therefore implied either a period of virtual non-existence until the Last Judgement, the dawning of the New Age and their ultimate consignment to hell, or else an interim time of preparation for that Judgement, perhaps in the form of exposure to some kind of purgatorial fire.

The concept of temporary non-existence being altogether too difficult for the Western mind to grasp at the time, the doctrine of Purgatory therefore came firmly into its own.

But this Purgatory, it now seems to have been realised, was tantamount to a more or less indefinite experience of hell itself — indefinite to the extent that the duration of the necessary purging could not be even remotely assessed, while the Last Judgement itself seemed to be an inordinately long time coming. Which in turn had to mean, in effect, that the souls of the wicked were as surely already judged at the moment of death as were their righteous counterparts.

Almost inevitably, therefore, the tendency to look forward — whether with longing or trepidation — to the coming Millennium started, in Church-influenced circles at least (and there were, of course, few others), to fade inexorably into the background. In its stead there arose a new emphasis on the soul's immediate prospects on passing over to the 'other world' which, it was now assumed, in some sense already existed. The very phrase

Thy will be done,
on earth as in heaven

specifically suggested, after all, that the long-expected Kingdom, whose very definition had always been the performance of the divine will, was already in full swing at the celestial level.

The results of this new perspective are most clearly exemplified by what followed in Europe during the Middle Ages. The whole of society became almost obsessively guilt-racked and doom-orientated. Since nobody could claim to be perfect, everybody — from the highest to the lowest in the land — became subject to a veritable nightmare of dread about the torments which awaited them in the world beyond. The gruesome paintings of the later Hieronymus Bosch still preserve for us today a taste of that dread. Impelled by irrational apprehensions that eventually reached a kind of fever-pitch, society turned inwards on itself in a frenzy of mutual suspicion and collective mortification. There arose a kind of mass psychosis which was as responsible at the popular level for the village witch-hunt as it was at the official level for monstrosities such as the Inquisition.

The Church's more mercenary elements were quick to take advantage of this situation. Thanks to the doctrine of Purgatory, there was an obvious chance for the Church to grow fat on the sale of indulgences (guarantees of a given number of purgatorial days' remission for the souls of the living) and of masses (supposed to have an equivalent effect for those of the dead). It was this sordid traffic that, perhaps more than anything else, was so to enrage Luther at the time of the Protestant Reformation.

But that the Reformation itself ever took place at all is in large measure due not so much to the medieval Church's exaggerated emphasis on the fate of the soul at death, as to its corresponding neglect of the concept of the coming Kingdom of Heaven on earth. Understandable that change of emphasis may have been. Barring apocalyptic accidents, after all, personal death was inevitable. The longer the apocalypse itself was put off, on the other hand, the more unlikely did it seem that it would ever actually happen at all.

So that the point has eventually been reached in our own day when, even with the traditional signs of the apocalypse all around us — the wars and upheavals and pestilences and famines and earthquakes, the threat of planetary annihilation by nuclear weapons, the return of the scattered Jews to their homeland, the healing of the sick and lame and blind and deaf, the resuscitation of those who would formerly have been classed as dead, even (it could be argued) the coming of man (in this case from outer space) 'in the clouds of heaven'[41] — nobody within the churches but the members of a few fundamentalist Christian sects seriously expects either the Last Judgement or the Kingdom of Heaven to materialise on earth at all. The right place for the Judgement, it seems to be generally assumed, is before the celestial Judge; and the right place for the Kingdom of Heaven is — where else? — *in* heaven.

Just, indeed, as the Roman Church in particular has been at pains to suggest, albeit mainly by implication, ever since medieval times.

But this neglect of the earthly millenarian ideal was to have dire consequences. Somewhere in the human psyche, it seems, there lurks — whether inbuilt or conditioned by social myth over many millennia — the expectation that one day a new Golden Age will dawn *on earth*. Any model of human destiny which ignores that expectation risks being discredited and abandoned in the face of almost any new view which comes along to offer an alternative, millenarian hope.

It was just such a view that, in the course of the fifteenth century, was eventually to shatter the Church's former hold on the imagination of European society. The new view was to have such profound and far-reaching effects on the Western psyche that we still refer to it, even today, as the Rebirth, or Renaissance.

And it had the effect not only of contradicting all previous models of human destiny, but of transforming the reigning despair regarding the restoration of the long-lost Golden Age on earth into a new and shining hope — a hope to which 'Old Agers' and 'New Agers' alike are even today the direct, if often unknowing, heirs.

PART II
THIS LAND OF EDEN

PART II

THIS LAND OF EDEN

9
Onward and Upward

Ah, love! could thou and I with fate conspire
To grasp this sorry Scheme of Things entire,
Would we not shatter it to bits — and then
Re-mould it nearer to the Heart's Desire!
Rubaiyat of Omar Khayyam (tr. Fitzgerald)

So closely is the phenomenon of the European Renaissance nowadays linked with the concept of classical rationalism that it comes as no little surprise to realise that the movement's origins were almost purely Romantic in character. When the imminent fall to the Turks of Constantinople — the last surviving bastion of the ancient Roman Empire — first brought its Greek scholars to Italy in the late fourteenth and early fifteenth centuries, bearing with them the precious manuscripts and scholarly traditions which had been preserved in the city since classical times, the effect was to present the medieval European mind with a veritable revelation.

Here, it seemed, were tangible proofs that there had indeed been some kind of Golden Age on earth as little as a thousand or so years before — and here in Europe, at that.

For the general picture of the classical world which inevitably emerged was of a venerable civilisation attuned to nature and devoted to the arts and sciences, to philosophy and politics — in short, to open-minded enquiry of all kinds, unshackled by dogma or authoritarianism, whether academic, religious or political. The whole of classical antiquity seemed bathed in the light of an almost ideal blending of natural justice and civilised behaviour. Suddenly it seemed that humanity was, after all, capable of establishing a golden Age on earth *by its own efforts*, and quite independently of any outside influence on the part of stars or planets, numerical cycles or even the Deity. Indeed, it was quite clear that the ancients had achieved most of what they had achieved without even believing in that Deity by name, whatever minor gods and goddesses they might have associated with the natural world about them.

And if it had been done once, then it could be done again. As the Italian poet Petrarch had put it, 'Our grandsons will be able to return to the pure radiance of the past.'

It seems completely to have escaped the notice of those concerned that the supposed Golden Ages of both Greece and Rome had had to be sustained in their day by a combination of armed violence abroad and institutional slavery at home — and, in Rome's case, had led to one of the most corrupt, sadistic and tyrannical regimes that the world had ever known. Ignorance, however — as the saying has it — is bliss. And certainly, in this case, it left the new enthusiasts for antiquity free to see classical civilisation in a Romantic, idealised light which owed at least as much to imagination as to history.

As a result there arose a view of human destiny which totally contradicted almost every previous model. Instead of the picture of everlasting cyclic decline and renewal which had characterised not merely Hinduism and Buddhism, but also traditions as disparate as those of ancient Greece, Babylon and Central America; instead of the picture of a single, long decline to world-destruction followed by an everlasting Golden Age, as painted by Zoroastrianism, post-exilic Judaism and latter-day Islam; instead, equally, of the broadly similar outlook offered by Christianity, modified only to the extent of being capped by an eternity of bliss not on earth, but in heaven — instead of all these earlier models, none of which had so far succeeded in producing the promised millenarian goods, or now seemed even remotely likely to do so, the new Renaissance paradigm offered the optimistic prospect of a broad, continuous, *upward* slope (if a backward one) to the eventual Millennium, and one which it was entirely within the capability of humanity to construct and crown by the sheer sweat of its own collective brow.

It was truly a conceptual revolution of the first order, and one which was to condition the shape of human thinking and society for centuries to come. Indeed, just such a model remains basic to much of New Age teaching to this very day.

* * *

There had, of course, been contacts between Western Europe and classical Byzantium ever since the time of the Crusades. In the twelfth century, too, Italian scholars had been among those who visited the translators' school at Toledo, in Spain, to participate in its often-overlooked work of rendering the ancient Greek texts — and particularly the scientific writings of Archimedes, Hippocrates, Galen, Euclid and Ptolemy — from their Arabic translations, via

Hebrew and Spanish, into Latin (which, thanks to the Church's influence, was the scholastic *lingua franca* of the day).

One by-product of that work, incidentally, had been the long-delayed entry of Pānini's zero and its accompanying numerals — which had been imported by the Arabs directly from India — into Western European mathematics.

That these sparks of ancient knowledge failed to ignite the full fires of the Renaissance at the time probably indicates that the contemporary European intellectual climate was as yet unfavourable for combustion, or that the potential fuel of the human mind was still far too soaked with the steady rain of Church dogma to respond with any flame of its own. Certainly the Church of the day did its utmost to stamp out the new lights of learning wherever they sprang up — whether in the law-schools of Bologna or Paris, or in the influential cathedral-school of Chartres. And the seductive, rationalistic teachings of Aristotle seem at the time to have been its particular *bête noire*.

By the mid-fourteenth century, however, both social and intellectual conditions were much more propitious. In Italy, especially, the recently-founded merchant-states of Milan, Florence and Venice, with their energetic money-economies and bourgeois values, were starting to provide fertile ground for the seeds of new ideas to sprout and take root, especially where these offered the heady prospect of breaking out of the oppressive prison of long-outdated papal dogma. The very founding of the three city-republics had, after all, resulted from a popular revolt against the tyranny of the papacy at a time when the latter was locked in conflict with the so-called Holy Roman Empire based in Germany. It was entirely natural, then, that the new city-fathers such as Leonardo Bruni should seek to compare themselves with the founders of the apparently ideal ancient city-states of Greece and Rome, which had arisen under broadly similar circumstances.

The hunt for precedents was on.

And so the still-existing resplendent classical civilisation of Constantinople, with its arts and sciences and scholastic traditions, presented an almost irresistible attraction and model.

As it happens, it was at about this very time that Constantinople itself was starting to come under heavy pressure from the invading Turks. By 1354 they had established their first foothold on the European mainland at Gallipoli. Soon it was clear that the writing was on the wall for what was, in effect, the last surviving example of the former, classical way of life. There remained but a few years during which those Italian scholars with the means to do so could visit Greece, while the Byzantine scholars, for their part, could transfer themselves and their various artifacts and manuscripts via Mistra in south-western Greece to Italy, sure of protection and support from their admirers in the newly-fledged city-states. By 1422, Constantinople itself was under attack. And finally, after a second campaign and a year's further siege, it succumbed to the Asian invaders in the summer of 1453.

* * *

Of all the rulers of the Italian city-states, none was more enthusiastic for the revival of ancient classical civilisation in his own backyard than Cosimo de Medici, who held effective political power in Florence at the time. Anxious to collect and preserve all the classical manuscripts that he could lay hands on, he built the still-extant library of San Marco to house them and serve as the intellectual power-house of his day. A regular industry of copying and studying these documents arose, conducted by a small army of dedicated scholars whose expertise soon ranged from the relatively intuitive and spiritual insights of philosophers such as Pythagoras and Plato on the one hand to the more hard-headed rationalism of the latter's pupil Aristotle and his successors on the other.

The result was a veritable explosion of psychic energy which was to have the most profound of effects on the minds of contemporary intellectuals, if comparatively little immediate effect on the shape and values of society as a whole.

Effects which, as we shall see later, were to be every bit as important for the arcane world of post-Platonic esotericism (and thus of subsequent New Age thought) as for secular art, science and philosophy.

At this point it is interesting to note that, by and large, the ideas involved tended to be expressed practically, rather than merely defined in words. The ancients' freedom to think for themselves, unrestricted by the straitjacket of imposed religious convention, was reflected in a similar practical exercise on the part of the Florentines, rather than in theoretical written expositions of the idea. The associated classical belief in the individual as a thinking being in his or her own right was similarly reflected in a revaluing of the individual as capable of unlimited independent achievement, given only the willingness and opportunity to use that inborn power of reason freely and independently. And if the well-known contemporary thinker and architect Leon Battista Alberti expressed the idea in the words 'A man can do all things if he has the will to,' he also expressed it in a life of quite extraordinary vigour, variety and achievement — such as we still associate, even today, with the true 'Renaissance man'.

It was out of such ideas as this that the concept which we today regard as above all typical of the early Renaissance came into being — that of 'man as the measure of all things', as the true yardstick in terms of which the whole of creation ought to be gauged. Gone was the depressing religious concept (the fruit of medieval guilt rather than of true biblical scholarship) of the human individual as a mere insignificant worm, the unworthy by-product of God's creation. In its stead came a revival of the ancient mystical concept of macrocosm and microcosm — the notion that the whole of the universe was somehow mirrored in the human organism, and the human organism in the universe, so that by mastering itself and attaining inner and outer harmony humanity could hope, as it were magically, to gain control of the cosmos itself and so ensure that eventual harmony would reign throughout the whole of creation.

An almost alchemical notion, admittedly, but one which had the effect of enabling contemporary humanity to see itself not merely as the *measure* of the universe, but as its master too — a master who could thus create a new Golden Age on earth by sheer act of will.

It was of course a daring concept, and one which flew in the face of the salvationist dogma of the Church, which still wielded considerable power and influence. Yet this fact did not prevent the entry of the new humanistic ideas into Church circles themselves. Within a few years, one of Alberti's own friends and co-enthusiasts had been installed in Rome as Pope Nicholas V, and he and his successors seem to have been perfectly capable of reconciling the various themes of classical paganism with those of Christianity in the art which they now chose to commission for their massive new buildings.

This very massiveness, meanwhile, was itself significant. In harmony with the idea of relating everything to human proportions, the early Renaissance architecture of Florence had been built on what often strikes modern visitors as a remarkably small scale.

It was, in effect, human-sized.

With the spread of the movement to Rome, however, and the consequent influx into the city of its leading protagonists, the latter were suddenly confronted with all the megalomaniac grandeur of the still-surviving ruins of the ancient Roman capital. What had hitherto been seen — or rather overlooked — as inconvenient eye-sores, overgrown and crumbling heaps of stones of no great human significance, useful mainly as handy stone-quarries for later builders (particularly now that major building-works were once again in hand), suddenly turned out to be sophisticated feats of civil engineering. Bridges, aqueducts, palaces, amphitheatres — all were revealed for what they were: not merely examples of a highly-advanced technology, but edifices built on a truly colossal scale.

The resulting impression was therefore almost inevitable: the ancients had been a veritable race of giants.

Not that there was anything new in this idea. It had been sub-scribed to in its most literal sense ever since the Middle Ages. But in the new climate of psychological self-confidence and belief in the power and dignity of the human being it accorded to a gratify-ing extent with the Renaissance view of humanity's role in the universe. Not, of course, in terms of actual physical stature, but rather of the innate potential of the human psyche to achieve any-thing it chose to.

The effect was to throw down a gauntlet before the pioneers of the new movement. No longer was it merely a matter of imitating the ancients and thereby flattering them as acknowledged super-iors. From about the year 1500 a new mood of heroic endeavour seems to have gripped the contemporary imagination. Whether in science, or engineering, or artistic beauty, or sheer size, the chal-lenge was on to *surpass* all that had been achieved before.

Which would have been all very well, left to itself. Even we today have inherited some of that spirit. But it has to be remem-bered that the leading light of the movement in Rome was initially the papacy itself. And it made no bones about hijacking the new heroic impulse for its own purposes.

The Church, it has to be remembered, had always had a vested interest in overpowering the individual with the greatness of God and the cosmic significance of its ritual. During the Middle Ages, it had unashamedly used cathedral architecture to rub the point in. On his accession in 1503, the new Pope Julius II was thus pre-sented with a golden opportunity to continue this tradition. In the name of the new spirit of confident gigantism, he decided on the dramatic step of pulling down the venerable and already-large basilica of St Peter, and commissioned the architect Bramante to build on the same site an even larger and more illustrious Renais-sance building of truly crushing proportions.

The project was financed by the self-same sale of indulgences which finally provoked Luther's Protestant Reformation in Germany. In the event, the construction took more than a hundred years. At the same time it became, with its associated structures, the natural focus for some of the greatest painters, sculptors and architects of the era.

To start with at least, their works continued to display all the aesthetic and philosophical breadth, tolerance and all-inclusiveness that had characterised the early years of the Renaissance. Inspired by surviving fragments of Greco-Roman sculpture, Michelangelo's Sistine Chapel ceiling is a triumphant celebration of the essential unity of the human body, mind and spirit, far-removed from the medieval tradition of horror of the body and mistrust of the intellect. In decorating the Pope's private library, similarly, the young Raphael was clearly under no pressure to emphasise the spiritual only, let alone the Church's particular view of it.

On one wall, for example, he painted the now-celebrated *School of Athens* — a representation, set within Bramante's vision of what the new St Peter's would look like, of all the major thinkers and philosophers of ancient Greece assembled as a group. What is amazing about this painting, however, is not so much its beauty and execution as the extraordinary aptness of the arrangement of the figures within it to what we now know about the workings of the human brain.

In the centre of the picture stand the figures of Plato and Aristotle, with Plato (on the left) gesturing on high in token of the source of his intuitive idealism — and no doubt, too, of the later, Neoplatonist ideas so popular in Alexandria during the third century AD, which were destined to supply a basis for what might be termed the esoteric, or even occult, side of early Renaissance thought. On the right, Aristotle, by contrast, extends his hand palm-downwards in a gesture of moderation, of playing down such high-flown notions in favour of a careful and deliberately circumscribed rationalism. Further to the left of Plato, a whole range of thinkers are depicted who likewise favoured the intuitional and emotional approach to reality, while on Aristotle's right are grouped those of a more analytical and purely intellectual frame of mind — among them, in the foreground, the geometer Euclid.

What is extraordinary about this arrangement is that it corresponds exactly to what the respective functions of the two brain-hemispheres would suggest. In the left-hand field of vision, which is now known to be the province of the right hemisphere, the representatives of intuition, emotion and the 'all-in' view (said to be

Raphael: The School of Athens

typical of the New Age approach) to which we nowadays refer as holism. In the right-hand field of vision, and thus appealing to the left hemisphere, the representatives of order and logic, of intellect and analysis — in short, of what we nowadays refer to as reductionism and see as the prevailing approach of Western society at large.

Precisely those areas of experience, in fact, in which each hemisphere tends to specialise.

We can be confident, of course, that Raphael himself had no direct knowledge of the neurological aptness of what he was about. What he was certainly aware of, however, was the fact that he had set all these figures within the framework of the most resplendent contemporary manifestation of the Christian Church — Bramante's vision of the new St Peter's. Could this have been a way of saying that he, and possibly his papal patron too, were confident that the Church was fully capable of absorbing the whole corpus of Renaissance ideas into a new, resplendent whole — a new dispensation in which the Christian religion and its pagan antecedents would join hands to build a true utopia on earth for the exclusive benefit of humanity?

If Raphael did entertain any such ideas, they were soon to be dashed. By 1527, with the Imperial sacking of Rome, the Italian Renaissance proper came to an abrupt end. In response to the attacks of northern Protestantism, the new Church which emerged from the temporary crisis chose to show its teeth by emphasising, rather than playing down, its former religious dogmatism. As a result of the Council of Trent, the sacred institution which had become the Renaissance's chief patron and benefactor seems suddenly to have ditched it in all but its trappings.

But then it has to be said that the Renaissance had always been a movement restricted to the tiniest of educated minorities. Its relevance to the labouring masses had always been virtually nil, except insofar as they were affected by various of the new practical ideas and techniques which had come out of it, or by what could be described as second-hand ideological fallout.

Under this latter heading, for example, we could place the rapidly-spreading Protestantism of northern Europe, facilitated (and indeed largely sparked off) by the newly-developed printing-press and the relative freedom of information which it permitted. To the resurrection of ancient geographical theories, similarly, we can trace the expedition of the Italian Columbus to the Americas in 1492, which was subsequently (as we have seen) to lead to the fall of the Aztec empire to Cortés in the early 1520s.

But what replaced that empire had little or nothing to do with the Renaissance or its values. What was imposed on the natives of Central America, as later on those of South America too, was a Church-dominated social and doctrinal orthodoxy that took no account whatever of the free-thinking and liberty of individual action which the Renaissance had encouraged among its privileged Italian devotees, let alone of the vast expansion of knowledge which had accompanied it. For all anybody in the Americas cared to acknowledge at the time, the Renaissance might never have happened, other than in the sphere of art and architecture.

In Europe, too, very little had changed on the surface. Most European societies continued to function in almost exactly the same way as before. *Ideas*, however, have a certain life of their own and, once started on their way, have an uncanny ability to escape all nets, undermine all prohibitions and disregard all frontiers.

Especially when assisted by the advent of mass printing technology.

And so it was to prove in the case of the new — or rather very old — ideas which the Renaissance had let loose upon the world.

For a start, of course, there was the newly re-affirmed assertion of the right of individuals to consult the evidence for themselves and make up their own minds on that basis, rather than having them made up for them by authorities 'out there', however well-informed or well-meaning. With the now-widespread availability of the writings of those authorities, after all, it was possible to compare the written word with the actual facts on the ground — a process from which the 'authorities' did not always emerge with unalloyed credit.

One of the most obvious results of the application of this idea was the Reformation. Examination by the new breed of lay Greek scholars of the actual text of the original Greek New Testament made it perfectly clear that the scriptures on which the Church claimed to base its authority provided a far from sufficient basis for a good deal that was being advanced as essential Christian belief. Moreover, anybody with sufficient education to consult the writings of these scholars could now personally confirm the fact. No longer could the Church hide behind its own monopoly of scriptural exegesis.

When, therefore, the papacy embarked upon its flirtation with classical paganism — adding insult to injury by financing its greatest monument to that flirtation through a sale of indulgences which clearly had no basis whatsoever in scripture — the die was truly cast. There arose a general outcry of protest which in due course became focused in the person of Martin Luther. If true authority lay in the Bible, he pointed out, then clearly it was to the Bible, and not to the Church of Rome, that the faithful must in future defer.

To this attack the papacy, now in its new mood of defiant react-ion following the shock of 1527, responded by attempting to undermine the very basis of the new movement. Authority did indeed lie in the scriptures. But there was a greater authority still — namely the direct guidance of the Holy Spirit, which had inspired Christianity's founders to compile those scriptures in the first place and, thanks to the apostolic succession, could be held still to be guiding and inspiring it now.

A presumably inspired, if hardly new, thought to which the world already owed such divine miracles as the Court of the Holy Inquisition . . . .

Even within the Catholic fold, however, there remained a good many scholars and honest thinkers who were not to be bambooz-led by such exegetics. Erasmus, Colet and Sir Thomas More (who subsequently became Henry VIII's inconveniently conscientious Chancellor) remained unafraid to apply the Renaissance princi-ples of free enquiry to a whole range of subjects, not excluding the Church itself. Even in Italy, the reforming friar Savonarola had dared to voice similar views.

The Platonic (or rather Neoplatonic) aspect of the Renaissance, in other words — the whole area of intuition and free personal enquiry into spiritual truth — was every bit as ripe for investig-ation as its more purely intellectual, Aristotelian counterpart. And not merely by the Church hierarchy in isolation.

There were, of course, dangers in all this. Much depended on the free-thinker's ability to keep his head down, to avoid the lime-light, to couch what he had to say in language which — like that of Erasmus particularly — was susceptible to a number of differ-ent interpretations.

As poor Savonarola, who was eventually tortured, hanged and burned at the stake, discovered to his cost.

The same applied, indeed, wherever the thrust of the new scholarship threatened to cross swords with established ecclesias-tical dogma. And such clashes were liable to occur not merely in the sphere of religion itself, but in any area of knowledge on which the Church reckoned to have some prior claim.

Even the field of pure science was no exception.

It had been all very well for Leonardo da Vinci to exercise his vaulting scientific imagination within the secure environment of the Florentine Renaissance. But for others of a later generation things were to prove much less easy. Even in academic circles, a kind of *rigor mortis* had set in. The original atmosphere of freedom in which the ancient sources could be consulted as a basis for further, first-hand investigation soon gave way to a new climate in which those sources — and particularly the works of Aristotle — started themselves to be treated as a kind of incontrovertible Holy Writ, thus effectively stultifying all further enquiry.

Whether within or without the Church, in other words, breaking new ground was becoming a more and more difficult, if not distinctly hazardous occupation.

And so the Polish canon Copernicus, taking up an idea first mooted in ancient times by Pythagoras, felt obliged to wait until the year of his own death (1543) before finally publishing his *Revolutions of the Heavenly Bodies*, which mooted the heretical notion that the earth went around the sun instead of vice versa. In the event, any fears that he may have had of church persecution proved unfounded, since the ecclesiastical establishment (which had itself actually commissioned Copernicus's study in the context of calendar reform) chose to regard the idea as a convenient fiction rather than as an attack on biblical 'fact'. Later, though, the Italian mathematician Galileo only escaped being burnt at the stake by the skin of his teeth for supporting Copernicus's ideas and believing the evidence of his own telescopically-assisted eyes — and then only by virtue of having recanted everything that he had said and written on the subject.

In the new, Protestant areas of Europe, meanwhile, things might have been expected to be a good deal more propitious for the flourishing of true scholarship. But here, too, there were problems. Not, in this case, of fixed ecclesiastical dogma so much as of exaggerated respect for scriptural revelation. Once again the healthy Renaissance disregard for authority had led, through free and uncramped examination of the scriptures, to the elevation of those scriptures themselves into what was, in effect, a new authority. And so, while free scientific enquiry was encouraged in principle, any piece of thinking or research which could be shown to be in clear contradiction of scripture stood in just as great danger of public vilification and condemnation as it might have done under the former, Catholic dispensation. Indeed, it was from Protestant, rather than from Catholic, sources that Copernicus was to suffer his most violent criticism.

The books concerned, subsequently, were just as liable to be consigned to the flames as before, even if their authors were marginally less likely to join them.

The result of all this, very naturally, was to put a brake on the development of what has been termed the New Learning, even if it did not actually stop it in its tracks. Such new learning as did occur tended to take place more in the rapidly-growing field of foreign travel and discovery — the results of which were clearly difficult to contradict — than in that of original thought and science on native soil. If we except the founding of the Royal College of Physicians in 1518, when the Renaissance was still in full swing, it was only towards the end of the seventeenth century, when both Protestantism and Catholicism were beginning to lose some of their teeth, that European science truly started to get into its stride. Thanks to the new authoritarianism, mathematics in particular remained for many decades firmly stuck in the Pythagorean and Euclidean moulds, while it was at least a century before physics, astronomy and cosmology succeeded in finally escaping the clutches of Aristotelian dogma.

Stimulated by the astronomical work of the astrologer Kepler, however, mathematics at last started to make greater and greater strides, thanks largely to researchers such as Napier (the inventor of logarithms), Descartes, Pascal, Newton and Leibniz. This work duly bore ever more promising fruit in the fields of physics, botany, geology, zoology, medicine and of course astronomy itself — so laying the foundations for the new science and technology of the eighteenth and nineteenth centuries.

Once again, consequently, humanity started to be granted a glimpse — if a somewhat dim one — of the man-made Golden Age which the Renaissance had promised to let loose on the world, but which the Church in one or other of its guises had managed to sweep safely back under the folds of its all-enveloping cassock.

* * *

In the sphere of religion itself, meanwhile, things were — paradoxically, perhaps — decidedly less promising. The Kingdom of Heaven having been either put off indefinitely or, as we noted earlier, spiritualised and banished to outer space, there seemed to be little, if any, light at the end of the Christian tunnel. And there was little prospect, either, of alleviating the gloom with the light of original thought. For, just as Catholicism made no bones about dismissing all new ideas out of hand as damnable heresy (the word, significantly, means nothing more reprehensible than honest doubt, which is why the great Christian mystics have always been accused of it in their day), so Protestantism, for its part, allowed free thought only in so far as it could be shown to accord with the scriptures. And since, the scriptures being what they are, the number of possible interpretations of them was at least as great as the number of interpreters, every new religious idea, every fresh religious sect or splinter-group, was bound to be seen by somebody as contrary to the word of God. At which point, if that somebody wielded any sort of social or political power, the stage was set for a whole range of possible religious persecutions.

Those persecutions duly materialised.

And the result was a series of developments all of which were eventually to lead in one way or another — and however unexpectedly — to a view of society that once again offered some hope of a man-made Millennium on earth, with or without the aid of divine intervention.

The immediate reaction to persecution among the more determined of the new religionists was, very naturally, to fight back. But since defeat or even death was the almost inevitable consequence, the next best thing was to flee to some place of safety where their new religious insights could put down fresh roots in relatively uncontaminated soil. Where better, then, than in the newly-discovered lands on the other side of the ocean, which numerous reports had already described as some kind of El Dorado?

It is, of course, a well-known human characteristic to paint any newly-discovered land in glowing colours of unlimited potentiality. The tendency had been evident at least since the time of the Jewish exodus from Egypt, when the land of Canaan — much of it distinctly inhospitable to husbandry — had been optimistically portrayed as 'a land flowing with milk and honey'. No doubt the reports were a deliberate piece of public-relations propaganda. Certainly this was so in the case of the Viking Eric the Red's much later discovery of an ice-clad land-mass well to the west of Iceland — a positive hell on earth which, in order to encourage his Norse compatriots to settle it, he ironically christened 'Greenland'.

The Americas, similarly, had been advertised, even in Columbus's day, as a continent of virtually unlimited opportunity and potential, particularly in the matter of such worldly accoutrements as gold and silver. This was not entirely the Italian sea-captain's own fault. Wherever he landed — in San Salvador, in Haiti, in Cuba — he was assured by the natives that whole cities and mountains of gold lay further to the west. The eager Spanish adventurers who, spurred on by the rumour, eagerly joined the subsequent expeditions, were always given the same assurance. And it is true that gold was indeed to be found in the rivers of Haiti, and was displayed in profusion in the ritual ornaments of many of the mainland tribes.

Yet the almost monotonous regularity with which the so-called 'Indians' perpetuated this fiction of unlimited riches 'further west' suggests a deliberate subterfuge, a well-worn tribal ploy for persuading plunderers for whom such things were evidently so important to ignore the local, relatively impoverished towns and villages in favour of pressing on westwards in search of the real jackpot.

Unfortunately, the locals had forgotten, as most of us do at some time or another, that their own 'somewhere else' was somebody else's 'here'. And to this error of judgement, consequently, the Spanish rape of the great civilisations of Central and South America can in some measure be attributed.

To it can also be attributed, of course, the rapid propagation of the myth in Europe itself, especially when Francis Drake returned from his renowned round-the-world voyage loaded to the gunwales with concrete evidence to support it — gold and silver in abundance, looted first by the Spaniards from the Aztecs and the Incas, and then for a second time from the Spaniards by Drake himself in the course of his own officially-sanctioned exercise in international piracy.

The news, naturally enough, was a sensation. In no time the British writer Hakluyt was extolling America as a land 'of huge and unknown greatness', while John Donne was virtually equating it with paradise itself. In time-honoured fashion sailors who had visited it were soon embellishing their descriptions of the new lands in the most shameless way. And it was not long before the business community, too, became caught up in the general euphoria.

Not, of course, without good reason. For the fact is that a newly-discovered land *does* offer almost endless opportunities to start up afresh, free from all previous restrictions and prohibitions, whether commercial, political or religious. Yet people have an uncanny ability to take their own restrictions and limitations along with them wherever they go.

And so the promised paradise never turns out to be quite as expected.

Perhaps that was why Sir Thomas More, in setting the fictional paradise of his best-known book of 1516 in the new continent beyond the Atlantic, had cannily chosen the name *Utopia* for it. For the word is based on the Greek for 'nowhere'. And that 'nowhere', as time was to prove, was to be found just as inevitably in America as it was anywhere else.

The fact did not deter the new flood of would-be emigrants, however. Nor did the manifest difficulties which beset the earliest colonists, who found little to justify the poet Drayton's optimistic description of Virginia as 'Earth's onely paradise'. So that, when a group of religious refugees who had fled from eastern England to Holland became dissatisfied even with life in that relatively tolerant country, America still seemed to them to offer the obvious haven.

It was, of course, that same group that was to produce the by-now almost legendary Pilgrim Fathers.

Contrary to what is often supposed, though, this small band of humble religious dissidents had no illusions that they personally were about to inaugurate the Kingdom of Heaven in America. No such grandiose idea ever seems to have entered their heads. That vision was much more the creation of a later pioneering venture on the part of a group of English religious Puritans led by an aristocratic government lawyer named John Winthrop.

Disgusted by the corruption of the established Anglican Church and its failure to dissociate itself from what they saw as the pseudo-magical rigmaroles of the Catholic Church (whose true representative, in point of fact, the Church of England claimed — and still claims — to be), Winthrop and his followers sailed for America in 1630 at a time of increasing political crisis at home, with the stated intention of founding there a new social order of integrity and justice based on strict religious purity. On this he was quite specific. The role of the new colonists was nothing less than to found on American soil a 'city of God' — a specific reference, it seems, to the biblical vision of the New Jerusalem representing the new, millennial order.

No longer, in other words, was it merely a matter of founding a New England or New Spain. What was at stake was a veritable New World.

We still use the term today. What we are seldom aware of, however, is that it is a direct reflection of the term 'New-born World' which was (as we saw earlier) the expression used in Matthew's gospel for the expected Kingdom of Heaven on earth.[70]

The idea seems to have been contagious. When, over a century later, the fathers of the American republic sat down to draft its founding charter, it was still clearly very much in the back — if not exactly in the forefront — of their minds. The American Declaration of Independence was finally drawn up and promulgated in the summer of 1776, and its bold assertion of the God-given equality of all men and of their inalienable right to 'Life, Liberty and the pursuit of Happiness' — not to mention their right to be governed only by their own consent — not only struck what, to establishment circles back in Europe, must have seemed the most alarming chords of revolutionary dissent, but also clearly harked back to the somewhat idealistic Renaissance view of republican Greece and Rome as a kind of Golden Age of natural innocence and justice.

However, the deed having been done, there was now a new infant state to be invested with all the appropriate constitutional trappings. Among these, inevitably, would have to be a Great Seal for the validation of state documents.

The seal was duly designed and approved in 1782, and it displays some most remarkable features. On its reverse side it bears the image of an incomplete pyramid with thirteen courses of masonry (the number apparently refers to the then current number of states in the Union) about to be crowned — and thus completed — with a resplendent capstone incorporating a mysterious, disembodied eye. Above the image stand the Latin words ANNUIT COEPTIS and, enscrolled beneath it, NOVUS ORDO SECLORUM. The bottom course of the pyramid bears, for obvious reasons, the date '1776' in Roman numerals.

Not, you might think, particularly striking. Most people, indeed, never give the design a second thought. At first glance it appears to be no more than the customary piece of over-imaginative heraldic extravagance which often accompanies such amateur forays into state and civic symbolism.

But in fact the design is much more than that. Its central image is replete with the time-honoured symbols of Freemasonry — a fact which, seeing that a good many of the republic's founders are known to have had Masonic connections,[26,35] is not altogether surprising. The incomplete pyramid appears to refer, as in the case of the Great Pyramid of Giza itself,[44] to a world steeped in imperfection because of its neglect of the divine or cosmic laws. The descending capstone — itself, of course, a perfect pyramid, though here represented, curiously enough, as a mere two-dimensional triangle — begs to be identified with the Deity itself. The eye — a traditional decoration of the capstones of Egyptian pyramids — is apparently intended to refer to the all-seeing Eye of Horus. Horus having been the falcon-god of the sky (and thus the direct Egyptian equivalent of the Jewish Yahweh), the expression 'the Eye of Horus' was, naturally enough, the Egyptians' term for the divine sun itself, and in token of this fact their pyramid-capstones were often sheathed in gold. The capstone of the Great Seal deliberately reflects this symbolism in the effulgent aura with which it is surrounded.

But that is not the end of the mystery.

Further examination of the Seal's design makes it quite obvious that the capstone *will not fit* the pyramid as it stands. Only when the latter has been built up by a few more courses will the summit-platform have the same dimensions as the base of the capstone. The conclusion is obvious: further states, it seems, have to join the Union. Eventually the whole world must be transformed and perfected *by human hand* before the ultimate union of earthly and divine can be achieved. Or possibly some effort at reconciliation and atonement is to be expected of both parties. The symbolism is redolent of the New Testament imagery of Saint Paul, itself derived from Pharisaic esotericism, in terms of which the Church — the 'body of Christ on earth' — has to grow up to meet the head — namely Christ himself — before the Kingdom of Heaven can finally be inaugurated.

The Seal's Latin legends tend to confirm this interpretation. *ANNUIT COEPTIS* is generally translated to mean 'He looks with favour upon our undertaking' — the 'He' in question clearly being the owner of the eyes, i.e. God himself. And *NOVUS ORDO SECLORUM* (a quotation from the Roman poet Virgil) means — highly significantly — 'A new order of ages'.

Nothing could be clearer, in fact, than that the Seal reflects the determination of the republic's founders to found on American soil the definitive Kingdom of Heaven on earth. Whence, of course, the image of the phoenix (latterly transformed into an eagle) on the front of the seal, crowned with a cluster of stars, in token of the hoped-for rebirth of true humanity out of the ashes of the former, European civilisations — a humanity faithful at last to the demands of heavenly truth.

And just in case any American should ever lose sight of this would-be national vision, steps were subsequently taken to oblige every citizen actually to carry it around with him or her.

For it is reproduced on the back of every dollar bill, its patently religious message spelt out in unambiguous terms by the addition of the national motto 'In God we trust'.

Curiously enough, although very few Americans are even aware of this symbolic adornment of their currency, the idea seems to have taken root to a remarkable extent. It is almost axiomatic to many Americans — especially those of a religious turn of mind — that the United States is 'God's own country', and

The reverse side of the Great Seal of the United States,
as reproduced on the back of the one dollar bill

consequently that anyone who threatens or opposes it is *ipso facto* an agent of the Devil. In some right-wing circles particularly, American righteousness and virtue has become almost as much an article of faith as its counterpart formerly was for the Church of Rome — which similarly saw itself as God's only true representative on earth. This curious similarity of attitude was even to produce, in the anti-communist witch-hunts of Senator Joseph McCarthy in the 1950s, a tolerable imitation of the former Inquisition itself.

But the attempt to found a New World in America through sheer human effort aided by divine inspiration was to prove no more successful than it had ever been in the past. From the start, the new religious colonists imported with them not only their own particular religious sectarianisms, but also the very religious intolerance from which they were trying to escape in the first place. Only the Quakers seem successfully to have avoided this rather obvious trap. Not surprisingly, therefore, subsequent history has shown little or no evidence of the establishment of the hoped-for millennial dispensation on American soil, at least in any recognisable form. Freedom, justice and abundance have manifested themselves, admittedly, but only for those Americans who were not enslaved, discriminated against, persecuted or dispossessed (curiously enough, the rise of the United States was to be based as firmly on institutional slavery as the rise of Greece and Rome had been before it). Disease and death have been respectively combated and postponed, but between them, inevitably, they have always won in the end. Religion has been almost as widely practised in church as it has been ignored in the street and in the marketplace. Widespread lip-service to God-given values has too often served less as a guide to action than as a cover for the most insidious and self-seeking forms of personal and corporate corruption.

Great though the virtues of the American republic and many of its present-day citizens undoubtedly are — and one thinks immediately of the latter's typical generosity, their easy-going and outgoing attitude to others, their breadth of vision, their devotion to their own democratic ideals, their infectious self-confidence and (thanks possibly to Quaker influence) their extraordinary personal openness and frankness — the lamentable prospect remains that the Kingdom of Heaven is no more likely to materialise in America, either now or in the future, than anywhere else on earth where human attitudes persist in their present form.

By which I mean the continuing human trend towards divisiveness and rigid categorisation which, as we saw in our first chapter, goes right back to humanity's early and — as it has turned out — increasingly obsessive love-affair with language at the expense of directly-perceived experience. A love-affair, moreover, which the Church-influenced post-Renaissance penchant for Aristotelian logic, as opposed to Platonic inspiration and intuition, merely served to intensify.

The American experiment was a brave attempt. It has had remarkable effects on the contemporary world. And not only in the conventional, materialistic sphere. It was, after all, largely American money and energy that finally boosted today's multi-faceted New Age movement into its subsequent high orbit, possibly in the unconscious hope that it would succeed where the American secular endeavour has so far failed — namely in finally bringing about the 'New Order of Ages' so optimistically announced by the USA's original founders.

For the very conviction of national rightness with which the infant United States was endowed at birth has paradoxically served to ensure that the long tradition of human divisiveness has persisted unchecked both in its domestic politics and in its international relations. Indeed, it has possibly even been aggravated world-wide — to the point where, in our own day, it even threatens to destroy our very planet and so scupper the chances of the promised Kingdom for good and all.

The road to hell, it has been truly said, is paved with good intentions.

10
Once Reason Reigns

Reason is itself a matter of faith. It is an act of faith to assert that our thoughts have any relation to reality at all.

G.K. Chesterton: 'Orthodoxy'

Curiously enough, had John Winthrop and his followers been able to wait another hundred years before embarking on their colonial adventure, they might have found it to be unnecessary. For in the interim a slow change was to spread across the face of Europe — a change encouraged on the one hand by the slow yeast of the Renaissance ideas which were now being propagated far and wide thanks to the advent of printing, and on the other by the gradual rise of a bourgeois middle class and petty nobility with both the money to purchase the resulting books and the time, the education and above all the inclination to read them.

This latter phenomenon had a variety of positive effects. For a start, it tended to remove the virtual monopoly which the monarchy and the Church had between them formerly exercised over all serious thought and speculation. Whether in the seventeenth-century coffee-houses of London (the ancestors of today's gentlemen's clubs) or in the later salons of Paris, largely self-educated men and (in the latter case) women of intelligence could enter into lively discussion on virtually any topic under the sun without fear of imminent arrest or persecution. The veritable ferment of ideas which emerged from all this activity encouraged a new spirit of general curiosity and enquiry which was eventually to spread, in England at least, even to Restoration court-circles. For it was at the instigation of Charles II himself that the scientific research association known as the Royal Society was officially instituted in 1660, with celebrities such as Wren, Boyle (of Boyle's Law), Hooke (inventor of the microscope) and, later, Newton, Halley and Leibniz among its members.

Like their Dutch precursors in the world of science, however, virtually all these men were essentially amateurs. Often their academic appointments were in nothing more specific than philosophy. The professional description 'scientist' (the word, it has to be said, is an ungainly latter-day concoction of Latin and Greek elements) was not even invented until the nineteenth century. Wren's original expertise was in mathematics and astronomy, Leibniz's in law. But all proved themselves to be passionately interested in all areas of learning. To this extent they were true heirs of the spirit of the Renaissance.

And in the new climate of free enquiry that spirit now started to flourish once more.

There had, of course, been much earlier pioneers of free thought. Even in the previous century the French lawyer Montaigne had laid the foundations of the sceptical outlook on which the newly-revived freedom to question and explore was ultimately founded, and had invented the 'essay' as a suitable literary form for floating his ideas. His countryman René Descartes had gone on to develop this sceptical approach into a fully-fledged system of thought for investigating the very nature of perceived reality. Realising, however, that their work posed a potential threat to the values of the established order, whether religious or political, both had felt obliged to remove themselves from the reactionary firing-line — Montaigne by retiring to his country estate, and Descartes by emigrating to the comparatively permissive atmosphere of Holland.

When, in 1603, Montaigne's ideas came out in English translation, they found in England a much more receptive and tolerant climate for further growth. It was here, consequently, that they bore their earliest recognisable fruit. The politician Francis Bacon, indeed, seems already not only to have made their acquaintance, but also to have got wind of Montaigne's newly-invented vehicle for expressing them. His own collection of *Essays* on general philosophical topics appeared as early as 1597, to be followed by a treatise on the principles of empirical scientific enquiry. This he later elaborated (1620) into his celebrated *Novum Organum Scientiarum*, widely regarded as one of the seminal works of modern science. In 1610 he also published the *New Atlantis* — a vision of a kind of scientific utopia which bore witness, if nothing else, to the fact that the millenarian ideal still lurked, if somewhat in the shadows, beneath the surface of much contemporary activity in the scientific and philosophical spheres. Indeed, his title even suggests that the ancient occult and alchemical traditions, too, were still sufficiently alive in the minds of the scientific pioneers of the day to be regarded as worth taking seriously.

Which might account for the fact that the later Newton was to write at least as voluminously on such subjects as he did on what we should nowadays regard as 'proper science'.

The stage was now set, then, for a whole succession of scientists and thinkers to exercise their minds on the problems of the day, whether scientific, social, philosophical or religious. Once again the struggle for a better world was on.

* * *

To start with, though, progress was slow. Both the Pilgrim Fathers and John Winthrop's pioneers had felt obliged to seek sanctuary in the New World long before Descartes's ideas started to exert any serious influence. In Britain, Protestant Puritanism — so convinced of its own rightness that it proposed to impose its ideas on everybody else by force if necessary — was still rampant until the middle of the seventeenth century, and was proving at least as intolerant of free thought as the Roman Church had been before it (and indeed still was over much of continental Europe).

What seems to have freed up the process of discussion and re-examination more than anything else was the English Civil War and temporary Republic of 1642 to 1660. At last the forces of popular dissent had dared to come out into the open. Nobody was under any illusion, of course, that the process had been a pleasant one to live through, but at least it had succeeded in finally exorcising the dogma that royal authority, being God-given, was absolute and not to be questioned. Put together with the similar lesson which had been learned in the religious sphere from the Reformation, Cromwell's republican experiment, disastrous though it had proved in many ways, had removed the final straitjacket of superstition from contemporary thought. Even the Restoration regime of Charles II, which enacted more than its fair share of repressive religious laws, was under no illusion that the old authoritarian dogmas could now be restored. And the lesson had not been lost, either, on the common people who, whatever their particular loyalties in the conflict, had inevitably been caught up in it in the most direct and traumatic of ways.

It was no accident, then, that it was under Charles II's patronage that the Royal Society, originally founded in 1645 as the 'Invisible College', was able to come out into the open and receive its official charter in 1660. Already, in other words, the new spirit of liberation was starting to make itself felt in the scientific sphere.

During the next three decades Newton in particular was, with Halley, to revolutionise mathematics, physics, mechanics, astronomy and optics. His mathematical work was to be complemented on the continent by that of Leibniz. By 1704 the first scientific encyclopaedia had been published by John Harris. The more general *Cyclopaedia* of Ephraim Chambers followed in 1728, and this in turn gave rise to the great French encyclopaedia of Diderot and d'Alembert which appeared between 1751 and 1772 — itself a product of the literary salons of Paris, which owed their own particular freedom of thought to their remoteness from the bored and apathetic court at Versailles.

The actual title of this encyclopaedia was the *Dictionnaire Raisonné des Arts, des Sciences et des Métiers* — a fact which should remind us that this was also the age of the first great dictionaries. That of Dr Johnson, in fact, was to appear contemporaneously with the French work in 1755, while the first *Encyclopaedia Britannica* followed in 1768-71.

The purpose of all this activity was no secret. Indeed, it was explicitly stated. It was, quite simply, to conquer ignorance and so advance humanity. This aim, it is evident, marked the resurgence of the former Renaissance ideal of building a new order on earth by sheer human effort and achievement. True humanism was once again in the air, and the power of human reason was once more being accorded a value which far transcended the spiritual dogmas of the established Churches.

Even if, in establishment circles at least, the equally important emotional and intuitive aspects of the Renaissance were just as cheerfully being ignored.

All this was, of course, a considerable revolution of attitude, and one to which it is difficult to assign any one cause. We have already cited the British Civil War and subsequent Republic, as well as the geographical remoteness from Paris of the French court. But the Churches themselves seem to have started to suffer a distinct lack of confidence from about the year 1725. And the reasons for this are to be found more in a general sense of malaise and rebellion, ably fostered by the writings of a series of remarkable thinkers, than in any particular set of political circumstances.

What was above all needed now, it seems to have been felt, was an alternative to the seventeenth century's tradition of almost obsessive extremism, especially in the religious sphere. Dogma had had its day and proved itself wanting. British society had been torn apart, continental Europe devastated by a whole series of bloody religious wars. Now it was time for a period of reasonableness and tolerance.

The feeling was reflected not only in the so-called 'English Revolution' of 1688, when Britain finally turned its back on the authoritarianism of the Stuart monarchy, but also in the Toleration

Act of 1689, which at last permitted religious freedom to Protestant dissenters.

And so it is surely no accident that historians nowadays feel able to describe the century which followed as the Age of Reason.

* * *

The rise of rationalism, as we saw earlier, seems to have started in France with the sceptical works of Montaigne and especially the strict rationalism of Descartes. But France, inevitably, had not been the most favourable environment for the propagation of such ideas.

In Protestant Holland, on the other hand, things of this kind were much more in order. Long the printing-centre for allegedly seditious literature from all over Europe, Holland had duly provided sanctuary for Descartes, and had itself developed a tradition of amateur scientific observation and realism which can be seen reflected to this day in Dutch paintings of the time.[12]

It is perhaps no accident, then, that the mid-seventeenth-century Dutch philosopher Spinoza was one of the first (if we except such early religious revolutionaries as Peter Abelard) to apply the techniques of rational analysis to the words of the scriptures themselves. His British contemporary John Locke took the processes of reason even further — even, one could say, to the point of self-destruction — in that he managed to use reason itself to show that there were very definite limits to what human beings could ever hope to find out by the use of reason alone, and even more definite limits to what they could hope to find out through sensory experience. At the same time he felt free enough to float the truly revolutionary idea that governments had the right to govern only with the consent of the governed — a political bombshell which, as we have seen, was finally to explode at the time of the American Revolution, and which has continued to reverberate around the world's political arena ever since.

Not an idea, moreover, which could easily have been expressed at the time anywhere other than in post-Cromwellian England.

The fact is significant. Shortly after the publication of Locke's ideas, for example, the British political atmosphere was already open enough to permit a whole rash of pamphlets, newspapers and periodicals to start appearing on the streets. True, the political establishment was well aware of their possible dangers, and in 1713 attempted to dampen the public's enthusiasm by imposing a stamp duty on them. But the attempt was a total failure. By 1776 there were fifty-three regular newspapers in London alone, many of them not only decidedly free in their views, but often personally scurrilous, even by today's permissive standards, about members of the establishment itself.

'At last the old fool is dead,' the *Morning Post* later felt free enough to exclaim on the death of George III in 1820.

The results of what might be termed the 'Information Revolution' were both profound and inevitable. Thanks both to the rise of the newspaper industry and to the ever-increasing availability of comprehensive dictionaries and encyclopaedias, what might formerly have been regarded as privileged information for the ears of the political and religious elite only was rapidly becoming common knowledge. People could increasingly base their judgements on what was actually the case, rather than on what the various authorities told them was the case. Consequently there was a new public awareness, not merely of bread-and-butter scientific, philosophical, geographical and historical facts, but also of blatant social ills and inequalities.

It was all very well for the religiously idealistic Leibniz to attempt to reconcile his Roman Catholicism with the demands of reason by suggesting that all was for the best in the best of all possible worlds. The idea, as we shall see later, may actually have been remarkably close to the truth of the matter in absolute terms, yet the brute facts of popular experience repeatedly suggested otherwise. The great British essayists and social commentators of the day — Addison, Steele, Defoe and Swift among them — were quick to remark on the fact. And it was not long before their 'subversive' ideas — most of them perfectly innocuous by today's standards — crossed the Channel and started to gnaw their way into the comparatively conservative French body politic.

The chief French agent of this important development was, in the event, to be the now-celebrated Voltaire. An almost perversely rebellious and anti-authoritarian character from his youth up, he spent the years 1726-9 in England, and soon became a firm admirer of the English and their institutions — and especially, of course, of their freedom of thought and expression. But when he tried to emulate the great British social critics and promulgate their ideas in his own country he quickly ran into trouble, and eventually had to beat a hasty retreat, first to Germany, and then to his idyllic château at Ferney, close to the safety of the Swiss border.

Even from here, though, his influence remained immense, to the point where he is nowadays regarded as the father of what is generally referred to as the Enlightenment.

Voltaire's main ideological plank was, quite simply, reasonableness. In his eyes, there really was no excuse either for religious intolerance or for political repression. Given a responsible and critical use of man's God-given reason, there was absolutely nothing to prevent the creation of an ideal society on earth — a society in which everybody's rights and freedoms would be respected, and justice and natural law would finally reign supreme.

In short, a firmly humanist — if deistic — version of the long-awaited Golden Age.

The views of Voltaire and his British antecedents were later echoed, if less stridently, by the German critic and playwright G.E. Lessing, especially in his play *Nathan der Weise*, whose theme was, quite simply, religious tolerance. Lessing, moreover, was himself a friend of Moses Mendelssohn (grandfather of the composer) who, by dint of applying similar ideas to the inevitably dogmatic teachings of his own Jewish religion, became the father of what we now know as Reformed Judaism.

* * *

Yet even while the philosophers of the Enlightenment were pursuing their quest for a moderation based on reason, the very ground was being cut from beneath their feet.

Already we have seen how John Locke had applied the processes of reason to reason itself and discovered its potentialities to be strictly limited. By the mid-eighteenth century the Scottish philosopher David Hume was taking the process even further. Since our reason is based on the evidence of our senses, he argued, and since there is no objective guarantee, outside what the senses themselves tell us, that that evidence is accurate — or indeed that there is even an 'outer world' to be experienced or a self to experience it in the first place — we are left in something of a quandary. For the upshot — it is quite evident — is that any attempt to use reason as a tool for reforming that world amounts to using one unknown quantity to operate on another. The prospects, in consequence, are far from encouraging.

The German philosopher Immanuel Kant took up the same theme, only to extend the argument. If we do not perceive the objective world, he pointed out, but only our own perceptions of it, then the world we perceive is essentially *our own creation*. The world mirrors the mind, not the mind the world. It follows, therefore, that if an ideal world is ever to be created, then it is the human mind that has to create it.

The point is remarkably close to what is believed by many of today's New Agers, partly under the influence of Norman Vincent Peale's ideas on 'positive thinking'.

At this point, however, Kant seems to have fallen foul of his own initial postulate. For Kant's whole edifice of argument, it needs to be remembered, was based upon Hume's demonstration of the unreliability of reason as a tool for dealing with our perceptions. Yet Kant now went on to suggest that reason was the very tool whereby the mind could proceed to work towards a better world through the observation of reasoned law, a reasoned morality and even a reasoned transcendentalism.

The weakness in Kant's approach is thus apparent. If reason is of limited validity, then it hardly qualifies as a valid tool for reforming perceived reality.

A point which finds distinct affirming echoes in a good many modern New Age circles.

Between perceived reality and the mind, after all, there is (as Kant himself recognised) not a jot of difference. Tempting it may be to suggest that, in view of this, a totally reasonable mind would produce a totally reasonable perceived reality — i.e. an ideal world. But we all know that the mind is *not* totally reasonable. There can be nobody who has not, at some time or other, been surprised and even taken aback by its inherent irrationalities and inconsequentialities, its periodic insistence even on working against what, in our supposedly saner moments, we conceive to be our own best interests. The eighteenth-century thinkers were certainly aware of such things, even if they did not admit to them, and no doubt regarded them as mere mental aberrations.

But this does not alter the fact that they occur for all that.

Consequently there can no longer be any question of using reason to reform either the supposed objective world or our own experience of it. Admittedly a revolution in the mind is needed — but a revolution in perception, not in reasoning. Only such a revolution can hope to produce that ideal world which can only ever be its own creation, and so bring about (by whatever name) the long-awaited Kingdom of Heaven on earth.

What is required, in other words, is a veritable *volte-face* that has nothing whatever to do with the exercise of logic, and everything to do with the way in which we view the world.

* * *

The point seems to have been lost on the mainstream philosophers of the Enlightenment, however. It took a rank outsider — though one who, as it happens, had close associations with Hume himself — to take on board the full, revolutionary implications of the Scottish philosopher's conclusions.

And the name of that outsider was Jean Jacques Rousseau.

Not that Rousseau was averse to using the fashionable tool of reason to criticise the society of his day. His very insistence on doing so caused him to be ostracised and persecuted by Church and State alike. Like Voltaire, therefore, he too was forced to retire from the fray. After taking refuge in several foreign countries, including a spell with Hume in England, he eventually settled on a lake-island in Switzerland. And it was while there that the full implications of what were, in effect, Hume's arguments seem to have struck him like a bolt of lightning.

Suddenly, in the midst of his meditations by the lake, he became aware that all thinking and reasoning had ceased. Instead there was only perception — his own perception of the sound of the waves, his awareness of nature going about its work all around him. 'I realised,' he wrote later, 'that our existence is nothing but a succession of moments perceived via the senses.'

The senses. So long neglected, so long obscured by thought and obsessive ratiocination. It was the senses that now had to be the point at issue. Direct experience was all, not imposed dogmas and beliefs, nor third-person written authorities. And that meant experience *of all kinds* — physical, emotional, mental and spiritual. In short, it meant what New Agers nowadays delight in referring to as Being Here Now.

An attitude which, as we noted in our opening chapters, does seem to be a key prerequisite for any return to the type of consciousness which alone seems capable of producing a Golden Age on earth.

All this, of course, was at least as much a reaction to what had gone before as a spontaneous insight in its own right. Rousseau the social rebel was merely applying his natural rebelliousness to accepted philosophical assumptions. That, no doubt, was why mental, intellectual experience — which ought, under the terms of his new philosophy, to have been as valid and important as any other form of experience — tended to be as firmly played down by the new breed of 'Romantics' as it still is by a good many modern New Agers.

And in its place the sensations and emotions were exalted into virtual gods.

To be fair to the exiled Rousseau, however, he was not the first to edge in this direction. The English poets Thomson, Gray and Collins had for some time been writing about the natural world in terms that were no longer merely descriptive or didactic, but frankly emotional — an emotion which, in their case, was characterised by a kind of melancholy nostalgia, as for a world of former innocence now lost to humanity beneath the heavy trappings of civilisation (compare the quotation from Wordsworth's *Ode on the Intimations of Immortality* in Chapter One above).

Once again, in other words, the ancient vision of a former Garden of Eden was abroad — but in this case a kind of drop-out vision with a distinctly back-to-the-womb feeling about it.

But it was by no means entirely a matter of pie-in-the-sky. There was by now plenty of apparently hard, scientific — not to say rational — evidence to justify such views. Increasingly the great explorers of the day were discovering primitive societies which actually appeared to be living examples of the supposed primal state of bliss. The point was emphasised specifically by the French explorer Bougainville when he visited Tahiti in 1767. But then Bougainville was himself a disciple of Rousseau, and might have been suspected of having an axe to grind. When, however, even the hard-headed Yorkshireman Captain Cook, following in his footsteps two years later, found himself unable to avoid confirming the impression, and compared European civilisation distinctly unfavourably with life in Tahiti, the die was cast. Very soon Rousseau's ideas were all the rage, and the forces of rationalism were in retreat all over Europe.

The new Romantic ideal, then, was not so much 'thinking man' as 'natural man' — a humanity that would once again be fully in tune with the natural world, responding to it instinctively and emotionally. The self-same vision is still avidly pursued, almost as if it were the ultimate in human goals, by a good many New Age groupings. The aim of the Romantic movement's devotees was to be able to say, as Dryden had done almost exactly a century earlier,

> I am as free as nature first made man,
> Ere the base laws of servitude began,
> When wild in woods the noble savage ran.

* * *

The noble savage! That was the new watchword. Clearly, though, it was not a new thought. Even Montaigne had briefly considered the idea back in the sixteenth century in his essay *On Cannibals*. But now nature and natural man were actually being taken seriously. Before long they had come to occupy centre-stage in contemporary thought.

The trouble was that the rationally-inclined intellectuals of the eighteenth century were ill-equipped to cope with the unleashing of the new forces of feeling and emotion. As Pascal had put it over a century earlier, *Le coeur a ses raisons, que la raison ne connaît point* ('The heart has its reasons, of which reason knows nothing'). Almost inevitably, therefore, the artistic products of the new Romantic Revolution were, for the most part, wild and undisciplined. This is particularly noticeable in the early stage-dramas of Goethe, Schiller and the other representatives of the German *Sturm und Drang* movement — most of which were highly idealistic would-be imitations of Shakespeare. Some of them, in fact, were so wild as to be completely unstageable. But then this was only to be expected. With reason unceremoniously thrown out of the window, what discipline could there possibly be to exert, or authority to exert it? The sole guide now was the soul, the *daemon*, the 'inner genius', and this, by its very nature, was largely unconscious and, of course, totally unpredictable.

Dangerously unpredictable.

This fact soon became obvious when the new ideas started to make their transition from the purely artistic sphere into the political one. True, in the visual arts they were to inspire admirable work on the part of painters such as the nature-worshipping Constable and the later Turner, as well as the French artists Delacroix and Géricault. In music, they were to become dominant from the time of Beethoven and Schubert onwards, and notably in the music of Liszt, Chopin, Schumann and the later Wagner.

In literature, equally, following the astonishing outburst of the German *Sturm und Drang* movement led by the young Goethe and the even younger Schiller during the closing years of the eighteenth century, the new, Romantic ideas were soon motivating the school of English poets which included Wordsworth, Coleridge, Byron, Shelley and Keats, as well as helping to inspire the novels of Scott. A similar school of writers became active in Germany, while its French counterpart — which included writers such as Chateaubriand, Lamartine, de Musset, de Vigny, Victor Hugo and subsequently Baudelaire — had a certain exotic flavour added to its Romanticism when the French linguist and adventurer Anquetil-Duperron published his translation of fifty or so of the ancient Hindu *Upanishads* in 1804.

This particular work was also to exert an almost overwhelming influence on the German philosopher Schopenhauer. And for very good reason. Here, after all, was further concrete evidence of a contemporary culture — and one of great antiquity and sophistication, at that — in which the deep, inner realities so prized by the Romantics were apparently accorded greater respect than were the mere, superficial demands of Western rationality.

The Romantic ideal, in other words — or something very like it — could actually be shown to be working in practice, whether in the sophisticated climate of India or in the relatively primitive societies of the South seas.

The fact was important. The purely artistic manifestations of Romanticism were all very well, and all the while they remained securely confined to the artistic sphere they posed no threat to the existing social order. They could even be regarded as a useful way of 'letting off steam', especially of the adolescent sort. But even in Rousseau's time there had been, as we saw earlier, a strong social and political side to the movement as well. From the start, Rousseau's basic axiom had been the resounding clarion-call: 'Man is born free but is everywhere in chains.'

It is no accident, perhaps, that the self-same imagery was later to be echoed by Marx and Engels in the closing sentences of their *Manifesto of the Communist Party* of 1848: 'The proletarians have nothing to lose but their chains. They have a world to win.'

Almost inevitably, therefore, the general climate of opinion generated by the Romantic revolution tended to be one which assumed that all of humanity's ills were the result of the structure and organisation of contemporary society. Once dispose of these, and the innate nobility of the common man would ensure the birth of a new utopia, or rather a return to the state of primal bliss which humans had once enjoyed in the original Garden of Eden.

It was, of course, just such an initiative that had been undertaken by the followers of John Winthrop in America back in the 1630s. But in their case they had also had a positive vision to fulfil — namely the deliberate creation of the Kingdom of God on American soil through a sheer act of communal human will. In Europe at the end of the eighteenth century, on the other hand, the vision was inherently much more negative. *Ecrasez l'infâme!* ('Crush the Beast!') had been Voltaire's celebrated, if ambiguous, war-cry, and the vision of the later, Romantically-inspired revolutionaries was scarcely more specific or positive. The emphasis, as in the early *Sturm und Drang* plays, was on popular resistance to oppression, whether social or ideological, rather than on what was supposed to replace it — apart, that is, from vague ideals of 'freedom' and 'justice'.

And it has to be said that this basically negative attitude is also to be found among a good many of the would-be primitives and drop-outs who move on the more revolutionary fringes of the New Age movement even today.

Needless to say, the French Revolution, when it came in 1789, revealed little evidence of the common man's supposed primal innocence, once the old order had been overthrown. In place of the old aristocratic authoritarianism there merely appeared a new, bourgeois one — if admittedly modelled on classical precedents. True, there were hopes for a time that the military hero Napoleon might put the popular revolution back on the right rails (he was, after all, a true Romantic idealist whose favourite bedside reading was Goethe's lacrymose early novel *Werther*, the international best-seller of the day). But those hopes were soon dashed when he crowned himself Emperor in 1804, thus announcing to all and sundry that what they were in for was not a new order at all, but merely the old one in a new, if possibly more benevolent, disguise.

The general sense of public let-down was characterised by Beethoven's now-celebrated reaction. Having dedicated his new *Eroica* (i.e. 'Heroic') symphony to Napoleon, he promptly scratched out the dedication the moment he realised that the great French revolutionary saviour was going to be nothing of the kind.

Once again the elusive Millennium had slipped through humanity's fingers just at the moment when it had seemed to be finally within everybody's grasp.

The Great Search, it seemed, was far from over yet.

11
Come the Revolution

I will not cease from mental fight,
Nor shall my sword sleep in my hand,
Till we have built Jerusalem
In England's green and pleasant land.

William Blake: Preface to 'Milton'

By the early eighteen-hundreds, then, it was already obvious that Romanticism alone was not going to be the answer to all the world's ills. Merely overthrowing the existing social order would not of itself restore the long-lost Garden of Eden, despite all the fraternal fervour of Schiller's quasi-revolutionary *Ode to Joy*, so memorably set to music by Beethoven in his ninth symphony.

Inherently noble the ordinary human being might be, but that nobility was a tender plant, too liable to be crushed under the heavy feet of reactionaries and power-seekers — not to mention the juggernaut of popular authoritarian expectations — to be left to its own devices. What was needed now was not so much a movement back to the racial womb (strangely in tune though such a movement would have been with the original, underlying spirit of the Renaissance) as a forward-looking initiative fired by some clear and positive vision of a totally new future.

A vision, in other words, based on the hitherto virtually unknown concept of *progress*.

Strangely enough, just such a concept was even then starting to come into vogue — and this for reasons that apparently had no direct connection with the Romantic movement at all.

* * *

The first of these reasons lay in the development of science and technology. Not, in the event, as a result of anything so obvious and deliberate as Charles II's founding of the Royal Society in 1660, but rather because of a curious side-effect of the same king's anti-nonconformist legislation. The so-called 'Clarendon Code' of the early 1660s had had the effect of banning all non-Anglicans from posts in parliament, the professions and local government, as well as from attending the universities. As a result, able dissenters found themselves coerced into careers in trade and industry. And so the Quakers and Unitarians in particular soon set about founding schools of a totally new type to equip their youngsters for such careers. These establishments were not only much more practically oriented than their traditional counterparts. They also did their teaching in English instead of Latin, included science in their curriculum, and consequently tended to produce pupils who were, technically at least, a quantum leap ahead of their contemporaries elsewhere.

Almost inevitably, therefore, their impact on industrial technology was to prove immense.

And not least because they were the bearers not merely of a whole range of new technical and industrial skills, but also of a particularly well-honed version of what has since come to be known as the 'Protestant work-ethic' — that association of moral uprightness with worldly endeavour and success which was to fuel much of the activity of the age that was to follow and produce a whole crop both of benefits and of problems right down to our century.

It took a long time, though.

Admittedly, new techniques for using coal instead of wood to smelt iron were starting to be developed by around the year 1700. But the progression from coke-furnace to blast furnace, from iron to high-grade steel, from simple metal implements to complex industrial machines and machine-tools was, in the event, to prove a relatively slow one. It was 1733 before Kay came up with his Flying Shuttle, 1764 before Hargreaves produced his Spinning Jenny, and 1779 before Crompton's Spinning Mule finally helped bring the British textile industry to total world pre-eminence.

The technology of power-generation for the new industries was equally slow to take off. The textile industry had traditionally relied for the most part on water-power — a technology that went back at least as far as Roman times. True, Newcomen had devised a means of using steam-power to pump out Cornish tin-mines as early as 1705. But it was 1769 before Watt and Boulton produced a steam-engine efficient enough for more general use, and 1801 before it occurred to Richard Trevithick to use it as a mobile power-source. The following year William Symington produced the first steamboat, so realising at last the extraordinary vision first mooted by the millenarian Friar Roger Bacon back in the thirteenth century. And it was 1829 before George Stephenson, with others, finally re-used the technique to inaugurate the age of the railways.

By now, however, the long-hoped-for Industrial Revolution, with all its promise of a future Utopia for humanity, was at last in full swing.

* * *

It is a curious fact that, to start with at least, the newly-revealed wonders of science were regarded as truly Romantic — not merely because they promised ever deeper insights into the sacred marvels of nature, but also because their technological spin-offs held the promise of eventually relieving people of the need for manual labour (much as the human slaves of ancient Greece and Rome had done before them), so allowing the new, idealised, Romantic man the time and leisure to spend his days in paradisical contemplation.

Later, though, it came to be realised that the new technologies were beginning to produce a world that was far from paradisical. Instead of a return to the Garden of Eden, an entirely different vision was coming into manifestation. Its initial signs were smoky, overcrowded cities and ruthless, capitalist exploitation of the poor — and there was no telling where it would all end. Certainly not, it seemed, in the final foundation on earth of the long-promised City of God. In Blake's memorable, if sardonic words,

And was Jerusalem builded here
Among these dark Satanic mills?

To the high priests of the new technologies, however, all was undoubtedly well. With enormous energy and originality they set out along the path which their new, materialistic religion set before them, supremely confident that it at last offered people the opportunity that they had been seeking for so long — to build a new world of their own devising, an earthly paradise which, thanks to their own efforts, would at last offer virtually all the seemingly miraculous benefits which had formerly been held out before them by biblical Christianity in the name of the Kingdom of Heaven on earth.

Progress was definitely in the air. And this time it really *was* progress, not merely a return to some supposed former state of bliss. The new Millennium would be a phenomenon that had never been seen before in the history of the world.

And it would be an entirely human creation.

* * *

Strange as it may seem, it was out of the infant Industrial Revolution's need for an efficient national transport system that the second main reason for the new belief in progress first arose. And it did so in the most unexpected of ways — namely as a result of the associated development in Britain of a technology largely imported (like King William III himself) from Holland.

The technique of canal-building.

The roads of King William's time were, after all, still in a very poor state of repair, despite numerous official attempts to rectify the situation. The railways had not yet come into existence. Canals, on the other hand, promised an enormous increase in the amount of freight that could be carried from A to B at any one time, with a correspondingly enormous decrease in unit costs.

Accordingly, the first major canal was eventually constructed in 1757. By 1775 a whole network of major waterways was already connecting the main ports with every large coalfield in the country. As the work went on, there came into being a veritable army not only of itinerant manual labourers skilled in this particular work — mainly imported from Ireland, and known ever since as 'navvies', from the 'navigation' works in which they were engaged — but also of highly-experienced canal-building engineers.

The situation was extraordinarily reminiscent of the Middle Ages, when the great cathedrals — the vessels, if not the actual sea-lanes, of contemporary *religious* trade — were built by similar travelling gangs of specialised labour which were in time to give rise to institutionalised Freemasonry (see next chapter).

Soon the engineers, as well as knowing every trick in the trade, were accumulating an extraordinarily thorough knowledge of the types of rock through which they were cutting their canals, as well as of their national distribution. By the 1790s it was becoming clear that the earth's surface was made up of a series of 'strata', lying at all sorts of crazy angles, which emerged at the surface in more or less predictable patterns, and each of which contained its own characteristic mixture of fossilised plant and animal remains. Soon it even became possible to use these remains to identify the rocks concerned. And so the science of geology was born.

One of the acknowledged experts in such matters was the canal-builder William Smith, who between 1796 and 1814 (when he published his book *Strata Identified by Organised Fossils*), succeeded in mapping geologically the whole of England and Wales.

What was important about the work of Smith and his successors, however, was not so much what it did for canal-building as what it did for humanity's view of its place in the universe. For at a very early stage it became evident that many of the animal remains in particular were totally unknown to zoology. It began to seem as if there had been not one, but several different Creations — each corresponding, perhaps, to one of the 'days' of the biblical account, and each destroyed in its turn by its own particular Flood. But the lie was soon given to this idea by the fact that some of the creatures concerned still existed in modern times, while a good many of the fishes among them (presumably immune to destruction by floods, whether biblical or otherwise) had long since ceased to exist.

Meanwhile the dramatic discovery, during the 1820s, of ever-increasing numbers of identifiable dinosaur fossils merely served to sharpen the argument and to spark off widespread public interest in the whole affair.

By the time the botanist Charles Lyell published his three-volume *Principles of Geology* in 1830, it was already clear that the development of life on earth had in fact been a single, continuous process (albeit characterised by alternating periods of stasis and dynamic development) lasting not the mere six thousand or so years suggested by Archbishop Usher's seventeenth-century analysis of Bible chronology, but untold aeons of time. And the first discoveries of primeval *human* remains in the bed of the river Somme, apparently antedating the biblical Garden of Eden by thousands of millennia, seemed finally to put the scientific cat among the religious pigeons.

For now the very origin and destiny of the human race itself had been drawn into the argument.

A theology student and amateur entomologist by the name of Charles Darwin was one of those who were immensely impressed by Lyell's work. Quite coincidentally, he was also intrigued by Malthus's celebrated theories on the relationship between population and food supply, first published in 1838. Putting two and two together following his celebrated research-voyage aboard the *Beagle* and his equally celebrated visit, in the course of it, to the Galapagos Islands, Darwin eventually combined Lyell's and Malthus's ideas to establish what he believed to be the mechanism behind the whole process of what was evidently some kind of evolutionary process. He called it 'natural selection' — though we nowadays tend to refer to it by the railway-engineer Herbert Spencer's much more colourful phrase 'the survival of the fittest'.

Apparently apprehensive about the potentially explosive implications of his new theory — or perhaps merely anxious to ensure that all his details were correct before publication — Darwin hesitated for thirteen years before releasing news of it to his colleagues. Almost at the same moment he received word that a young naturalist by the name of Alfred Russel Wallace had reached almost identical conclusions as a result of his own researches in Malaya. It was this news that at last forced Darwin to publish his highly influential work *On the Origin of Species by Means of Natural Selection* in 1859.

The book's theme was that evolutionary change was inevitable — as it were an inbuilt feature of the whole of creation (for Darwin, contrary to common belief, still managed, despite occasional worrying doubts, to believe in one). This evolutionary change was in turn based on the constant struggle for survival, in which the species and the individuals best adapted to current conditions would always tend to triumph and consequently replicate themselves. The result was a constant upward slope towards perfection — a slope which had led to humanity itself, and might result in even further marvels yet.

For Darwin's contemporaries, the most controversial aspect of all this was, of course, that it seemed to allow no room for God — except, possibly, at the very beginning of the whole process. And in particular, it seemed to suggest that the appearance of *homo sapiens* was a mere accident, the result of purely mechanical processes. This view seemed totally incompatible with the traditional religious teaching that God had created humanity in his own image and with a definite spiritual destiny in mind.

The human species, it seemed, was reduced to a mere glorified ape. Materialism had been elevated into a new god. The religious foundations of traditional civilisation seemed to be threatened.

And so the great battle between science and religion was finally on in earnest.

Yet the battle was as good as settled almost before it had begun. True, there was for a time an effective spiritual backlash against the materialism of the Industrial Revolution and its indirect progeny of Darwinian ideas. Not only was there a new upsurge in the Free Church movement, especially among the industrial masses. There was also a powerful, if temporary, spiritual revival within the established churches themselves, as represented, for example, by the Oxford (or 'High Church') Movement within Anglicanism. At the same time new, alternative forms of religious experience started to become popular, notably in the form of the Spiritualist movement (founded in America in 1847) and the Christian Science movement of 1879 — to say nothing of the other, more exotic cults which we shall be considering in some detail later.

But the die was cast. The ancient preconceptions and 'final answers' of religion stood no more chance than the old, Newtonian dispensation of universal symmetry and stability against the new myth of progressism and human perfectibility, which was clearly an idea whose time had now come. The new, Darwinist view quickly gripped the contemporary imagination, and as it did so the assumption grew steadily more widespread that the inevitability of progress was nothing less than an inbuilt characteristic of the universal order, which it was therefore futile for humanity to resist.

To such an extent that, nowadays, the mere quotation of the trite adage 'You can't stop progress' is generally quite enough to silence any suggestion to the contrary.

* * *

Both Wallace and Darwin, meanwhile, had been profoundly influenced by the third major source of the nineteenth century's belief in progress — a source that was neither industrial nor scientific, but strictly academic in nature.

That source was philosophy itself.

Ever since the 1820s, the influence of the German philosopher Hegel on contemporary thought had been steadily growing. His teaching was centred on the idea that the whole universal order was engaged in an upward struggle towards what he called the Absolute, characterised by a dialectical process whereby each new idea or development engendered its opposite, and the reaction between the two produced a higher state to which both contributed.

In the idea's classic formulation: thesis, antithesis, synthesis.

This overall process was a direct function of the fact that the Absolute was in a sense already in existence in the realm of mind, so that observed reality — being likewise, as Hume had demonstrated, a function of mind — had no option but eventually to bring that Absolute, through the laws of reason, into concrete manifestation.

Everything, in other words, was in a constant state of creative becoming, and only absolute perfection could therefore lie at the end of the road.

Hegel's younger contemporary Arthur Schopenhauer had arrived at a similar conclusion — though, as it happens, by an entirely different route. Whereas the root of Hegel's insights lay in the teachings of Kant, and thus ultimately in Hume and Locke, Schopenhauer's ideas derived very largely from Anquetil-

Duperron's highly influential 1804 translation of the Hindu *Upanishads*, as well as from Buddhist teaching. Consequently it is no surprise to find him propounding the idea that the Universal Being, hidden though it is behind the impenetrable veil of sensory illusion, has an inexorable will of its own, which Schopenhauer called the 'life-force' (a notion which was to become something of an obsession among later German thinkers) and which he equated with the sex-drive (thus anticipating Freud by several decades). While his view of the consequences for the individual were decidedly pessimistic, he was profoundly convinced that the universe was thus continually evolving (though in this case unconsciously and irrationally) towards the highest possible form of existence.

This last view was in due course to be enthusiastically endorsed (and for largely similar reasons) by the various 'alternative' spiritual movements which grew up shortly after Schopenhauer's death, notably the Theosophical Society and its offshoots — and thus, by direct succession, the New Age movement of our own century.[42] The latter, in other words, can quite legitimately count both Hegel and Schopenhauer among its philosophical progenitors.

By the middle of the nineteenth century, Schopenhauer's book *The World as Will and as Representation* was already becoming popular among the intelligentsia, while Hegel's views had developed into something of an official orthodoxy in strictly philosophical and academic circles. The final, intellectual accolade had been set, in other words, on the fashionable idea of inevitable progress which both industry and empirical science already seemed to be validating ever more emphatically with each succeeding year.

No doubt it was largely due to this overwhelming constellation of progressionist influences that many of the movements for social change which characterised the mid-nineteenth century had a much more positive vision of what precisely they wished to achieve than, say, the French Revolution of 1789. Many of the social reformers who sparked off the revolutions in Austria, Hungary, Germany, Italy and France during the year 1848 actually did so on the basis of definite programmes for social reform.

Karl Marx's *Communist Party Manifesto* of the same year was a case in point. Taking as its basis both the apparent materialism of Darwinism and its affirmation of the absolute necessity for struggle as a prerequisite for progress, Marx's ideology also drew on Hegelian dialectic as a model for social evolution, and sought its motivation for social change in the brutal social divisions which had resulted from the Industrial Revolution — an explosive mixture of ideas which he finally topped off, for good measure, with a goodly dose of typical Hebrew millenarianism.

There was, it seemed, an inexorable historical process whereby the rule of the aristocracy must be superseded by that of the bourgeoisie, who must in turn be violently overthrown by proletarian revolution. Then must ensue the 'dictatorship of the proletariat' — a marvellously ambiguous phrase by which Marx presumably meant government by the workers, but which has in practice been interpreted by successive revolutionary leaderships to mean government of the workers by a largely self-appointed caucus of party leaders. And finally this arrangement, too, must disappear as the state 'withered away', to leave a kind of benevolent anarchy very much reminiscent of the traditional Jewish vision of the final Kingdom of Heaven, in which each man would at last sit unmolested under his vine.

But Marx was not alone in his indebtedness to the typical progressist assumptions of the nineteenth century. In America, the self-same influences — the supremacy of materialist values, the conviction of the necessity for struggle, the belief in the survival of the fittest and in the consequent inevitability of social progress — were largely responsible for the typical American belief in self-reliance, ruthless competition and success-through-strength which still characterises the typical outlook of much of America to this day. The main difference was that, where Marx had applied these ideas to an entire social class, the American social pioneers applied them to single individuals — much as the original terms of Darwinian theory actually required.

It was the same nexus of ideas which, in Germany, was eventually to produce a national obsession with racial purity and dominance, a belief in the necessity for national struggle against degenerate enemies, and a conviction of the eventual triumph of the German nation as alone embodying the true human spirit — a truly *racial* application of Darwinism which was, of course, to become the basis of twentieth-century Nazism.

As for the eventual New Age movement, it too was to become suffused with enthusiasm for the idea of human progress and evolution. In its case, however, the evolutionary sequence was to be seen in terms very different from Darwin's. Thanks to the extraordinary writings of Madame Blavatsky in the 1880s, supplemented by those of Rudolf Steiner some forty years later, the general evolutionary scheme was to be seen in the form of a cyclic 'descent' of spirit into matter and back out of it again. The associated development of life from mineral to vegetable and vegetable to animal was no more than the material context for this underlying process. Evolution there therefore was, even at the material level, but the *real* evolution, the *real* progress lay in the lessons cumulatively learned by an essentially spiritual humanity from the ever-repeated round of earthly experience.

The importance of the general idea of evolution to this theory may be gauged from the fact that the term is mentioned no less than thirty-two times in Madame Blavatsky's celebrated and (for New Agers) truly seminal book *The Secret Doctrine*.[5] And the present-day relevance of its argument in this regard lies in the assertion that the great cycle is currently in its 'upward' mode, so assuring the progress of humanity for millions of years to come. And not only of humanity. For the apes, too, are destined to share in this resplendent future, having actually *descended from man* in the first place.

So, at least, Madame Blavatsky made bold to claim. And even if this last conviction was not to be widely admitted to by later 'New Age' heirs to her ideas, that of humanity's almost inevitable progress towards a shining future destiny of spiritual light and truth most certainly was.

* * *

Between them, then, science, technology and philosophy had conspired to ensure that, in whatever form, progressism would be the reigning myth of the late nineteenth and early twentieth centuries. It took a hundred years and two world wars before the conviction that 'You can't stop progress' started to run into severe problems — and even then the idea was to die hard.

Despite the mass slaughter of the trenches during the First World War; despite the mass unemployment of the inter-war period; despite the Jewish holocaust and the mass destruction which resulted from Hitler's Nazi experiment; despite the shock to traditional values administered by Hiroshima and the growth of the world-wide nuclear threat — despite all these, it seemed, there were always brighter things to point to. Medicine had improved by leaps and bounds. Standards of living in the industrial West had risen for all classes of society. To those who could afford them science and technology offered a growing cornucopia of hitherto unheard-of marvels to sweeten the pill of daily life.

Yet by the 1960s it was starting to become starkly clear to all those who cared to think honestly about things as they were (and these, as ever, were mainly the young) that actual experience just did not back up the grand, progressist assumption.

In whatever direction one looked, it was becoming increasingly obvious that what passed for progress was not necessarily anything of the kind. Far from solving the world's problems, the achievements of science and industry, of politics and social engineering, were merely shuffling them around. It was almost as if there were a fixed amount of *problema* in the world — a *problema* which no amount of planning or problem-solving could do anything about, and which was actually a direct function of that human consciousness which had presumably produced it in the first place.

It was not merely that modern civilisation, having removed all the environmental pressures which ensured that only the fittest would survive, had effectively stopped the biological evolution of the human race dead in its tracks. It was not merely that the various socialist revolutions showed not the slightest sign of producing true communism — i.e. Marx's ideal, stateless society — let alone a better world. Science and technology, too, actually appeared, on a world scale at least, to be making things worse rather than better.

In the Western, developed nations the continuing development of industry and consequent urbanisation was leading to an ever-growing divide between the rich and the poor, to mounting problems of crime and drug-abuse, to pollution of the environment and dangerous over-exploitation of the world's natural resources. Greater material expectations among the populace at large were producing greater demand, and so leading, in a context of resource shortages, to rampant inflation. At the same time growing industrial efficiency was resulting in greater unemployment, both among the customer-nations of the Third World and eventually at home too — not to mention an ever-more-dehumanised working environment. This in turn, along with inflation, was providing a fertile breeding ground for increasing industrial and social discontent, to more and more frequent confrontations between unions and managements and — where the latter came under the direct control of left-wing governments — between workers and the state itself.

An important aspect of the industrial scene, meanwhile, was the manufacture of ever more sophisticated arms, whether for use at home or for export. Not surprisingly, this exporting of the technology of conflict tended to encourage the world-wide proliferation of warfare, which in turn supplied further incentives for the development of still more deadly armaments. And the eventual result of all this was, of course, the development of nuclear weapons so powerful, and delivery systems so deadly, as to place the very survival of humanity under a dark cloud of deepest doubt.

Supposed advances elsewhere were having no less deadly effects. The apparently innocent activity of improving health-technology was not merely making life longer and more pleasant at home, but also reducing the rate of infant mortality in Third World countries. This in turn was resulting in a massive explosion in the world's population — and in those parts of the world which could least afford it, at that. The consequently increased demand for commodities in those countries was resulting, paradoxically, in a turning over of ever scarcer fertile lands to cash-crops in order to pay the interest on vital foreign loans. These were being used to buy food and industrial machinery from the richer countries — both of which naturally had to be paid for at First World rates. Moreover, this very development tended to push up the prices of those self-same foods, so rendering the plight of the Third World even more hopeless.

Even such attempts as were being made to solve the various problems were merely producing new ones. At home, wage and price controls worked for a time, but merely served, in the end, to fuel further explosions in inflation. Social reforms to help the poor merely made them more dependent and estranged them from the rest of society. Minimum-wage legislation merely tended to decrease the number of jobs available.

Alternative strategies proved no more successful. Monetarist policies brought down inflation, only to drive the weakest to the wall. 'Targeted' social welfare benefits created unforeseen poverty traps. 'Pricing yourself into a job' too often meant selling yourself into near-slavery and exploitation. Market freedom meant freedom to make money, but it also meant freedom to starve.

Attempts to help the Third World were having similarly unforeseen effects. Loans merely made the recipient nations even more indebted than they had been before. Cash-grants were often either made conditional upon purchases being made from the wealthy nations, or were misappropriated by Third World government-officials intent on achieving for themselves a First World lifestyle. And even direct gifts of food tended to produce increased dependency and helplessness, and a consequent need for even further gifts of food.

The cycle of problems seemed never-ending, and the long-revered processes of reason were clearly no longer capable of solving them. Indeed, it was reason's brainchild, technology, that had apparently caused most of the problems in the first place. It seemed highly unlikely, then, that it could be of much help in discovering suitable antidotes.

Even the reassurances of eminent futurologists such as Herman Kahn that the problems could still be solved at some future date by a combination of further technical marvels seemed to leave two vital questions unanswered: For whom? And at whose expense?

The sole eventual beneficiaries, it began to seem, would be the marvellous machines themselves, almost as if humanity's sole role in cosmic evolution were to act as midwife to some kind of superior, self-replicating, artificial intelligence — a new brand of 'fittest' that would keep human beings more or less as pets, while itself going on to think thoughts and to experience experiences that would be forever closed to humanity itself. (Curiously enough, this would accord perfectly satisfactorily with the book of Daniel's description of the coming Saviour [7:13] merely as 'one like a man'. It could even be held to explain why, although the Genesis account places human creation on the sixth day, the creation-week is not counted as complete until a further day — specifically described as a 'day of rest' — has elapsed on the seventh.)

As for the ultimate losers in the process, it is difficult to avoid identifying them with the bulk of humanity itself — and notably the inhabitants of the Third World — whether through injustice, inequality, starvation or simply brute nuclear extinction. To say nothing of all the other nasties that have long been predicted by a whole range of psychics and mystics for the 1990s and beyond.[41,44]

And so it is that the realisation is now dawning among the public at large — and not before time — that, for humanity at least, material 'progress' is as likely to lead to hell as to heaven on earth.

Which is not altogether surprising. For the literal meaning of the word 'progress' is 'stepping forward'. And whether that stepping-forward will lead you to anywhere better depends entirely on your initial choice of road.

12
When the Light Dawns

Truth is within ourselves; it takes no rise
From outward things, whate'er you may believe.
There is an inmost centre in us all
Where truth abides in fullness . . . and to know
Rather consists in opening out a way
Whence the imprisoned splendour may escape,
Than in effecting entry for a light
Supposed to be without.

Robert Browning: 'Paracelsus'

When you reach an impasse, it is only natural to assume that you have taken the wrong road. And certainly there were many who, even as early as the last quarter of the nineteenth century, were convinced that Western humanity had made a fatal mistake in taking the road of Darwinist materialism in the first place.

Rationalism, it seemed, had been weighed in the balance and found wanting. The Kingdom of Heaven was not, after all, in the gift of science.

Indeed, it was increasingly evident by now that reason, far from being the godlike embodiment of truth and justice that it had once seemed to be, was no more than a convenient tool for making sense of experience, and one which was fully capable of justifying any position whatever — a fact which was (and still is) perfectly apparent no less from a comparison of the conflicting statements of succeeding generations of scientists than from those of any single generation of lawyers and politicians.

Yet the result of this realisation was not, as might have been expected, the final abandonment of the idea of progress and human perfectibility altogether. Still less was it the reinstatement of the official religious dogmas which Darwinism was, in the event, doing so much to undermine at the time. For the Church's views, too, were totally flawed. That much had been equally evident to a good many thinkers and doubters ever since the time of the Renaissance.

Instead, what emerged was yet another progressist movement, but one which was to base its evolutionary ideas on essentially *non*-materialistic foundations.

We have already referred to it on numerous occasions. For it was at this point that what has nowadays come to be loosely referred to as the 'New Age' movement started to come into its own.

Yet 'New Ageism' did not spring up overnight, as it were out of nowhere. Like every movement, it had its roots. And it is to the time of the Renaissance that we need to return in order to discover the most vital of them. Indeed, it is to the wisdom of classical and even pre-classical times that (as we hinted earlier) the movement owes many of its characteristic ideas.

It is therefore to the story of their subsequent growth and development that we now need to turn our attention.

* * *

We have already seen how, at the time of the High Renaissance, a veritable flood of ancient classical lore had poured into Italy. Contrary to what is often believed, however, the information involved was far from being purely rational and scientific in character. Indeed, the chief inspiration behind Cosimo de Medici's founding of his famous library in Florence seems to have been rather his passion for the specifically *Platonic* aspect of classical learning, as augmented by the gnostic and hermetic insights of the Neoplatonic philosophers of third-century Alexandria. It seems to have been as a result of a series of lectures by the Byzantine scholar Georgios Gemistos (better known as 'Pletho'), the Mistra-born rediscoverer of Plato, that Cosimo then went on to found his Platonic academy and to commission other scholars such as Marsilio Ficino to translate not only the works of Plato, but also the *Corpus Hermeticum*, a compendium of extremely ancient teachings handed down not only from Pythagoras and Plato, but also allegedly from such shadowy figures as the mythical Orpheus and the Egyptian Hermes Trismegistus. Ficino's pupil Picco della Mirandola added further works to the list, and in his *Nine Hundred Conclusions* even managed to incorporate Kabbalistic elements into the general scheme of things.[50]

With the shifting of the centre of gravity of the Italian Renaissance from Florence to papal Rome, this tradition of classical all-inclusiveness continued. Astonishing as it may now seem, the contemporary Roman Church gave every sign of being prepared to accept the whole corpus of pagan classical and neo-classical tradition — both Aristotelian and Platonic — as of value to the advancement of contemporary humanity.

As we saw earlier, however, the honeymoon proved to be short-lived. With the rise of Protestantism in northern Europe and the sack of Rome in 1527 the Church was placed very much on the defensive, and its reaction was to beat a hasty retreat from its former position of relative tolerance. The chief effect of what is now known as the Counter-Reformation, as set in train by the epoch-making Council of Trent, was a period of severe retrenchment. As a result of it the teachings of Aristotle, insofar as they posed no threat to Church doctrine, were henceforth to be regarded as virtually on a par with Holy Writ, while the Platonic and Neoplatonic teachings were seen as rivalling, and therefore threatening, the traditional spiritual teachings of the Church. There was, it seemed, only one spiritual truth and one way of attaining it — and to that heavenly dispensation the Church, by definition the heir to the mantle of St Peter, held the only key. Such, at least, was the gist of the official position.

The result was inevitable. The much broader insights of Platonism and Neoplatonism were quickly driven underground. The gnostic and hermetic traditions came to be seen as pertaining to the same subversive, esoteric realm as magic, witchcraft and medieval alchemy. Yet, as with all movements driven underground by official repression, the resulting tradition of broadly-based, dissident, alternative spirituality soon started to acquire ever-increasing strength and popularity among those of independent mind.

* * *

After eighteen years of intermittent wrangling, the Council of Trent finally came to an end in 1563. Perhaps it is no accident, therefore, that it was within only a few years of the promulgation of its repressive conclusions that the first 'alternative' spiritual groupings started to make their presence felt. And, naturally enough, the first stirrings emerged within the relatively secure Protestant milieu of countries such as Germany.

Germany, after all, had long had an alternative mystical tradition of its own, based both on its own version of the Arthurian legend and on a whole succession of decidedly eccentric flesh-and-blood mystics such as 'Meister' Eckhart, Nicholas of Cusa, Agrippa von Nettesheim and the celebrated Paracelsus. Among the themes most characteristic of this general tradition were not only the idea of a mystic brotherhood of idealists serving humanity *incognito* behind the scenes, but also that of a great leader, long since fallen asleep, who would one day reappear to lead the world to its ultimate fulfilment — i.e. to the long-awaited Golden Age.

Clearly, this latter part of the tradition — represented by the legends not only of King Arthur, but also of Charlemagne and the emperor Frederick Barbarossa — had direct thematic links with the Jewish and Christian Messianic teachings, as foreshadowed in turn by ancient Zoroastrian lore. As for the tradition's 'secret brotherhood' aspect — as represented by the legendary Grail-quest of King Arthur's knights — this seemed to have a special relevance at a time when a new body of behind-the-scenes ideal-ists felt themselves to be the sole bearers of a now-banned spirit-ual inheritance which, in their own view at least, could yet prove to be of inestimable benefit to a hard-pressed humanity in search of heaven on earth.

And so it was that, with the approach of the year 1600, condi-tions were ripe for a ferment of 'occult' millenarian speculation along these general lines. Much of it was to take for its starting-point the writings of the immensely influential twelfth-century Italian abbot and mystic Joachim of Fiore. For Joachim, basing his speculations largely on Old Testament chronology, had put for-ward a view of history which envisaged a succession of three great ages — that of the Father (based on Old Testament Law), that of the Son (based on faith in the Christian Gospel) and that of the Holy Ghost (an age of perfect freedom based on direct spirit-ual revelation, as foreshadowed by the prophet Jeremiah and already taken up by the Essenes themselves as a model for the final Kingdom of Heaven[41]). Since each of these ages apparently lasted 1260 years, it followed that the final, post-gospel age would start in around the year AD 1260, after a grim but brief period of world purification instigated by the expected Antichrist and last-ing some three-and-a-half years.

As ever, Joachim had of course assigned the advent of his Millenn-ium to a date shortly after his own time. As ever, equally, he was to be proved wrong. In consequence, numerous later scholars and speculators were to revise and elaborate his datings and general scheme of things — all in their turn assigning the New Age to a date just in advance of their own times.

Thus, in his *Prognosticum Theologicum* of 1588, a scholar by the name of Adam Nachenmoser advanced the view that the 1260 years of the Gospel Age should instead be counted from the death of the emperor Constantine in AD 327, so giving a date of 1587 for the final inauguration of the Golden Age. Since this figure seemed rather untidy, however, he proposed that the intervening time of troubles was destined to last not three-and-a-half, but thirteen years — so putting the inauguration of the Millennium back to the numerically more satisfactory date of 1600. Moreover, in keeping with the last verse of the book of Malachi, it was to be expected that a new reincarnation of Elijah would duly appear to proclaim it.

And in the event Nachenmoser's proposed scheme turned out to be yet another idea whose time had come.

* * *

In the year 1614 esoteric circles in Europe were suddenly electrified by the publication of an extraordinary German pamphlet entitled *Fama Fraternitatis, dess Löblichen Ordens des Rosenkreutzes* ('The Legend of the Brotherhood of the Worthy Order of the Rose-Cross'). Allegedly first circulated in manuscript as early as 1610, it related the story of one Christian Rosenkreuz, who had ostensibly lived during the fourteenth and fifteenth centuries and, after acquiring much of the secret knowledge of the East, had founded a secret Brotherhood whose members, working behind the scenes, went about healing the sick and dispensing the hidden wisdom to those worthy of receiving it.

Rosenkreuz, it was alleged, had lived to the remarkable age of 106, and had then been buried in a vault which had only recently been discovered and reopened after an interval of 120 years, so giving rise to the present document.

Since the opening of the tomb was supposed to have occurred in 1604, this would give Rosenkreuz's dates as 1378-1484, and the period of his occupation of the hidden, underground chamber as 1484-1604.

The actual message of the document was no less startling than the alleged circumstances of its publication. Anybody interested in participating in the Brotherhood's work had only to make their interest known in any way for the Brotherhood to hear about it: by whatever mysterious means, actual contact would then follow. And the eventual upshot of the whole initiative would be the final establishment of a new era on earth.

In the words of the *Fama* itself, 'We know that after a while there will now be a general reformation of things both divine and human after our desire.'

In the following year a further document followed. This one was entirely in Latin, and entitled *Confessio Fraternitatis* ('The Confession of the Brotherhood'). But its basic message was much the same. Thanks to the exalted wisdom of the purported Brotherhood, the world would shortly be reformed and the tyranny of papal

Rome finally overthrown. The *Fama*'s millenarian theme, in other words, continued unabated. Soon, proclaimed the *Confessio*, 'the world shall awake out of its heavy, drowsy slumbers, and with an open heart, bare-headed and barefoot, shall merrily and joyously go to meet the new sunrise.'

The documents' author, as the text makes evident, was fervently anti-Catholic, if not specifically Protestant. Moreover, both the language of the *Fama* and its place of publication (Kassel) showed him to be German, while its general tone made it apparent he was convinced that Germany was destined to play a leading role in the establishment of the expected New Order.

In 1616 the third of what are now known as the Rosicrucian Manifestos was published. This took the form of an extraordinary novel entitled *Die Chymische Hochzeit Christiani Rosenkreutz* ('The Chemical Wedding of Christian Rosenkreuz'), in which Rosenkreuz himself purportedly describes his fantastic experiences at the wedding of a mythical king and queen in terms replete with occult and alchemical symbolism.

The true meaning and purpose of this work have never been conclusively established, and so it is open to an almost unlimited number of possible interpretations. What *is* known about it, however, is the identity of its real author. As he himself later admitted, he was a young Protestant theologian from Tübingen by the name of Johann Valentin Andreae. Moreover, it now seems evident that he had had at least a hand in the other two works as well.[50]

Yet why should a Protestant theologian, or even a group of them (as seems possible), choose to unleash such a seductive philosophical bombshell on an unsuspecting world? What were they seeking to achieve? And did they have any inkling of the practical effects their initiative might have?

In answer to the first of these questions we can only speculate. Any one of a number of reasons might apply — from mere youthful rebellion and high spirits, through a desire to provoke the Protestant establishment into a real effort at world-reform, to a genuine feeling that dry, Bible-based Protestantism, no less than rigid Catholic dogma, was currently ignoring the deeper aspects of humanity's psyche and spirituality on which alone the prospects of ultimately bringing heaven down to earth truly rested.

Possibly, indeed, their purpose was purely satirical.

To the last of the above questions, however, a more definite answer seems possible. For it seems quite clear that Andreae and his colleagues failed completely to anticipate the flurry of spurious claims, over-literal interpretation and general self-delusion to which their efforts would in due course lead.

True, they had been careful at the time to make it quite clear that what they had produced partook somewhat of the nature of a 'Devil's Advocate' argument. This they had done by binding with the *Fama* an extract from an allegorical satire entitled *News from Parnassus* by the Italian author Trajano Boccalini. In German translation this extract was entitled *Allgemeine und General Reformation, der gantzen weiten Welt* ('The Universal and General Reformation of the Whole Wide World'), and its eventual moral was that all systems and formulas for reforming society were inherently invalid, and that only a renewal of human love and goodwill could hope to bring the final Millennium into being.

The contents of the Manifestos, in other words, might be exciting stuff, but it was all pretty incidental to the serious business of restoring the world to rights. Perhaps, indeed, the real implication was that all such speculations are inherently invalid.

The gullible, however, were not to be fobbed off. What they wanted was certainties. Determinedly refusing to notice the true meaning of the Latin word *Fama* ('Legend' or 'Rumour'), they persisted in clinging to the Manifestos' apparent assurance that there was another order of reality, a realm of existence that was as immune from the dry-as-dust literalism of Protestant theology and the down-to-earthness of post-Renaissance intellectualism as it was from the superstitious tyranny of Catholic dogma.

The Brotherhood, in other words, with its marvellous knowledge and semi-magical powers, was a fact, and it was therefore of paramount importance to seek it out, to emulate its powers, even — if necessary — to appoint oneself to its ranks.

In vain did Andreae and others attempt to point out that the Manifestos' contents had been purely symbolic, if not intentionally downright spurious. 'Harken, you mortals,' he wrote in his suggestively-entitled *Turris Babel* of 1619. 'You await in vain the coming of the Brotherhood. The comedy is at an end.' Even the circumstances of Christian Rosenkreuz's alleged life should have made the true state of affairs perfectly clear to all concerned. Not only was 'Rosenkreuz' a totally non-existent German surname, but the combination of his two names into an expression meaning, quite literally, 'Christian Rose-Cross' was just as clearly allegorical as the name of Mr Valiant-for-Truth in Bunyan's somewhat later *Pilgrim's Progress* — and apparently a direct reference to the design of Martin Luther's coat of arms to boot. Indeed, even Rosenkreuz's supposed dates had a clear symbolic significance — for the dates assigned to his life fell comfortably within the period of the High

Renaissance, with its remarkable tolerance of the whole range of classical 'alternative' (not to say pagan) spiritual traditions; while the period of his entombment comfortably covered the period not only of the Reformation, but also of the Counter-Reformation and its aftermath, when those traditions had similarly had to 'go underground'.

But it was all to no avail. The deed had been done. The comedy was most emphatically *not* at an end. Soon a whole army of enthusiasts were promulgating and elaborating the message of the Manifestos. The Brotherhood's alleged wisdom was traced back to the earliest biblical times, or said to include the secret of transmuting base metals into gold. There was a positive stampede to form new Rosicrucian societies, or to join those already in existence, as though doing so would somehow confer on those involved something of the Brotherhood's own supposed wisdom and power.

The lure of the Brotherhood, indeed, has continued to exert its spell to this very day, and not least within the New Age movement itself.

* * *

But then it has to be said that there seems in any case to have been something of a mania for joining secret societies in northern Europe at around the turn of the seventeenth century. Andreae himself seems to have become a member of a semi-secret organisation called the *Fruchtbringende Gesellschaft* ('The Fructifying Society'), which was founded in 1617 on the model of an earlier Florentine equivalent.[50] This group was to become linked with a further secret order called the *Orden der Unzertrennlichen* ('The Order of Inseparables'), which had been founded in 1577 and concerned itself mainly with alchemy and smelting-technology. Among its alleged accoutrements were a hidden chest of secret documents and an equally secret alphabet which included alchemical symbols, and its organisation was based on a system of five grades designed to lead to the mastery of spiritual alchemy for the transformation of humankind.

The similarity to later Rosicrucian practice is of course striking, and it may well have been from either or both societies that Andreae drew his original model for the Manifestos' 'hidden Brotherhood'.

In Britain, meanwhile, there had arisen a similar vogue for joining secret organisations. Here, though, the process seems to have been sparked off by what, in effect, was a sudden vacuum in the British trade union movement.

Ever since the Middle Ages, the masons involved in building the great gothic cathedrals had constituted a basically itinerant fraternity whose members were of necessity largely unknown to each other. The result had been the development of a Catholic guild of masons characterised by a system of secret signs and forms of speech designed to mark out the qualified craftsmen from what we should nowadays call the 'cowboys'.

With the completion of Cambridge's King's College Chapel in about 1512, however, the gothic building programme virtually came to an end. It left behind it a guild without a purpose, an antique and semi-secret society whose private rituals and ceremonies no longer served any real purpose, an organisation largely bereft of active membership.

Quite suddenly, it seems, educated private gentlemen with nothing much better to do took to joining the lodges of the now largely defunct guild (for obvious reasons an exclusively male preserve), possibly as a mere, harmless pastime which promised to offer them some escape from the humdrum daily routine of business and family-life. Possibly, too, the exercise partook somewhat of the nature of the similar exercise whereby some members of the modern middle classes have taken to drinking in working-class pubs, or to buying up former peasants' cottages in an apparent attempt (rather like Marie Antoinette in her miniature dairy-farm at Versailles) to recapture the presumed rural bliss of a life close to the soil — though without actually committing themselves to any of its real-life disadvantages.

Whatever the reason, the numbers of the new, so-called 'speculative' (as opposed to 'operative') masons rapidly grew. The Edinburgh Lodge was already accepting 'speculative' members by 1600. In 1646 Elias Ashmole, founder of the Oxford Ashmolean Museum and himself a Rosicrucian enthusiast, was admitted into the movement. By 1670 the Aberdeen Lodge had nearly four times as many 'speculative' as 'operative' members. And in 1717 the Grand Lodge of England (itself entirely 'speculative' in character) was founded, incorporating within its organisation the old masonic tradition of three grades of membership — those of Apprentice, Fellow or Journeyman and Master Mason.

Now that Freemasonry (as we nowadays call the movement) had effectively freed itself from its Catholic working-class origins, opportunities for considerable change presented themselves. By the 1730s the organisation's essential Catholicism had been first watered down and then thrown out of the window in favour of a vague, typically eighteenth-century deism, while its internal rituals and ceremonies were being elaborated on the basis of what appear to have been largely Rosicrucian models.

And so it was that in 1813, after the new brand of Freemasonry had (as we have already seen) made a not inconsiderable mark on the founding institutions of the American republic, the United Grand Lodge of England was founded in more or less its present form. And a notable feature of the new organisation was the acceptance of the so-called 'Royal Arch' rite, which not only incorporated into its ritual its own version of the Rosicrucian legend of the discovery in a hidden vault of secret knowledge (in this case the 'lost name of God'), but also added thirty superior grades to the original three, each with its own special qualifications and initiation procedures.[35]

* * *

Rosicrucianism, meanwhile, had likewise been going from strength to strength, and its fame had been rapidly spreading. Even as early as the turn of the seventeenth century, Francis Bacon had certainly been familiar with the original Manifestos, and his younger contemporary Robert Fludd wrote copiously in support of the movement. Even the later Descartes made a vain attempt to contact the supposed Brotherhood. Indeed, the very foundation of Charles II's Royal Society in 1660 may have been influenced by the notion of the hidden Rosicrucian Brotherhood, as its former designation as the 'Invisible College' seems to hint.[50]

At the same time the movement was also widely attacked for its occult leanings by contemporary churchmen. Especially at issue was its apparent preoccupation with alchemy, whether inner or outer (i.e. whether concerned with magically transforming human nature or merely with transmuting base metals into gold.) This preoccupation was particularly rife among the eighteenth-century continental nobility — possibly as a reaction against the typical, dry rationalism of the time — and it was above all the German Rosicrucian order known as the *Gold- und Rosenkreuz* which appears to have pandered to it.

In due course, indeed, the very success of the 'Gold and Rosy Cross' was to lead to its own demise. This seems to have been largely due to its merging of the Rosicrucian tradition with a particularly exotic form of Freemasonry known as the 'Scottish Rite', which had been imported into France by Jacobite exiles and had subsequently made its way into Germany. The result was a movement which combined the idea of an elite equipped with secret knowledge, a distinct ethical and political conservatism, a pseudo-religious function and, perhaps above all, an appeal (very much in line with the original Rosicrucian Manifestos) to German nationalistic feelings. All this seems to have made the movement altogether too popular and powerful for the authorities, and in 1766 it was banned throughout the Austrian Empire and discredited in Germany as well.

The result was the founding of a new form of Rosicrucianism — or rather a version of Freemasonry with a goodly topping of Rosicrucian icing. Candidates for admission to the new order had already to have passed through the first three grades of orthodox Freemasonry before embarking upon the nine new Rosicrucian grades which followed. The notion of the Brotherhood was retained, however — now in the form of the *unbekannte Oberen*, a group of near-superhuman beings supposed to be in charge of human destiny. And the movement's aims were 'to activate the hidden forces of nature, to release nature's light which has become buried deep beneath the dross emanating from the curse, and in this way to light within each brother a torch by whose light he will the better be able to know the hidden God . . . and thereby become more closely at one with the primal source of light.'

Later versions of the order were to promulgate aims that were similar, if somewhat less imbued with obvious alchemical imagery. The Qabalistic Order of the Rosy Cross of 1888, for example, had as its stated purpose to study the classics of occultism, to enter into spiritual communion with the Divine through meditation and to spread the resulting wisdom to the uninitiated. With this we may compare the rather less dramatic ideals of conventional Freemasonry — the preservation of the order's own ancient secrets and rituals, mutual intellectual, social and moral improvement and the exercise of brotherly love to Masons and non-Masons alike.

* * *

The comparison is not an idle one, however. For in due course the two streams of idealism — the one often extravagantly occult, the other more urbanely idealistic — were to come together once again in response to an unfulfilled need deep within the human psyche. And the eventual child of the union was to be the modern New Age movement.

We have already seen how, during the third quarter of the nineteenth century, the rise of Darwinism dealt a body-blow to conventional religion. Educated people particularly — and especially members of the relatively open-minded Church of England — felt increasingly that the bottom had been knocked out of their religious world. With the very universe apparently reduced to a mere process of blind, mechanical chance, and humanity deprived of what previously had seemed to be its divine purpose, the whole of existence seemed to be reduced to meaninglessness, all hope of personal immortality and redemption to be dashed for ever.

Nature, it is often said, abhors a vacuum. And the principle was no less applicable than ever in the present case. In the lack of any coherent or convincing view of humanity's purpose and destiny (for the idea seems not yet to have sunk in that the Darwinian scheme of things actually implied that the human race itself could expect to evolve yet further), there was a golden opportunity — indeed, a pressing need — for some suitable substitute view to move in on the Western psyche.

One potential candidate was, of course, the model advanced by the new brand of Rosicrucian Freemasonry, with its conviction that humans could somehow pull themselves up by their own bootstraps through the exercise of hidden powers, liberated by ancient and arcane techniques of however uncertain a pedigree. Just such views, indeed, were even then being vigorously promoted by the Frenchman Alphonse-Louis Constant who, as 'Eliphas Lévi', had undertaken a massive exploration into magic and 'occultism' (his own word) and duly committed his copious and intriguing findings to print. Lévi's views in turn were being popularised by one of his leading disciples, the British novelist Lord Edward Bulwer-Lytton, whose novel *Zanoni* purported to describe the work of the same secret Brotherhood which Rosicrucianism supposed to be behind the task of bringing these occult views to eventual fruition.[85]

Another, equally powerful potential substitute for the now largely defunct Christian scheme of things was the oriental view based on the concepts of *karma* and reincarnation — a view which was even then starting to make itself felt in the West, thanks largely to the new translations of the Hindu scriptures by Anquetil-Duperron and the later Max Müller of Oxford. Popular awareness of the Eastern tradition was also being promoted by the ever more widely-circulated works of Schopenhauer, as well as being given added impetus by the recent establishment of the British Raj in India.

Perhaps it was inevitable, then, that in 1875 — the same year in which Max Müller published the first of his massive, fifty-one-volume *Sacred Books of the East* — a society was formed in New York which was to unify all these influences under one roof. Led by the formidable and perennially controversial Madame Helena Blavatsky and her colleague Colonel Henry Steele Olcott, the Theosophical Society's proclaimed purposes were to promote human brotherhood throughout the world, to encourage the comparative study of world religions and philosophies with a view to the establishment of some kind of unified world religious ethic, and to discover and develop hidden aspects of nature and the human psyche. The findings of modern science, too, were to be included in the general scheme of things.

It was not long, either, before the Rosicrucian 'secret Brotherhood' also entered the Theosophical picture in the form of a group of allegedly Himalayan 'Masters' whose sole intermediary Madame Blavatsky suddenly claimed to be. Among these supposed luminaries, curiously enough, there now figured both the Buddha and Jesus (later to be referred to almost exclusively as 'the Christ'). The latter, however, was stripped of his divine sonship and salvationist function, not least because, in the new, post-Darwinian climate, the very idea of God in the Christian sense could naturally find no place in the system.

Soon whole cosmologies and models of planetary destiny were being worked out — notably in Madame Blavatsky's already-mentioned work *The Secret Doctrine* of 1888.[5] Based largely on somewhat bowdlerised versions of the Hindu and Buddhist traditions, these proposed a version of the familiar cyclic model of world destiny which, as we saw earlier, actually offers little or no hope for the inception of a new Millennium within any conceivable human timescale, yet which in its new, Theosophical form at least made available a possible path to world transformation through the gradual spiritualisation of humanity at the instigation of the hidden Hierarchy, assisted by its duly initiated — if self-appointed — servants.

The impact of this fresh set of variations on the old teachings was both sudden and dramatic, and within a few years the influence of the new Society and its ideas was being felt virtually world-wide. Some of the most respected members of the European and American intelligentsia were soon committing themselves to its work, and the Society consequently achieved a remarkable degree of official respectability.

As later investigation was to reveal, however, that respectability was in many respects somewhat ill-founded. The story of the Society's internal growth and development (which I have chronicled elsewhere[42]) was, in the event, to be a stormy and even scandalous one. The extent and range of its influence was nevertheless to prove quite extraordinary, and was to reflect with great aptness the astonishing mixture of idealism and delusion, of selfless labour and personal egotism, of religious tolerance and esoteric dogmatism, of shared insights and vicious backbiting, of genuine research and deliberate hoodwinking which characterised the organisation's inner workings during its early years.

Thus, the Society had a profound and benign influence on the young M.K. (later 'Mahatma') Gandhi, being largely responsible for his discovery of his own national religious heritage. Both the young Jawaharlal Nehru and the young Krishna Menon later passed through its hands, no doubt to their general benefit. Its leaders played an important part in the Indian campaign for Home Rule, which was eventually to result in the nation's independence in 1947. It was in large measure responsible, too, for the new respect which Hinduism was to find both in India itself and, latterly, in the West as well. At the same time, thanks to the almost single-handed efforts of Olcott, it helped to bring about a powerful revival of world Buddhism — a revival which was likewise to have later repercussions in the West.[30]

But this was not all. In its efforts to initiate a new world order, it deliberately trained the young Jiddu Krishnamurti to be the future World Teacher, or Messiah — only to have him eventually turn around and reject their whole tottering edifice of belief. Mainly as a result of a series of internal crises, and not least a scandal concerning an alleged immoral incident during the young Messiah's training, it also helped generate a whole series of splinter-groups and occult movements of varying degrees of respectability, many of their founders being not only members of the Theosophical Society, but leading Rosicrucians and/or Freemasons as well.

Among these groups were the highly influential Order of the Golden Dawn of 1887 (best-known, much to its misfortune, for the lurid magico-sexual practices of its most celebrated member, the infamous Aleister Crowley); Max Heindel's Rosicrucian Fellowship of 1909; Rudolf Steiner's Anthroposophical Society of 1913, which deliberately concerned itself more with the innate wisdom of Western humanity than with that of supposed Eastern Masters; Spencer Lewis's well-known California-based Ancient Mystical Order of the Rosy Cross (AMORC) of around 1916; the obscure German magical/occult organisation EBDAR, set up by J.A. Schneiderfranken ('Bô Yin Râ') in around 1922; the remarkably serious and responsible Arcane School founded by Alice Bailey

(inventor of the very term 'New Age') in 1923; the correspondingly dubious Oriental Templar Order of the early 1920s; and the
Nazi party's occult organisation known as the Thule-Gesellschaft.
This last group was at least in part responsible for Adolf Hitler's
own vision of the New Age, to which he even referred specifically
by name — *die neue Zeit*. (Hence, no doubt, the fact that modern
German alternativists much prefer to use the safer *English* term
'New Age'!) The Nazis' thousand-year *Reich*, or Kingdom, was to be a
glorious, if harsh and puritanical, version of the Jewish millennium, ruled over by Germany in the name of the supposed Aryan
race — notwithstanding the fact that the latter's existence had
originally been mooted by Max Müller as a mere linguistic working hypothesis before it was taken up as an article of faith by
Madame Blavatsky.[5,42]

And not only these, but a whole host of other organisations and
groups were spawned, either directly or indirectly, by the Theosophical initiative, virtually all of them dedicated in some way to
the central Theosophical proposition that humanity had it within
its power to transform itself and so bring about a new era on earth
— an era of peace and toleration, of universal brotherhood, of
hitherto undreamt-of powers over both psyche and nature.

The old dream of human mastery over the universe, in short,
had been born again, if in a new, essentially non-rational form.
And it was out of that reborn dream that what we nowadays
know as the New Age movement was to take its genesis.

13

The Other Side of Change

It matters not how strait the gate,
How charged with punishments the scroll,
I am the master of my fate:
I am the captain of my soul.

W.E. Henley: 'Invictus'

The term 'New Age movement' is necessarily a vague one. Typically it could be said to refer to the whole family of movements, groupings, communities and networks of non-conventional millenarian idealists that have grown up out of the Theosophical initiative and its associated splinter-groups during our own century, and particularly since about the 1950s.

In view of this wide range of antecedents, it is no surprise to find that the movement is something of a many-headed monster. Indeed, its various Theosophical heads are not even its only ones. Which is just as well, since virtually all of those heads grew directly out of ancient bodies of tradition and practice many of which have already had two thousand years and more to produce worldwide results, without ever showing much sign of doing so.

(It is the very antiquity of these traditions which evidently lies behind the conviction, shared by many Rosicrucians and Masons alike, that their two movements were actually founded in very ancient times — the truth being, of course, that it is their adopted *traditions*, rather than the movements themselves, which can be traced back to such ancient beginnings.)

Other strands in the fabric of the New Age movement have been supplied by the dream-insights of the great Swiss psychologist Carl Gustav Jung (many of which, it has to be said, can likewise be traced back to ancient Greek initiatory practices); to more recent developments in applied psychology; to the indirect influence of thinkers representing most of the world's major religions (not excluding Christianity itself); to the growing public awareness during the 1960s of increasing problems of world pollution, raw-material depletion and environmental destruction posed by the very nature of advanced industrial societies; and to the general youth-revolt of about the same time, together with a more general movement for individual and social liberation — the combined result, it seems, of the social levelling brought about by two world wars, and of their destructive effects on the older generation's confidence in its rigid, traditional values.

Moreover the movement's millenarianism, as we observed at the outset, is far from unique. In fact it is the product of the whole range of earlier millenarian models, and of the philosophical and social developments which duly arose out of them — no less than are the purely materialistic forms of society which it seeks to replace.

Within its over-all framework it is thus forced to try and reconcile a host of apparent irreconcilables. On the one hand the cyclic cosmological models proposed by Hinduism, Buddhism, astrology and, latterly, Theosophy and Anthroposophy; on the other hand, not only the straight-line religious views represented by Zoroastrianism, Judaism, Christianity and/or Islam (each with its own particular dramatic eschatological conclusion), but also — and at one and the same time — the parallel secular alternatives advanced both by the backward-looking Renaissance and by the forward-looking scientific optimism of nineteenth-century evolutionary Darwinism.

On the one hand, in other words, a variety of views which see our planet's destiny as subject to the regular workings of an inexorable cosmic fate, or to the equally *ir*regular will of a capricious deity; on the other a similar range of views which place human destiny generally in the hands of humanity itself, or specifically in those either of a semi-divine Saviour or of a chosen (or even self-chosen) elite — variously seen either as human or as superhuman — which is either already in place or, conversely, yet to appear.

On the one hand, consequently, the conviction that the long-dreaded Last Times are already upon us and the world about to be reduced to ashes; on the other the contradictory view that the promised New Age can be achieved through positive human action without the need for any such 'purification' at all.

Moreover, the inherited, conventional conviction that this much-to-be-desired consummation can be achieved at least partially through the exercise of reason, backed up by the findings of modern science, is counterbalanced (indeed, in practice — and hardly surprisingly in the circumstances — largely outweighed) by the equally firm conviction that it is reason and science that got us into our present mess in the first place, and that a basically *ir*rational approach is consequently the sole guarantee of humanity's posterity.

It is a desperately explosive and incompatible mixture of ideas, and one that becomes all too clearly apparent to anyone visiting any of the various well-known jamborees — be it the Psychics and Mystics Fair or the Festival of Body, Mind and Spirit — at which the New Age movement regularly (and somewhat daringly) puts itself on public display. But then perhaps the New Agers are to be forgiven for trying to eat their conceptual cake and have it too (for all the obvious risk of severe digestive problems). Even more to be sympathised with, possibly, is the opposite tendency — the urge to eat only selected parts of the icing, while leaving the bulk of the cake untouched (for all the risk of subsequent philosophical mal-nutrition and dental decay).

For the upshot is that the whole movement has come to be char-acterised by an extraordinary mish-mash of ideas, a positive fer-ment of beliefs having little obvious connection with each other apart from a common conviction that sweeping changes are need-ed — changes not merely at the surface level, but in the whole corpus of assumptions which have hitherto underlain both individual behaviour and the structure of society, and Western industrial society in particular.

Whence, of course, the umbrella term commonly applied to the movement as a whole, together with its various hangers-on — the 'alternative society'.[249]

* * *

The result has been inevitable. Types of commitment and levels of involvement have varied enormously. At one end of the spectrum there are now permanent, 'intentional' communities of fully com-mitted individuals who could justifiably be described as social and/or spiritual revolutionaries. At a slightly less committed level there are national and international networks of home-based activists devoted to one or the other 'alternative' cause, whose self-imposed task is to link members of local groups who them-selves meet regularly to compare notes and give each other moral support. Then there are more loosely-knit groupings of individuals who rarely meet, but who are members of national or international organisations with which they keep in touch by correspondence, through news bulletins and magazines, or through infrequent general gatherings and festivals. And finally there are remarkable numbers of apparently isolated individuals who are intent on pur-suing their own personal 'New Age' quest through private medi-tation, thought or study — whether as a regular activity or merely in a relatively desultory way — but who rarely, if ever, make contact with other 'seekers' or with any of the wider organisations.

If there is a wide variation in the level of commitment involved, there is no less wide a variation in the degree to which 'spirituality' enters the picture. At any one of the levels that I have just listed there are some enthusiasts who are committed totally to a particular religion, cult-group or guru; others who are merely attracted to a particular *type* of path or religious philosophy; yet others who respond positively to almost any 'path' of this general type, without becoming particularly partisan about any one of them; and a goodly number who either were never attracted by religion or religions in the first place or who have, in a sense, already 'gone through' religion and come out again on the other side — and who are thus committed simply to the general movement's social and psychological aspects or, at best, to its philosophy of planetary transformation.

Thus, at the community level, there are a whole range of 'spiritual' establishments and foundations — from the innumerable Hindu ashrams of India[54] and, of recent years, those set up by itinerant Indian gurus of varying respectability in Europe and America as well[2]; via the Western Buddhist centres set up mainly by Japanese Zen Masters in California or by refugee Tibetan lamas all over the Western world — much after the style of the Samye-Ling community at Eskdalemuir in Scotland[2]; to centres of a more catholic and all-embracing nature such as the Findhorn Foundation in Moray, Scotland.[28] (It has to be said that traditional Christian monasteries and convents, which are of course extremely similar in general type and orientation, tend — with the exception of the particularly youth-oriented one at Taizé in France and the highly ecumenical ashram of the Benedictine monk Bede Griffiths near Madras — not to be thought of as 'New Age' communities at all, presumably because of their traditional, 'establishment' connotations in the West, and because of the virtual exclusion of Christianity from the early Theosophical thinking on which 'New Ageism' has thus far tended to be based.)

At a less overtly 'spiritual' level there are a number of centres devoted to a whole range of more specifically psychological therapies, one of the best known being the Esalen Institute near Big Sur in California — perhaps the seed-centre of what has since come to be known as 'humanistic psychology'. (This term implies a creative, living approach to the human psyche and its growth, rather than a purely analytical approach based primarily, as in the case of Freud, on studies of the mentally ill or, as in the case of the Behaviourists, on the conviction that the human being is no more than a kind of organic machine.) Another, quite different community typical of the less religiously committed approach is the Centre for Alternative Technology at Machynlleth in Wales, whose emphasis, as its name implies, is on developing and demonstrating new, low-energy technologies designed to lessen society's voracious demands on the planetary environment — and thus at the same time to help ease (both directly and indirectly) the energy problems of the Third World.

Religious or not, such communities still clearly have an identifiable ideal in mind. They are still committed to the creation of a new society, a new humanity and thus, eventually, a new world.

Yet there are 'New Age' communities who would disown even such generalised claims as unnecessarily grandiose. Typified by the so-called 'commune', and generally associated with the hippie movement of the 1960s (despite the fact that their ancestry goes at least as far back as the pioneering socialist communes of the 1920s), these groups of people, often living as 'family groups' in large, converted houses or farm complexes, generally seek merely to 'live lightly on the earth', and in the process to prove nothing more earth-shaking than that alternative lifestyles and forms of society are possible — indeed, that they offer a potential antidote to the get-rich-quick attitudes, social alienation, confrontation, polarisation and general tribal attitudes which threaten to undermine contemporary Western civilisation, if not actually to lead to ultimate planetary disaster and destruction.

And this despite the potential criticism that the very ethos of the commune, and indeed of the 'alternative' movement in general, can all too easily lead to its own form of tribal, 'us-and-them' attitude, and is itself dedicated, almost by definition, to the destruction of Western society in its present form . . . .

Meanwhile it is interesting to note how many 'New Age' communes and communities revolve specifically around the cultivation of a garden, or even a full-blooded 'return to the earth'. In the case of Findhorn the cultivation of its garden was one of the community's original points of focus and the cause of its initial rise to international fame.[28] It would be difficult, surely, to find a clearer symbol of what such institutions are really about — namely the re-creation of the original Garden of Eden on earth, an aim which has of course always been synonymous with the inauguration of the final, long-awaited Golden Age.

* * *

In the associated realm of movements, networks and communications, meanwhile, there is no less variation in the level of 'spirituality' involved than in the case of actual communes and communities. At the one extreme there are, of course, the various traditional religions often associated with the movement — Hinduism (and especially Vedanta), Buddhism (and especially the Tibetan form of Mahayana Buddhism, with its wide range of esoteric beliefs and practices), Taoism, Sufism and 'esoteric' Christianity. Indeed, it is specifically the level and range of their 'esoteric' content (not to say their *exotic* content) which seems to determine the extent to which each of these religions is regarded as a legitimate 'New Age' phenomenon. In their stricter, more purist forms — let alone their forms as actually practised in their countries of origin — they scarcely seem to qualify at all.

Following closely on their heels in the 'spirituality' stakes come the numerous cult groups, many of them based loosely on the major religions themselves, or on more or less unpromising amalgams of two or more of them.[2] Here we may mention the Rajneesh meditation movement; Maharaj Ji's Divine Light Mission; the Reverend Sun Myung Moon's controversial Unification Church (the so-called 'Moonies'); the science-fictionist L. Ron Hubbard's equally controversial Church of Scientology[17]; Leon MacLaren's somewhat secretive (and confusingly named) School of Economic Science, together with its various satellite schools of philosophy world-wide[29]; Swami Prabhupada's Krishna Consciousness movement — prominent through its young, enthusiastic devotees, saffron-robed and shaven-headed, joyfully dancing through the streets with their chant of 'Hare Krishna'[59]; the Sikh 'Healthy, Happy and Holy Organisation' (3HO), with its emphasis on Kundalini Yoga; together with a number of movements of a more overtly ecumenical nature such as Subud (which presents itself as a vivifying adjunct to *any* religion)[4] and the avowedly universalist Bahá'í faith mentioned earlier.[16]

Naturally enough, the native American and European organisations often tend to take as their starting-point the Western, rather than the oriental esoteric tradition — and notably, of course, the Rosicrucian inheritance of magic, gnosticism and inner alchemy.

In this connection we have already mentioned Rudolf Steiner's Anthroposophical Society, Alice Bailey's Arcane School and the various pseudo-knightly and Rosicrucian organisations set up in Europe and America during the first two decades of this century. To these we could add the numerous groups currently dedicated to spreading the inspirational messages of alleged occult Masters and Higher Beings, such as the Atlanteans, the White Eagle Lodge and Benjamin Creme's Tara Centres; others who claim Ufonauts as their source of knowledge, such as the Aetherius Society[2]; together with groups oriented towards ley-lines and earth-magic such as the Gatekeeper Trust.

Not all of these groups are necessarily as blinkered in their outlook as my brief description may have made them seem, however. Most are also concerned with wider questions of spirituality and human development, and it is in this area that their aims start to merge with those of more all-embracing organisations such as the Theosophical Society itself; Sir George Trevelyan's highly-respected Wrekin Trust; RILKO (Research into Lost Knowledge Organisation); the American Lindisfarne Association; and even groups which claim to have no specific spiritual pretensions, such as Maharishi Mahesh Yogi's Transcendental Meditation movement.[2,65]

* * *

All of these groups and organisations naturally publish their own magazines and broadsheets, and these in turn are supplemented by a number of widely-circulated magazines with no fixed allegiance, but which themselves reflect the by-now familiar spectrum of spiritual commitment. Currently these range from publications such as *Shambhala*, the *Science of Thought Review* and Findhorn's popular *One Earth*, together with the American *New Age Journal*, *East West Journal*, *Parabola* and *Brain/Mind Bulletin*; through less overtly spiritually-oriented magazines such as the *Journal of Humanistic Psychology* and *Re-Vision*; and *I-to-I* to the simple informational leaflets, counter-culture directories[60,67,68,86] and mail-order catalogues designed to make the whole range of 'New Age' information available to as wide a public as possible.

And in this the periodical industry is backed up by a growing number of book publishers who are devoting their lists either partially or wholly to books concerned with spiritual or 'New Age' topics in the broadest sense.

Certain of the magazines, meanwhile, have taken it upon themselves to adopt a semi-political stance, seeing it as their function to attempt to influence events directly, rather than merely by attempting to transform human consciousness in a general sense. Typical of these are Satish Kumar's *Resurgence* and Johann Quanier's *New Humanity*. Indeed, even some of the more mainstream 'New Age' periodicals are nowadays tending to venture tentatively into the political arena.

* * *

But then the tendency towards politicisation has long been apparent in other 'New Age' spheres too. Among the groups already listed, for example, the School of Economic Science has for many years had pretensions — if mainly covert ones — to exercising political influence behind the scenes, apparently through a process of infiltration.[29] The Transcendental Meditation movement, for its part, has even gone so far as to set up its own notional 'world government', as it were in exile, and has mounted expensive advertising campaigns offering hard-pressed national governments worldwide a kind of trouble-shooting service.

Political concerns are less often apparent at the purely networking level, however. Especially at the 'spiritual' end of the spectrum, most networks exist purely in order to bring together groups, organisations and centres with interests and fields of endeavour in common. The Findhorn Community runs its own networking service to this end. The endeavour is a timely one, not least because New Age groups often show a surprising tendency to isolationism, rather as though each believed that it alone had the 'right' answer.

(In addition, there are one or two networking organisations which have even taken it upon themselves to 'network the networks' — i.e. to bring all the various 'grapevines' under one roof with the aid of computers, so allowing those interested to have all the information they require instantly at their fingertips, and thus to link up with anybody else world-wide with similar interests and concerns. Hence the very name — Link Up — of one of the magazines designed to assist in this process.)

Nevertheless, political concerns (in the broadest sense) are well to the fore in a number of the avowedly 'spiritual' New Age organisations. Here we could mention Donald Keys's Planetary Citizens, based in New York, with its 'Planetary Initiative for the World We Choose' (a concept which entirely begs the question of whether we do not already have the world we choose, and might not do better to concentrate on promoting the world we need); national or regional grapevines such as the Wales One Earth Network, the British Business Network and the latter's American equivalent, Briarpatch — all of which also share some degree of 'spiritual' involvement; along with more overtly 'down-to-earth' organisations such as Friends of the Earth; the Soil Association; the Men of the Trees; Green Deserts; the Alternative Technology movement (based largely on the late E.F. Schumacher's philosophy of 'small is beautiful' and 'economics as if people mattered'[72]); Greenpeace; and even the national peace movements, the 'Green' political parties and the world-wide Women's Movement.

Most of these movements naturally have their own national and/or international headquarters, and these centres are in turn supplemented by others which do a minimal amount of actual networking, but are still concerned with bringing together the various movements and issues. Especially is this so in the field of futures research, which is represented, among other centres, by the London Teilhard Centre for the Future of Man and Willis Harman's Institute of Noetic Sciences in California — not to forget the already-mentioned Wrekin Trust, which is based in Gloucestershire.

* * *

The sphere of politics, though, is by no means the only area of 'old age' culture within which the New Age and its values seek to make their influence felt. In education, for example, the theories and writings of Rudolf Steiner have led to the foundation of numbers of so-called 'Waldorf' schools, as well as of teacher-training centres after the style of Emerson College at Forest Row, Sussex.[2] Very much concerned, like the New Age magazine *Educare*, with fitting the education to the child, rather than the child to the education, these schools are supplemented, thanks to the unstinting efforts of devoted idealists, by other establishments which have simply grown out of local needs (not least an official policy of closing down small local schools for alleged economic and even educational reasons). These schools consequently use a variety of teaching methods ranging from those of Maria Montessori to home-grown methods geared to particular local skills and situations. A typical example is The Small School founded by Satish Kumar and his colleagues at Hartland in north Devon. And even Ivan Illich's revolutionary ideas on 'de-schooling' are not without their influence.

Another educational movement — though this time with somewhat cultic overtones — is that represented by the already-mentioned School of Economic Science based in Kensington, London, which seeks to inculcate in its students world-wide (including those attending its associated day- and Sunday-schools for children) a lifestyle and philosophical attitude that derive mainly from Hindu Vedanta on the one hand and the teachings of George Gurdjieff and P.D. Ouspensky on the other.

As for adult education *per se*, 'New Age' ideas are once again reflected both in America's extensive 'Free University' movement and in the special courses run in Britain by organisations such as the Wrekin Trust and the Human Development Trust[2] at the many private conference centres which are now available for such activities. And even the official British Open University may yet prove far from immune from such influences.

The world of commerce, similarly, has of recent years seen an influx of so-called New Age businesses, most of them involved in activities specifically compatible with the 'New Age' ideal. These extend not merely to writing, publishing and bookselling, but also to horticulture and farming, home arts and crafts, the mounting of festivals, architectural design and community planning, home insulation, alternative technology and — astonishing as it may seem at first sight — even accountancy, banking and building societies (in this case seen as a means of providing much-needed funds for worthy and life-enhancing initiatives at non-exploitative or even zero rates of interest).

By far the greatest practical involvement of the New Age movement, however, is in the field of health, healing and what has been called the 'human potential' or 'consciousness' movement. (Indeed, its involvement in this field has produced a situation in which the words 'this New Age business' may be applied in their most literal and mercenary sense — for participation in the various therapies offered is often far from cheap.) And here once again we find the familiar, wide spectrum of 'spiritual' involvement.

To take the 'consciousness' movement first, the number of available techniques and therapies, and of organisations to promote them, is truly overwhelming[2] — to the point where one is tempted to ask in bewilderment, 'Which is the *right* one?' The answer, as ever where asking the way is concerned, depends entirely on where one is starting from. And this will vary according to one's previous experience, psychological make-up and general orientation — and in particular according to whether one tends to be spiritually inclined, primarily at home with one's emotions (as few in the so-called White Anglo-Saxon Protestant countries are), intellectually oriented or most comfortable in the physical sphere.

The familiar, broad 'spectrum of spirituality', in other words, can be a decided advantage here, as elsewhere in the New Age movement.

In point of fact, few of the available techniques are restricted solely to any one of these types of approach, though many do tend to concentrate on one aspect of human experience in particular. Thus, techniques such as Zen meditation[84] and Silva Mind Control could be said to relate primarily to mental and psychological work. Approaches which go on to combine this with an emotional component include Encounter Therapy (originally pioneered at Esalen); Co-Counselling; Transactional Analysis[27]; Fritz Perls's Gestalt[76]; Psychodrama (the improvised acting-out of the major themes and concerns of one's inner life); Insight; and the Forum, or est ('Erhard Seminars Training' — but also, not by accident, the Latin for 'it is', i.e. the realisation, surprisingly often forgotten within the New Age movement, that things are simply as they are).[7] Even the somewhat notorious Scientology movement could possibly be included in this category.[17]

A large number of further techniques take the range of applications even further by involving physical experience in the process.[2] These include traditional Raja Yoga (together with the familiar exercises of Hatha Yoga which are designed to serve as its physical preliminary); Arica; T'ai Chi Ch'uan and the other, more energetic oriental 'martial arts'; Bioenergetics and other Reichian therapies concerned with the built-in feedback mechanisms between *psyche* (mind and/or spirit) and *soma* (body); Rebirthing; the various approaches of humanistic psychology generally; Rolfing; the Feldenkrais and Alexander Techniques[3]; 'Growth Games' of various descriptions[40,46]; and even a number of new approaches in the everyday musical, artistic, sporting and leisure fields — not excluding self-immersion in the true, primal wilderness-experience. The main role of this last activity (a major component in many a de-stressing programme for harassed business executives) seems to be to allow participants to re-live the pre-linguistic wholeness and oneness with nature which seems, as we saw in our first chapter, to have lain at least partially at the basis of the long-since mythologised 'Garden of Eden' experience to whose recovery humanity's continuing 'Golden Age' initiative seems always to have been dedicated.

And finally there is a range of approaches which claim to be all-embracing, in that they are concerned with spiritual, psychological, emotional and physical experience alike — though most of them tend to ignore the intellectual aspect of experience somewhat, on the ground that this is currently over-emphasised in Western society already. The point may be a valid one, but it does incur a risk of lack of clarity — a point to which we shall be returning later.

Such techniques include Roberto Assagioli's Psychosynthesis; Transpersonal Psychology (i.e. psychological work involving every level of human functioning); so-called Life Training; Neuro-linguistic Programming ('NLP'); a variety of forms of meditation (including Tibetan, 'Dynamic', Theosophical, Anthroposophical,

Transcendental, Kabbalistic, Kundalini and simply 'Guided'); a similar range of Sufi exercises involving such activities as chanting and 'sacred dance'; and a number of related exercises based on the teachings of George Gurdjieff — teachings which, despite their often startling originality, can at least be absolved from the charge of lack of intellectual rigour.[56,62,77]

On the purely remedial front, meanwhile, a whole armoury of 'alternative' healing remedies are waiting in reserve, all designed to replace the allopathic treatments of orthodox medicine which are often more concerned with the removal or masking of symptoms than with the curing of disease. In point of fact, though, the same criticism can often be levelled at the 'alternative' treatments too. Frequently they are used by would-be healers merely as a kind of 'spiritual chemotherapy'.

Nevertheless, in the hands of responsible practitioners (who are possibly rather rarer than is often assumed within the movement) most of these techniques do involve treating the patient as a whole organism in distress, rather than merely as a collection of parts or symptoms. Among these approaches are, at the purely physical level, various dietary therapies; the 'New Era' tissue-salt remedies; remedial massage; Touch for Health; Chiropractic (normally involving gentle manipulation of the spine) and its now almost 'respectable' cousin Osteopathy; Biofeedback (involving the used of electronic self-monitoring equipment); oriental techniques such as Shiatsu, Acupressure and Acupuncture; and Reflexology and the Metamorphic Technique (both of them acupuncture-related techniques involving the application of pressure at selected points, generally on the hand and/or foot). At a level involving psyche and emotions, the available treatments include Jungian psychotherapy[32] and other, related forms of dream-therapy; hypnosis; and so-called Autogenic Training (based largely on autosuggestive techniques).

The picture is completed by a range of further techniques which, at their best, also involve a spiritual, or at least whole-person-oriented dimension — notably Homoeopathy, Naturopathy and Herbalism; the Bach Flower Remedies; various forms of astrological counselling[69]; Radionics and other work involving crystals and pendulum-diagnosis; musical therapies of several types[25]; 'one-off', mixed approaches such as the Course in Miracles[14]; Christian Science; mediumistic healing; and traditional 'laying-on of hands' and absent healing, as practised both by the Pentecostal churches and by members of Britain's National Federation of Spiritual Healers.

The range of 'New Age' activities, in summary, is truly vast. And yet the above is merely the 'official' tip of the New Age iceberg. For of recent years it has become increasingly apparent that the New Age has, so to speak, 'escaped' from its founding groups and institutions into the world at large.

Since about 1983 in particular, growing numbers of independent individuals with patently 'New Age' attitudes and convictions (many of them the 'private seekers' already mentioned above) have been emerging from the woodwork in the most surprising of places — in the 'official' medical establishment, in exalted Court circles, in the Church, in the State education system and in politics both national and international. They have also infiltrated the media, which as a result have been devoting more and more time and attention to serious consideration of 'New Age' topics.

And meanwhile ecological ideas and recycling principles are already starting to influence the agricultural and energy industries; a new awareness of atmospheric pollution and consequent global warming has begun (appropriately enough) to excite a fever of apprehension and debate among politicians and governments world-wide; the back-to-the-earth ethic to affect public eating habits and thus the priorities of much of the food industry; the return to traditional forms of wisdom to bring about a return to natural methods of childbirth; sheer human compassion to bring the world's peoples together at the grass roots level perhaps as never before.

For the New Agers, consequently, the auguries seem to be remarkably promising . . . .

* * *

The foregoing is, of course, merely a sample of the enormous range of activities and organisations characteristic of the New Age movement. If sales of New Age books and magazines or the claimed membership of the various New Age organisations are anything to go by, the number of people involved world-wide must already be into the millions, if not into the tens of millions. And all of them are in some sense 'doing their own thing'.

At the same time it is by no means easy to establish just where the 'New Age' begins and the 'Old Age' ends. Several of the organisations that I have included in my account, for example, would probably not recognise themselves as part of the movement at all, despite the conviction of many New Agers to the contrary.

The task, consequently, of nailing down exactly what 'this New

Age business' — this apparently crazy bedlam of frenetic and dis-organised activity — is all really about is an exceedingly daunting one, as numerous New Agers have discovered to their sudden consternation when asked the question by 'outsiders'.

Nevertheless, the various aspects of the movement do seem to have certain basic principles in common. And the most obvious of these, as we saw earlier, is sheer 'alternativeness'.

Wherever one cares to look, the movement tends to stress the opposite side of the coin of accepted wisdom. In place of hatred, love; in place of isolationism and alienation, togetherness in every sense; in place of confrontation, cooperation; in place of competition, mutual supportiveness; in place of reductionism, holism (i.e. all-inclusiveness); in place of negative and destructive attitudes, positive thinking; in place of guilt, self-affirmation; in place of self-righteousness and bigotry, tolerance; in place of the rigours of the Protestant work-ethic, a gentle, process-oriented attitude to work, with people and their needs put well before targets, schedules and organisational structures.

It is all rather reminiscent of the celebrated prayer of St Francis of Assisi.*

Thus, gigantism is 'out', to be replaced by human-scale thinking. Individuals are above all encouraged to be themselves and to develop to the full every aspect of their inner and outer being. At the same time, the needs of the planet as a whole are put before mere individual, factional or national interests. The apparent paradox has been aptly summed up in the slogan 'Think globally: act locally'; and within the movement itself it is reflected on the one hand in the move towards decentralisation and an emphasis on local interests, and on the other hand by the world-wide proliferation of networking.

Meanwhile the needs of the inner person are accorded far greater importance than is usual in conventional society. Dry rationalism is widely dismissed in favour of intuition, emotion and the workings of the unconscious. The receptive and holistic qualities supposedly typical of the 'feminine' aspect of the psyche (both in men and in women) are emphasised at the expense of their hitherto dominant, highly-focused 'masculine' counterparts — much, indeed, as seems already to be happening in the role-playing assumptions of Western society at large.

* 'Lord, make me an instrument of Thy peace; where there is hatred let me sow love; where there is injury, pardon; where there is doubt, faith; where there is despair, hope; where there is darkness, light; and where there is sadness, joy.'

And of course, thanks to the more spiritually-orientated members of the movement, the demands of 'spiritual truth' are generally placed firmly before the seductions of materialistic illusion, and the power of meditation, invocation, ritual and ceremonial magic are held to be more effective than conventional reason or mere brute force.

And if such principles were truly to hold sway the world, surely, would be a far better place. How can one say anything but good about ideals which apparently bid so fair to reform our society and transform the Old Age into the New?

'Transformation', indeed, is one of the New Agers' favourite concepts — transformation, that is, both of the individual and of humanity collectively. And yet just how effective is that transformation likely to be? What, indeed, is there to transform, and who is it who is trying to transform it?

* * *

Even in reading the last few pages, the reader may have been struck by what appear to be a number of strange contradictions — contradictions which merely add to those even more basic ones already listed at the beginning of this chapter. Certain worrying philosophical points also insist on rearing their heads — whether ugly or otherwise — and it is of no use to ignore them in the hope that they will go away.

Possibly the most basic worry of all is the fact that nearly all the above ideas are clearly based on dualistic, or analytical, thinking — that very dualistic thinking which, as we saw in our opening chapters, seems to have been responsible for the apparent 'loss of bliss' which is synonymous with humanity's original 'expulsion from Eden', and thus also with the current *absence* of the New Age, or Kingdom of Heaven on earth.

For if there is one thing that the most ancient spiritual traditions insist on — those same spiritual wisdoms on which 'New Ageism' generally claims to base itself — it is that the universe is one and indivisible. Research into modern high-energy physics, neurology and cognitive psychology points inescapably in the same direction.[42]

Every part of the perceived universe — ourselves included — is a direct function of the rest of it. Every atom carries within it the imprint of the whole of reality.

More than that, every part of that universe *is also the whole of it*, and the whole of it *is also every part*. The proposition may seem nonsensical — even though the now familiar (and significantly named) hologram provides a clear analogy with it* — but it is nonsensical only when we approach the idea through the habitual categories of our *separative* consciousness. In terms of the *pre*-separative, pre-linguistic consciousness of humanity's 'Garden of Eden' whose re-attainment seems, as we have seen, to have been the aim of all New Age movements that have ever existed, the proposition is literally self-evident. On whatever scale (and scale, inevitably, is a purely relative concept), reality is reality is reality.

And so the microcosm *is* the macrocosm. In the words of the well-known Hermetic axiom, 'As above, so below'. In the phrase so dear to the Upanishadic philosophers, TAT TVAM ASI — 'Thou art That'.

Both phrases, indeed, are frequently quoted by would-be New Agers. Which makes all the more surprising their proneness to ignore in practice what the phrases actually mean.

* * *

The New Agers' favourite word 'love', for example, implies far more than a mere warm, cosy, sentimental feeling. Especially in the context of high endeavour which is characteristic of New Age thinking, it has inevitably to refer to total will-to-union. Yet that very will-to-union implies an initial separateness. The very basis of the concept, in other words, lies in a duality-consciousness which denies the total oneness of the whole of the universe. Consequently any attempt to put 'love' into practice must also imply the presence of its opposite — a hatred which, presumably, has to be concealed or suppressed, or possibly diverted into other channels, with consequences that hardly bear thinking about.

To put it another way, if the lover and the beloved are truly one, then the injunction to love is irrelevant: if they are seen as separate, then no attempt at love can hope to bridge the gap. Indeed, the very attempt itself is a denial of the fact that ought to make it unnecessary — namely that there is no separation in the first place.

Much the same could be said about such familiar 'New Age' concepts as 'togetherness', 'cooperation' and 'supportiveness'. All of them presuppose a world of separate individuals who need to

---

* A hologram is a three-dimensional image formed on a photographic plate by the interference-effect between two laser-beams. If the plate is then broken into small pieces, the entire image is found to be present in each piece, but some of its three-dimensionality is lost. The implications are clear. They are that (a) while the whole image is present on every part of the plate, conversely (b) the whole plate is needed to store any single part of the image in its totality.

be brought together. All of them, consequently, operate out of the very duality-consciousness which actually prevents their long-term fulfilment — whatever short-term rewards they may bring within the relatively sheltered context of New Age groups and communities.

Even the commitment to positive thinking is not free of this particular danger. Commendable it may be to discourage people from concentrating solely on the negative aspects of existence. And certainly there is no doubt that positive thinking can work wonders — whether for Norman Vincent Peale, Dale Carnegie or anybody else — at least on a local and temporary scale. But there can be a price to pay for affirming that the world is as one wants it to be, especially if that is not the way it is. Ignoring the seamier side of life — pretending, for example, that pain and illness do not exist — is all very well, but disaster can all too easily result and all sorts of unforeseen side-effects ensue, as numbers of would-be Christian Scientists in particular have discovered to their cost.

And this for a very good reason. For the notion of positive thinking as opposed to negativity is dualistic to its very foundations. It implies allying oneself with one side of a universe that is perceived to be divided down the middle. But the universe is not dualistic. It is not divided down the middle. It is whole, and any philosophy or life-ethos which assumes the contrary is based firmly on illusion, and must therefore ultimately fail.

True, there seems to be at least a subliminal awareness of this within the New Age movement. The recent emphasis on 'holism' (a word coined, curiously enough, by Field Marshal Jan Smuts of South Africa) seems, on the face of it, to be an encouraging development. Until, that is, one looks more closely at how the idea is being applied. For the term 'holistic' has, in practice, too often tended to be devalued into a mere New Age buzzword. It is commonly stuck by New Agers in front of any word which refers to a concept of which they hope the listener or reader will approve. In New Age circles, in other words, 'holistic' more often than not means simply 'good', or even 'fashionable'.

Perhaps this is not surprising in view of what a true understanding of the term would necessarily imply. For 'holistic' really means 'applying to the whole'. Not the whole individual, nor the whole group, but *the whole*. The universe, the Reality, the totality with which both individual and group are inseparably and indissolubly one.

And so there can be, for example, no 'holistic' healing of individuals, despite what a good many 'New Age healers' would dearly love to believe. And this for the reason that there are no individuals; or rather there is only one individual — and we are all It. Any healing that is truly holistic, consequently, has to operate (as healers such as Joel Goldsmith long ago perceived[74]) out of the realisation that healer, patient and universal reality (or 'God') are one. And once that realisation — and not merely the intellectual awareness of it — is attained, healing automatically follows as does night the day.

It is no accident that the words 'holism' and 'healing' are — etymologically at least — one and the same.

Much the same goes for the New Agers' emphasis on promoting the free development of the individual, while at the same time insisting that the interests of the planet as a whole are paramount. The former proposition, clearly, has much to be said for it — conventional society too often forgets that people matter — yet the latter point seems (for all its equally obvious validity) to deny all that it stands for. The standard 'New Age' response to this apparent dilemma is that it is not a matter of either/or but of both/and. Duality-consciousness and universal consciousness, it seems, can somehow be maintained at one and the same time.

Humanity is to be conceived of, in other words, as a collection of separate individuals working together for the sake of Planet Earth.

The idea may seem attractive. Yet a moment's reflection reveals it to be untenable. It is no use claiming that you and the universe are one if you then insist on thinking and behaving as though you and it were two. You can have unity, or you can have duality. (In other words, it is possible to interpret your experience in a holistic or in a dualistic way.) But if you then try to have both, all that you are left with, necessarily, is duality.

And so you are back where you started.

Only when the realisation dawns that *you are* Planet Earth, just as you are the whole of the rest of reality too, does the problem resolve itself. Only then does it become apparent that the cherished individuality to which you were formerly so committed is no more than a mask of personality largely imposed by those around you. The *real* 'you' is already one with Planet Earth, and there is therefore absolutely nothing to be done. There is nothing to transform, and nobody independent to transform it. And so there is no need, either, for well-meaning injunctions such as 'Think globally: act locally', since at this level there is absolutely no distinction between the two.

And all networks — all attempts, in other words, to join together that which is presumed to be separate — become, in the light of this realisation, totally irrelevant.

* * *

Such, then, are some of the conclusions to which an examination of the typical tenets of the New Age movement inevitably leads. That such conclusions are not widely drawn by New Agers — or that those who do draw them tend to stop being 'New Agers' as such in fairly short order — is not too surprising, however, given the widespread mistrust of rational thought within the movement. Or possibly it is the desire to hang on to the 'approved' beliefs and illusions which is actually responsible for the widespread mistrust of rational thought.

Certainly there is an extraordinary 'in-group' attachment to what, to 'outsiders', seem to be irrational beliefs — an attachment which may in turn be responsible for the typical 'New Age' toler- ance of the religious and spiritual beliefs of others. The game involved here seems to be one of 'You accept my illusions and I'll go along with yours'. It all sounds splendidly civilised. Probably, too, it is a way of bearing practical witness to the fact that truth can never be tied down to a single set of words or ideas. But the result, of course, is a group of New Agers who are all staggering around bearing a huge burden of communal illusion on their shoulders.

And truth, needless to say — or even clarity of thought — simp- ly flies out of the window.

The results show up in a number of practical applications. Typ- ical 'New Age' scholarship, for example, is quite often shallow or even frankly spurious, as we have already noted in connection with the former Essenes. Biblical scholarship, in particular, tends to suffer a terrible mauling in 'New Age' discussions of compara- tive religion, as does philology in philosophical discussions.

Thus, garbled versions of statements by a whole range of biblical figures from Moses, through King David, to Saints Paul and John (not to mention others entirely unknown to Christianity) are fre- quently attributed to 'Jesus'. At the same time the memorable declara- tion 'The Kingdom of Heaven is within you' is almost universally treated as a kind of biblical proof-text justifying New Age spiritu- ality's characteristic concept of 'the God within', notwithstanding the fact that the declaration appears nowhere in the Bible.

In the philological context things are little better. The typically New Age term 'community', for example, is often interpreted as though the word were simply a combination of the words 'common' and 'unity'. Yet not only are the words 'community' and 'unity' totally unrelated etymologically (for all their apparent resemblance); the original meaning of 'community' was something much more like 'serving together' — a far more dynamic concept whose true implications for New Agers could thus prove both salutary and enlightening.

Again, we have already referred to New Age thinking on education. At almost every 'New Age' discussion of the topic the point is dutifully made that the English word 'educate' comes from the Latin *educare*, which means 'to lead or draw out'. The conclusion is then drawn that true education involves applying just such an approach to pupils — not filling them with facts as empty vessels might be filled with water, but leading them gently out of ignorance into knowledge, out of childhood into adulthood.

The idea is clearly a good one — so good that it is already applied almost universally even in the State education sector, at least at the primary level (which is the one which seems to concern New Agers most at the present time).

But the point is that the Latin *educare* does *not* mean 'to lead or draw out'. The Romans' word for this was *educere*. *Educare*, by contrast, was a horticultural term meaning 'to nurture', and involved giving growing plants everything they needed — light and love and warmth and water and air. There was no implication of 'moulding' them or 'drawing them out' — an idea which sounds perilously like pulling them out by the roots.

And it has to be said that the true derivation seems to be much more in line with what most New Agers would approve of than the 'Daddy knows best' attitude which seems to be predicated by the conventional explanation.

The point, of course, may be regarded as mere hair-splitting. But a similar lack of attention to facts tends, in other spheres, to lead to much more serious consequences. Practical decisions regarding lifestyles, psychological therapies and communal rituals, for example, are frequently taken on the basis of largely bogus accounts of the teachings of Jesus or the Essenes, or on equally dubious suppositions about ancient Greek or Egyptian practices derived from alleged psychic sources. Indeed, much of 'New Age spirituality', too — with its Masters and angels, its devas and over-lighting presences — is based on similarly shaky factual foundations.

But then any kind of spirituality which involves a belief that you can influence, or alternatively be influenced by, independent, 'spiritual' powers of whatever kind is so basically and obviously dualistic that its relevance to the establishment of a New Age of wholeness on earth has to be next to nil, whatever it may do for the egos or security-feelings of those who practise it. The very notion of 'spiritual truth' — almost as though there were two entirely different kinds of truth, the one spiritual, the other material — is inherently nonsensical from the outset. As a well-known Hindu aphorism puts it: 'Truth is One: it is our ignorance which divides it.'

And certainly we can be sure that, if a New Age does eventually dawn, the last thing that it is likely to be based on is illusion, whether dualistic or otherwise.

It is no surprise, then, to find a similar lack of attention to facts affecting the conduct of 'New Age' businesses. Here, however, the facts in question are not so much historical or spiritual as present and actual in character. Intent on their entirely reasonable commitment to 'putting people first', many such businesses (though fortunately not all of them) are entirely oblivious of the actual practical results of their policy. Their particular blind spot is that they fail to ask themselves, 'Which people?' As a result, while employees and colleagues are encouraged to tailor their work to their personal needs — to take a day off whenever they feel unable to cope, for example — deadlines are left unmet and customers consequently fuming. Process-oriented, rather than goal-oriented work attitudes often have a similar effect. With the result that it is often far more satisfactory for 'outsiders' to do business with an Old Age concern than with its New Age equivalent.

All of which suggests that even the modern New Age movement, with its high ideals and often marvellously supportive, tolerant and committed membership, is ultimately no more likely to deliver the millenarian goods than its many and varied precursors. It is not merely that it is based on insecure philosophical foundations and is therefore *potentially* untrustworthy as a force for true change. Practical results also tend to show up its actual impotence.

True, experiencing life in New Age communities such as Findhorn can be not only a valuable catalyst for self-development, but also extremely rewarding and fulfilling in its own right — so much so that it is all too tempting to join them purely because of their sheer 'niceness'. In part this may have more than a little to do with the fact that most of their members tend to be highly-motivated representatives of the educated and relatively affluent American and European middles classes, among whom 'niceness'

is nowadays regarded as something of an 'approved quality'.
Even allowing for this, however, there does appear to be a new
spirit abroad in such communities, a feeling that 'this is how the
world ought to be'. And so it could be argued that, here at least,
life has been transformed.

But then much the same kind of observation could be made
about many aspects of advanced Western society generally. There
can be little doubt that life is far better for many in the industrial
West than a hundred, or even twenty years ago. But the question
has to be asked: 'At whose expense — and what about the world
as a whole?'

And here it would be a rash observer who claimed that the
world situation has shown much general improvement during the
twenty years or so since the modern New Age movement started
to make itself felt. True, East-West confrontation has become more
muted of late, but the nuclear threat is still with us. And with
spreading pollution of air, sea and land, vast third world poverty,
and growing famine, international terrorism, unemployment,
drug abuse and social disruption world-wide, it is difficult to
draw any conclusion other than that things generally have got
considerably worse. The international politicians have admittedly
started to agree more often, but it really amounts to little more
than agreeing on how to let things get worse more nicely. More
nicely for the affluent North, that is.

But the New Agers have an answer. Typically they explain that
the apparent worsening of the general world situation is merely
the reverse side of the coin of the hidden, spiritual changes that
are abroad in the world. The Old Order, in other words, is in its
death throes, and the new spiritual order about to supervene.

Apart from remarking that this seems to be a curious example
of arguing that black is white, one has to admit that the prospect,
if valid, would be an exciting one. Certainly there can be little
doubt that the Old Order — both East and West — is in many
ways on its last legs. This fact, however, seems to be merely the
inevitable consequence of its pursuit of its own dualistic principles
of reductionism and confrontation to their ultimate conclusion,
rather than anything to do with the covert operation of presumed
'spiritual powers'. And in any case, whether the result of its eventual and undoubted demise will be the flowering of a glorious
New Order seems very much in doubt. Or at least, if something of
the kind does occur, then the New Order, based as it will still be
on the same dualistic attitudes which themselves produced the
Old Order, will certainly not be the final Golden Age of unbroken

wholeness which has been predicated and hoped for by the millenarian crusade throughout the centuries.

Even life at communities such as Findhorn, as their own members are often the first to confirm, is by no means all a bed of roses.

No doubt it is partly this realisation which lies behind the
movement's recent tendency to play down the word 'alternative'
in its typical 'job-description' in favour of the word 'complementary', especially in the medical sphere.

An improved Old Age such a new order may be — and not
before time. Certainly any society prepared to devote itself to the
fulfilment of current 'New Age' ideals cannot help but be a better
society. But, as ever, there is many a potential slip between in-
group theory and world-wide practice. For a good many centuries
now, after all, Westerners have generally thought it A Good Thing
to be in favour of righteousness and Christian values, but to very
little effect as far as actual practice is concerned.

One is rather reminded of St Augustine's celebrated prayer:
'Lord, give me chastity and continence — but not yet.'

And so even the New Age movement, for all its patent nobility
and positivity and dedication to all that is whole and loving and
good, seems as destined to ultimate failure in its quest to inaugurate Earth's ultimate Millennium as all the other, similar movements that have gone before it. Many of its members, indeed, are
already beginning to realise as much. No longer really believing in
the promised Kingdom as advertised, they have started to play
down the very term 'New Age'. As well they might. For it is more
than ever evident that we can no more enter the Kingdom of
Heaven with all our assembled baggage of inherited beliefs, concepts and traditions — be they rationalistic, spiritual or occult —
than can the proverbial camel pass through the eye of the equally
proverbial needle.

Somehow, it seems, the world is not for improving.

And perhaps it is that very realisation which — strange as it
may seem — is capable of leading us at last to the real heart of the
matter.

14

Apocalypse Now

The kingdom of God is among you.
Jesus of Nazareth (Luke 17:21)

'Old Agers' or 'New Agers', it seems, we all have failure staring us in the face.

Despite (or perhaps because of) the titanic calculations of the Hindu and Buddhist mathematicians; despite the inexorable cyclisms of the astrologers; despite the cosmological modelling of the ancient Greeks, the Babylonians, the Maya and the Aztecs; despite the confident apocalyptic assertions of Zoroastrians and Jews, Christians and Muslims; despite Renaissance attempts to retrieve the Classical Golden Age from the past, and nineteenth-century attempts to create a new, technological one in the future; despite even the generous commitment of modern New Agers to building a new Garden of Eden here on earth through semi-occult means by the dawn of the twenty-first century — despite all this, it appears, the long-hoped-for Golden Age resolutely refuses to dawn.

Why should this be?

Is it some kind of accident, some abstruse irony of fate? Or is it the result of a basic flaw in our understanding, a fundamental problem of human consciousness?

* * *

Certainly the evidence from all quarters seems increasingly to suggest that the answer does indeed lie on our own perceptual doorstep. Basic flaws of understanding are at issue. And not merely basic ones: there are some rather more superficial ones as well.

To take the latter category first, many of our problems in achieving a new World Order seem to spring from a simple failure of understanding in the realm of expectation, prediction and prophecy.

In my book *The Armageddon Script*[41] I distinguished between three distinct types of spectacles through which we habitually try to peer into the future. The most familiar of these are the relatively short-focus glasses of forecasting, familiar to us through the common-or-garden weather forecast and the official government economic prediction. More mysterious in their operation are the binoculars of clairvoyance, which somehow seem able to descry future events in spontaneous and often disconnected flashes of intuitive insight, though with a relatively limited ability to gauge true distances in time.

In the case of prophecy, however, the predictive tool is more in the nature of a telescopic rifle-sight, in that prophecy seems to be able to intervene directly in the future on its own account. It is, in other words, either a creative or a destructive tool which actually contributes to fashioning and conditioning the future which it describes. This it apparently does by influencing the psyches of those to whom it is addressed in such a way as to cause them to perceive reality in a new light, thus indirectly causing them to bring to pass whatever events have been prophesied.

Thus, while predictions can, in time, start to operate in the role of prophecies, this is less likely to happen in the case of mere forecasts, as most of these operate on far too short a timescale to have any fundamental transformative effect on the psyches and perceptions of those concerned.

(This link between perception and apparent reality is a point of some importance, and one that is of considerable relevance to our general discussion, as I hope to demonstrate shortly.)

In the course of my subsequent enquiry into the historical applications of these various aspects of futurology, I went on to propose a set of eight basic laws which seem to govern their operation. These can be briefly summarised as follows:

1. The Law of Surprise Fulfilment
The most likely outcome is the one that nobody has anticipated.

2. The Law of Thwarted Expectation
The most obvious expectation is likely to be the wrong one.

3. The Law of Prejudicial Interference
Preconception and prophecy do not mix.

4. The Law of Self-Fulfilment
Prophecies tend to be self-fulfilling.

5. The Law of Diminishing Accuracy
A prophecy's accuracy decreases as the square of the time to its fulfilment.

6. The Law of Divided Functions
Prophecy and interpretation are incompatible activities.

7. The Law of Prophetic Foreshortening
Clairvoyance foreshortens the future.

8. The Law of Non-Existent Impossibility (rider to Law Four)
If it can happen, it will: if it can't happen, it might.

To the extent that they are valid, it can readily be seen how most, if not all, of these laws are directly applicable to traditional 'Golden Age' speculations. But the one which is possibly most potent — and indeed most widely recognised to be so — is the Fourth Law: *Prophecies tend to be self-fulfilling.* Yet this being so, why is it that the persistent millenarian tradition (which, after all, has had several millennia now to accumulate sufficient psychic momentum to bring about its own fulfilment) is seemingly still unable to come up with the goods? Why does the Kingdom of Heaven not dawn? Why, indeed, has it not dawned long since?

The answer appears to lie partly in the obvious vitiating effects of all the other laws except the last one, and partly in the traditional form of prophetic statements themselves.

What, after all, has been the prime concern of speculators about the coming of the Golden Age ever since the idea was first mooted? Inevitably, 'When will it happen?' The various answers have been couched in similar terms: 'The New Age will come after *n* thousand years,' or 'when the Messiah comes,' or 'when technology finally solves all our problems,' or 'when the Masters finally return to live among us' . . . .

Always *will*. Always in the future.

Yet the future, by definition, never comes. Even more than the past, which is admittedly non-existent, but at least persists in memory, the future is always a mirage, an illusion, a reality only in the imagination.

The result is inevitable. The Golden Age, having been relegated to an uncertain future, insists on staying there. Joining hands with mañana, the Kingdom of Heaven becomes transformed into a mere *utopia* — literally 'nowhere'.

The Fourth Law of Prophecy, in other words, may indeed have done its psychic work. The prophecy may indeed have been fulfilled. But since we are alive *now* we have no means of checking the fact. The Kingdom of Heaven, in other words, *will come*. And it will continue to 'will-come' until such time as the form of the prophecy is changed in such a way as to insist that it actually comes *now*.

It is just such a task that the Essenes of ancient Palestine seem to have undertaken some two thousand years ago, and which led to the extraordinary phenomenon of the Jesus-initiative, with all the after-effects (largely unforeseen!) which have continued to plague — and sometimes bless — the world ever since. That the initiative failed to achieve its intended aim seems to have been due partly, as we saw earlier, to pure accident, and partly to the fact that, rooted as it was in the most obvious form of Zoroastrian-influenced duality-consciousness, it never stood the slightest chance of bringing about a New Order of wholeness, peace and harmony in the first place.

As the Essenes, who knew a thing or two about prophecy, should have realised all along.

Any new millenarian initiative to redress the situation, consequently, has to operate out of a truly *holistic* consciousness. And above all it has to operate on a new prophetic basis entirely — namely the realisation that, if the Kingdom of Heaven comes at all, it comes *now*.

* * *

At this point we are faced with the next piece of misunderstanding which has so far bedevilled all attempts to inaugurate a New Age on earth. And this is the assumption that the expression 'New Age' necessarily refers to a period of time at all.

We are all familiar with the idea, for example, in connection with archaeology and studies in prehistory. The Old Stone Age, we are taught, lasted from the dawn of prehistory until about 5,000 BC, and the New Stone Age from 5,000 BC until sometime after 3,000 BC, with the succeeding Bronze Age giving way to the Iron Age in about 1,000 BC.

It is interesting to note how each of these notional ages is shorter than its predecessor, almost exactly after the style of the ancient Hindu scheme of things. Much the same could be said of the various epochs of Western cultural history to which we also habitually refer: the Classical Age, the Dark Ages, the Middle Ages, the Renaissance, the Age of Reason, the Romantic Age, the Industrial Age, the Atomic Age, the Space Age . . . . And who can be sure that it will not also apply to the Post-Industrial Age to which our futurologists are already starting to turn their attention[11] — to say nothing of the 'New Age' itself?

Possibly this phenomenon of ever-increasing brevity is a direct function of the gathering pace of social and technological change. It may also be a function of our greater awareness of the details of events and phenomena nearer to us in time or space. This is reflected, for example, in our persistent tendency to foreshorten the distances between remoter objects and ourselves by assessing those distances against a larger scale. The tendency is apparent not only in astronomy, but in everyday geography too. People from the south of England often tend to think of Scotland as a small piece of land 'stuck on the top of England' — when in fact the north-south length of both countries is more or less the same. The British as a whole, similarly, often tend to think of New Zealand as being about as near to Australia as Ireland is to England — when in fact the distance is more like that from Scotland to Greenland, or from London to Bucharest.

Nearer, in other words, is bigger. And so even quite short periods of recent time seem to us to qualify as 'ages'.

But I digress. The point at issue is not that the 'ages' into which we divide past history tend to become progressively shorter, *but that they are thought of as periods of time at all.*

A moment's reflection reveals the falseness of this assumption. The Stone Age did *not* finish five thousand years ago. Not universally at any rate. In many parts of the world — among certain of the aborigines of Australia and Indonesia, for example, as well as among some of the remoter Indian tribes of South America — it is still very much with us. Much the same applies to the Bronze and Iron Ages.

The various cultures of China, Japan and Central and South America, similarly, have each known what might be described as their own Classical, Dark and Middle Ages — none of which necessarily corresponded in date exactly with its European equivalent. And if it is difficult in their history to identify any of the subsequent ages that I have listed, that is partly because of European cultural contamination from the time of the Renaissance onwards, and partly because terms of this kind have in any case such specific connotations for us in terms of dress, scholarship, political institutions and so on as to make any such comparison not merely difficult, but ultimately meaningless.

But if an 'age' in this sense does not mean a period of time, what *does* it mean?

Inevitably, it seems, it has to mean a particular level of human consciousness — a level of consciousness which then, of necessity, goes on to produce a culture which reflects it.

As anthropological investigation of 'culture-shock' in indigenous populations has shown in our own day, these differing levels of consciousness are almost totally incompatible — so incompatible that true communication between any two of them is next to impossible. Either the 'lower' level totally rejects the 'higher', or the 'higher' modifies, corrupts or even destroys the 'lower', with the result that any communication that does eventually take place does so only *on its own terms*.

The point, as we shall see, is of direct relevance to our general enquiry.

But if this is so of the Stone Age, the Bronze Age and so on, it seems inevitable that it must also be true of any New Age that may dawn. That, too, has to represent an entirely different level, or form, of human consciousness. And if a new society and form of culture arises, then it has to be as a direct result of this change of consciousness.

The moral for the millenarians is clear. Not only is it actually counter-productive to place the expected New Age in the future. It is also counter-productive to regard it as a period of time at all.

Instead, what has to take place is a total revolution within the human psyche. *And it is that revolution that will automatically bring about the various social reforms and personal changes for which so many social activists — and not merely the New Agers — are currently striving.*

To give them due credit, there are a good many New Agers who already realise this. If they still tend to fall down on the job, it is because they too often imagine that the necessary change of consciousness can somehow be brought about by force — as it were by pulling themselves up by their own bootstraps, while undertaking some kind of 'missionary activity' to drag the whole universe aloft with them.

In the case of the New Agers, then, it is the old bugbear of dualism — whether internal or external — that once again frustrates the whole exercise. A dualism which imagines that there is something to be done, something separate to do it to, and somebody independent to do it.

But this point is the cue for us finally to turn our attention to deeper matters altogether . . . .

* * *

For at this juncture we need to confront a number of much more basic realisations which not only reveal the utter impotence and pointlessness of all such would-be reforms, but are at the same time so revolutionary as to seem, at first sight, contrary to common sense.

As, indeed, expressions of deeper truth often do.

The first of these realisations — astonishing as it may at first seem — is that *the universe is absolutely perfect as it is.*

A point, you may feel, at which to stand back and take a deep breath. For the idea seems immediately to beg a good many important questions. Not the least of which is, 'What about Planet Earth?'

For while most Westerners seem able to accept the idea that the universe as a whole is basically perfect (at least as a working hypothesis), there is a strong feeling abroad that our own planet is somehow an exception. We are, in other words, a kind of fly in the universal ointment, very much as C.S. Lewis's science-fiction novel *Out of the Silent Planet* would have us see ourselves.[45]

A moment's thought reveals the dualistic fallacy involved in such a proposition. If, after all, the universe is perfect, then Planet Earth is necessarily perfect too. If, on the other hand, Planet Earth is imperfect, then so is the universe. For there is, as we have seen, no way in which the two can be separated.

And so the argument has to be pushed back into a historical setting — or rather a prehistoric, or even mythical one. The universe, as most of us would be prepared to agree, was perfect once upon a time. It was only when humans came into the picture that it suddenly became imperfect.

Immediately, of course, we are back to the old tradition of the Garden of Eden, Fall and Redemption — a tradition in which, as we have now seen, there is really no mileage whatsoever in terms of human hopes or prospects.

Quite apart from this, however, there is a basic oddity about this whole argument. If the universe was perfect, and it was humans who somehow spoiled it, how could this possibly have come about? If the universe was perfect, after all, then so, originally, was Planet Earth in all its multifarious aspects. So, originally, in other words, was that particular aspect of it known as the human race. But if the universe was perfect, and Planet Earth was perfect, and humanity was perfect, where could the supposed imperfection possibly have come from? Where else, indeed, than from *outside* the universe?

Yet this would be a contradiction in terms. Since the universe, by definition, includes everything there is, there can be nowhere 'outside' it for such imperfections to originate. Only by adopting the traditional Judaeo-Christian assumption that there is not only a God existing somewhere outside and prior to His creation, but also some kind of extracosmic Devil, can the idea possibly be entertained.

But at this point we are back once again to the old dualistic outlook which, it seems, got us into our present mess in the first place, and so offers us precious little prospect of getting back out of it again.

Once again, in other words, we draw a blank.

There seems to be no alternative but to accept the fact that the world was always perfect, humanity was always perfect, and *no imperfection ever entered into the picture at all.*

What, then, did enter the picture?

Here, at last — especially in the light of our opening chapter — the beginning of an answer does start to swim into focus. What entered the picture was *human consciousness* — not merely the generalised awareness of the right brain, but also the focused, analytical consciousness of the left. It was this latter form of consciousness that then started to divide up the world into categories which formed the basis of all subsequent thought and language. And if it divided up the world, what more natural than it should then find itself in the midst of a world that was divided — a world, in particular, that was subject to the very powers of good and evil which human consciousness had, however unknowingly, itself invented?

And so arose the idea that the world was at odds with itself, at odds with the rest of the universe, at odds with humanity itself. Here, in other words, was a situation which demanded efforts at improvement. It is thanks to those efforts that we in the Developed World now have modern civilisation, the arts, the sciences and most of the other benefits of twentieth-century living which we hold most dear. (It is surely no accident that the modern scientific tradition of dualistic reductionism and the myth of human perfectibility both had their beginnings at about the same time — namely during the European Renaissance.)

What we manifestly do not have, however, is an improved world in any general sense. And this for the very reason that no general improvement was either necessary or possible in the first place.

The imagined imperfection of the world was always a mere illusion from the beginning.

What had happened was that humanity had lost sight of reality as it was. And the only way to improve the situation was — and is — to put human consciousness back in touch with that reality, not least by re-establishing contact with our direct perceptions, uncontaminated by the entirely theoretical categories and judgements of our rampant left-brain consciousness.

* * *

Thus far, then, even a more or less conventional application of our left-brain's capacity for reasoned argument has allowed us to arrive at some kind of preliminary conclusion, even though we have made no attempt to use it to justify our initial premise of universal perfection. This latter idea is much more the result of a kind of 'natural intuition' or underlying gut-feeling (which I have therefore been careful to call a 'realisation') than a 'conclusion' (which would imply the result of some kind of logical argument).

It is nevertheless one which most of us share.

And the next realisation which we are going to have to face is likewise much more amenable to this all-at-once, gut-feeling type of approach than to the rationalistic kind of argument with which most of us are — thanks to our addiction to duality-consciousness — much more at home.

Except that, this time, it is a gut-feeling which all too few of us share.

The realisation in question arises directly out of what we have already said about the universe as a whole. Indeed, we have more or less expressed the gist of it already. But now it needs to be put more bluntly.

The world as we know it is exactly as it has to be.

Perhaps it is at this point that a good many readers will reach hurriedly for their discrimination — based in dualistic thinking though all discrimination necessarily has to be. To Western minds particularly, after all, such an idea is little less than heresy.

'What,' it is likely to be asked, 'about the nuclear threat, the menace of international terrorism, the scourge of unemployment and the various other ills to which you have already referred — including the population explosion, Third World poverty and famine, the depletion of the Earth's natural resources and worldwide environmental pollution? What, indeed, about AIDS? Surely all these are evidence that things are seriously wrong and that something drastic needs to be done to put them right?'

The suggestion that the world is as it has to be, in other words, is nothing more or less than fatalism, and pretty dangerous fatalism at that.

And it is this supposed fatalism that is of course the heresy.

Now it has to be said at once that the accusation of heresy is always a sure sign of the presence of dogma. And in this case the dogma in question is the belief, nowadays accepted almost universally in the Western world, that problems can be solved and the world improved — indeed, not only that they can be, but that they must be. It is the dogma, in other words, of action-at-all-costs.

And it is perhaps best summed up in the popular expression: 'Don't just sit there — *do* something!'

Implicit in this attitude is the familiar assumption that the world is imperfect. The assumption, of course, is in no way new or remarkable, particularly when we bear in mind the dominance in the West of left-brain thinking — and thus, necessarily, of duality-consciousness as well. What is remarkable is the degree of fanaticism involved in the commitment to action — a fanaticism which seems to have more than a little to do with the by-now familiar Protestant work-ethic.

It is assumed as a matter of faith, in other words, not merely that something must be done to right the world's apparent wrongs, *but that this 'something' will necessarily have the desired effect.* Help will assist. Intervention will bring about improvements.

Yet experience repeatedly demonstrates the contrary.

The typical Western response to perceived problems, for example, is to throw money and material goods at them. Whether in the case of mass accidents at the local level or of vast, world-scale disasters such as Third World famine, we tend to assume that the gods in which our own civilisation has put its faith will be effective in bringing salvation to others as well. No less than Christian evangelism, in other words, our attitude is an all-too-obvious version of the well-known missionary syndrome.

Though, of course, we apply the same assumptions to our own, home-grown disasters as well.

And so, when 116 children in the Welsh coal-mining village of Aberfan were killed in their school by an avalanche of coalmine waste in 1966, enormous quantities of money poured in from all over the country. Much the same happened some seventeen years later when the Cornish Penlee lifeboat was lost with all hands in the course of a desperate sea-rescue attempt, just as it has done in respect of a whole range of other tragedies since.

At the other end of the spectrum, there is a similar reaction when the media draw dramatic attention to some great catastrophe on a much larger scale. Even during the preparation of this book, for example, famines of almost unprecedented severity struck Ethiopia, Sudan and many of the other sub-Saharan countries of

Africa. Television pictures of the disasters drew an enormous response from the Developed World in terms of cash, food-aid, medicines and logistical support. Support which, it nevertheless needs to be said, would have been largely unnecessary had suitable help been forthcoming *before* the television pictures had had their devastating emotional effect.

There followed an almost audible sigh of relief from among the donors and contributory nations. 'At least something,' it seemed to say, 'is being done. I have done my best. My conscience is clear.'

The phenomenon is a familiar one where charity-donations are concerned. And there, all too often, the commitment to aid and support abruptly stops.

Now apart from remarking that this phenomenon raises the difficult question of just how far the donors are really interested in improving the lot of the sufferers, and how far in appeasing their own consciences and their almost religious faith in the efficacy of materialism, this whole phenomenon raises some absolutely basic questions. And not least because it is highly dubious whether the aid in question helps in the long run at all. Money not only failed to buy back the 116 children of Aberfan; its distribution also caused the most horrific social disputes and dissensions within the Aberfan community. Much the same happened in the case of the Penlee lifeboat, as well as in more recent disasters.

As for the great Third World famines, it has long since become evident that the aid offered has often had deleterious side-effects — even in the relatively few cases where it has actually been appropriate. Not only have corrupt government officials misappropriated both funds and food-aid for their own benefit, and merchants grown fat on the *sale* of food-aid which had been freely offered by the donor-nations and charities — while the local infrastructures have for the most part been hopelessly incapable of coping with the vast influx of goods in the first place. Even when the aid has succeeded in getting through to those for whom it was intended, the net effect (as we saw earlier) has frequently been to make them totally dependent on free handouts which, by the very nature of things, are unlikely to continue for ever. Except among a few particularly far-sighted individuals and organisations, it has scarcely occurred to the majority of those concerned that merely treating the effects is not the answer, and that tackling the real causes on a long-term basis is the only way of eliminating the problems.

Essential though the short-term aid is, in other words, its net effect in the absence of the longer-term view is merely to keep those at risk alive just long enough to condemn them to an even bigger and worse tragedy later on.

The road to hell, as ever, is paved with good intentions.

And so what has been exposed is the difference between the short-term, emotional response based on dramatic media exposure — a response which, for the most part, fails totally to *take responsibility* for the situation (for responsible we ultimately are, whether or not we currently recognise the fact) — and the long-term response based on a mature awareness of what is needed and (above all) appropriate.

The difference, in a word, between sentiment and compassion.

True, if my suggestion is valid that the world as we know it is exactly as it has to be, then there has to be a place in it for sentiment as well as compassion, for the eager first-aider as well as for the cool, dispassionate surgeon. There also has, presumably, to be a place in it for the common view that what is, in effect, the compassionate approach is somehow cold and heartless. For so, on the face of it, it has always seemed to be, whether as applied by the Buddha or by anybody else.

People who rush to pick up old ladies who have just fallen down in the street are no doubt profoundly convinced that they are doing the right thing, and no doubt afterwards feel a warm glow of self-satisfaction to match. The compassionate observer who waits for the victim to move of her own accord and helps her only to the extent that she asks to be helped may attract little admiration from the bystanders. But at least he or she is keeping matters sufficiently in perspective to realise that 'standing up' an old lady who may have broken one or more bones is liable to turn simple fractures into compound ones, and so may make a bad situation considerably worse.

True compassion, in other words, demands the long-term, overall view. Instead of attempting to operate on effects, it patiently seeks out an awareness of causes, knowing full well that, until the causes are satisfactorily dealt with, all that can possibly follow is a further bout of effects, many of which may be even worse than the existing ones.

Instead of 'Don't just sit there — *do* something', in other words, it may well be a question of 'Don't just do something — *sit there!*'

To give them full credit, the aid workers who try to gear their efforts at famine relief to the longer perspective are already taking a valiant step in the right direction. Yet hardly ever does this process go far enough. Usually it is still to the removal of *effects* that their efforts are chiefly directed — even if these are earlier, more far-reaching effects than the ones to the alleviation of which most aid is directed.

For the fact is that there is not one of the problems and ills referred to earlier which does not have its roots in the almost universal assumption that the world is imperfect, and especially in the rampant Western conviction that things are improvable. Not one of them, consequently, which is not based firmly in duality-consciousness. Scarcely one of them, for that matter, which has not actually been *caused* by the very efforts which we still insist on applying in a forlorn attempt to try and correct it.

Thus, to consider only the particular problems which I have already listed, the Aberfan disaster would not have happened had humanity never turned to coal-burning in the first place for the sake of ever-growing industrial efficiency and muscle, nor would the village's children have been buried in their school had not the world-wide effort to improve living conditions by founding complex societies necessitated the institution of mass education. The Penlee lifeboat tragedy, similarly, would not have happened had the urge to accumulate power and riches in the service of 'self-betterment' not resulted in the development of maritime technology and trading, and if the desire to improve the survival prospects of mariners had not demanded the foundation of the Royal National Lifeboat Institution.

On the larger scale, similarly, decades of East-West confrontation (however hopeful the noises that are currently being made to reduce it) would never have come about had the earliest peoples not come together in ever-larger groupings in an effort to improve their power, prestige and security vis-à-vis other groupings. Similar considerations of group advantage and power underlie a good deal of modern international terrorism. Partly fuelled by the same drive towards communal self-advancement, the nuclear arms-race would have been a non-starter but for our insatiable desire to discover what makes the natural world tick, rooted as that desire clearly is in the urge eventually to control the universe for our own benefit (almost as though we and it were ever separate in the first place).

By the same token, the world's current natural resources problems and the growing menace of environmental pollution can also be traced back directly (as can the current problem of mass unemployment) to the Developed World's unceasing quest for ever-increasing industrial power and economic efficiency in the service of its own self-enrichment and a supposedly better life for its citizens. And the drug-menace, self-evidently, is the direct result of individuals' forlorn attempts to make life more bearable or more exciting for themselves by chemical means.

Again not only the population explosion (mainly a Third World phenomenon) but also the Third World's perennial problems of poverty and famine can be traced back directly, in large measure, to the influence of Western colonialism — whether through its introduction of more effective medical techniques (which have resulted in higher survival rates) or through its local imposition of cash-crop economies and, later, the establishment of 'independent' regimes, mostly based faithfully on Western models and assumptions, who have tended to maintain those economies. It is, after all, those very forms of economy which have been responsible for forcing the mass of the people onto ever more marginal lands, with deforestation and eventual desertification the inevitable results. And all of this, as ever, in the service of 'making the world a better place' — whether overtly for the 'heathen savages', by bringing them the supposed benefits of Western religion and civilisation, or for the colonial powers themselves, by increasing ever further the power and supremacy of the white European nations for their own exclusive benefit.

Indeed, even such relatively 'minor' — or at least localised — disasters as airliner crashes or ferry sinkings (major though they inevitably seem to those involved) are clearly the direct result of our indulging ourselves with airliners and ferries in the first place. Mass deaths in football stadiums could never happen if we did not have football stadiums. Large-scale drownings in floods are often largely attributable to tree-felling further upstream in the interests of agriculture, fuel provision and the local economy generally. Future coastal flooding, similarly, may well result from a rising sea level that is ultimately attributable to our burning of fossil fuels and the large-scale destruction of the rainforests — both of them in the service of our economic growth. And deaths in earthquakes and hurricanes are nearly always the result of the collapse of the very buildings that we put up to *protect* ourselves from the elements.

And what of AIDS? Here we need to be quite clear about just what the problem is. The disease, heaven knows, is dreadful enough for those who are unfortunate enough to contract it — yet it is not AIDS that world health authorities are most worried about. It is not AIDS that has sexually active people from central Africa to California quaking in their boots. It is not AIDS that causes religious fundamentalists to flaunt all their self-righteousness and has the man and woman in the street reaching hurriedly for their hard-won and half-forgotten moral preconceptions, not to say their incipient bigotry. What concerns them all is not AIDS, so

much as the *spread* of AIDS. It is the sheer, exponential explosive-
ness of the disease that is the problem at issue — a feature which,
on the original basis of an approximate doubling of the numbers
infected every year, ought theoretically to mean that everybody on
earth should have the virus inside thirty-three years. Of course,
there is a large gap between theory and practice. Things are not as
simple as that. The rate of spread tends to reduce as those most at
risk die off or change their sexual habits. Medical preventive mea-
sures tend to have their effect, too — though most of these are far
too expensive ever to be likely candidates for application in the
Third World countries where the disease is most rampant. But the
spread is still the problem — a spread that remains quite exponential enough eventually to reduce the population of our planet (in
line with the apocalyptic Zoroastrian and biblical predictions) *by
up to a third*. The threat is truly gigantic — its scale still only half-
realised by politicians and others who have not yet learnt what
happens when you keep multiplying two by two.

But how does a disease such as AIDS spread? It is, after all, not
an airborne disease. So far, at least, it spreads only via direct
human contact and travel. The very fact that we have roads and
railways, ships and airliners, in other words, ultimately makes
that spread possible. Otherwise the spread from settled community to
settled community would be so slow as to be more than offset by
population increases elsewhere in the world — slow enough for
whole new lifestyles and moral codes to develop in time to fore-
stall it. Slow enough, possibly, even for a measure of natural
immunity to develop. But with AIDS we suddenly have a world
problem — a problem that is in the process of overwhelming our
whole planet virtually at once. Perhaps there are good reasons for
this. Perhaps such catastrophes always happen when human
numbers become too great or populations too concentrated. Perhaps, in other words, AIDS is actually some kind of planetary life-
line. Nevertheless, whatever the underlying merits of the case, it is
we who have helped promote its spread, and we have done so
precisely as a result of our past achievements in setting up commun-
ications-links between the nations of the world — a process whose
origins, you may recall, lay very largely in the efforts of the European colonisers to spread their religion, their culture, their trade
and — yes — their very medical technology itself world-wide.

* * *

Every one of the problems that I have mentioned, then, has its roots in the conviction that the world can somehow be improved — a conviction which of course implies that it is inherently imperfect. Every one of them, in other words, is based on an almost pathological commitment on the part of humanity as a whole — and especially Western humanity — to dualistic thinking.

It is that very dualistic thinking which actually makes it inevitable that our familiar world is as it is. The world as we know it is as it has to be *precisely because of the way in which we know it*.

Thus, to the traditional Native American, who sees the world in a holistic light, the perceived world is one and whole: we, on the other hand, see it dualistically, and so to us it is perpetually at odds with itself.

And so our own responsibility in the matter is clear. To put no finer point upon it, *we are responsible for the universe that we create*. And if that universe is not to our liking, then doing something about it is equally our own responsibility.

But it should by now be obvious that the action in question is not something to be carried out within the context of duality itself. The way *not* to solve the world's problems, in other words, is to see ourselves as confronted by them — to place them, as it were, on the other side of the fence and on the same level as ourselves. What has to be changed is not the problem, but the nature of our own awareness — not the effect, but the cause.

Which seems to be an invitation to see duality-consciousness in turn as a problem in its own right, and one which consequently demands to be tackled as it were 'from outside', in much the same way as we tend to try and deal with all our other problems.

But this, of course, is merely a recipe for yet more dualistic thinking.

And so it is possible to sum up in a few words what we have learnt about such would-be reforms from bitter experience so far. To many it may make for fairly brutal reading.

What it boils down to is that, if we wish to bring about a New Age of peace, harmony and light on Earth, then the following are definitely among the things *not* to do:

1. Place it in the future.
2. Think of it as a period of time.
3. Saddle God, the Messiah, the Masters, or higher beings from 'out there' with responsibility for it.
4. Imagine that you can achieve it by re-applying the failed techniques of yesterday.
5. Try to transform the Old Age.

6. Found or join New Age communities with a view to creating a new social order (whatever other reasons you may have for doing so).
7. Assume that 'spiritual truth' is the key to it.
8. Make it conditional upon the acceptance of any word-based belief whatsoever, or on the joining of any given group or organisation.
9. Distinguish between yourself as a 'New Ager' and others who are not.
10. Attempt to convert others to the idea (the missionary syndrome).

* * *

But if all these approaches are non-starters, what on earth *are* we to do? (The words 'on earth' are important. It is no use kidding ourselves that we can ever solve things by escaping into space. Like the original American colonists, we should merely be taking all our problems along with us. Nowhere in the universe can we ever hope to escape from ourselves.)

What is required, clearly, is a veritable quantum leap from the old form of consciousness to the new — from dualistic thinking to total, 'all-at-once' awareness. It is this alone — whether we describe it as holistic consciousness, universal consciousness, cosmic consciousness or God-consciousness — that seems likely to produce the New Age which humanity has been vainly seeking for so long.

The New Age, in other words, is not something that can be climbed up into — for the consciousness which predicates it (which, indeed, in the last resort *is* it, as we shall see) is as totally incompatible with our familiar, dualistic form of consciousness as the various kinds of consciousness associated with each of the preceding 'ages' evidently are with each other, if the anthropologists are to be believed. There is simply no ladder, or continuum, connecting the two.

Two caterpillars might as well endeavour to attain butterfly-consciousness via a process of mutual discussion, or one gorilla explain to another the principles underlying human nuclear physics.

On the other hand, neither is the New Age something that can be 'dropped out into' — for, if one thing is clear, it is that nobody who is incapable of coping with the Old Age has the slightest prospect of being able to cope with the much more exacting demands of the New.

Yet if duality-consciousness cannot produce the New Age or

evolve into the holistic consciousness which predicates it, neither can it explain or prescribe any route to it.

Not least because, by definition, there *can be* no route to it.

The fact, inevitably, puts anybody who attempts to discuss or describe the alternative form of consciousness — and this author in particular — in an extremely difficult position.

* * *

Nevertheless, the language which duality-consciousness has produced, and which makes the writing of books such as this possible in the first place, does have two useful functions to perform. It can outline analogies which at least help to point us in the right direction; and it can describe those approaches which are *not* appropriate — a process of elimination which, once again, can help to point us in the right direction, even if only by default. These two functions are well displayed in the frequent use by the world's great spiritual teachers of parable and paradox respectively.

A particularly relevant analogy, for example, can be drawn on the basis of the very story of the Garden of Eden which, in the event, has proved central to the theme of this book.

Let us imagine, for a start, a flesh-and-blood Adam and Eve living at peace in a similarly physical Garden of Eden. Everything in the Garden, as the saying has it, is lovely. And all life, necessarily, is there.

Our two mythical progenitors are at liberty to eat the fruit of all the trees in the Garden except one — and that one for very obvious reasons, since it is the Tree of the Knowledge of Good and Evil, the very symbol of dualistic thinking. Yet every mouthful they swallow sweeps to their deaths literally millions of the perfectly harmless bacteria which have made their home on the blissful couple's gut-linings. At the same time, further millions of skin-cells are dying every day in the ceaseless war between their living skin-tissues and the oxidising effects of the surrounding atmosphere.

Yet, curiously enough, neither fact is seen as a 'problem'. Both are seen as perfectly compatible with the paradisical perfection of the Garden. Or rather, they are not even seen at all.

And why? Because consciousness is operating not at the level of the individual cells or bacteria, but at a level which both transcends and literally incorporates them both. At the 'dualistic' level of cells and bacteria, admittedly, the inevitable mass-mortality might well be seen as a disaster of the first order, and all sorts of emotions of affront, pity and fellow-feeling might justifiably be evoked. But the body as a whole accepts it all, paradoxically enough, as an inevitable part of life itself — and even, in the case of the body-cells, as an essential prerequisite for its continued existence.

The moral, then, might seem to be that, seen from the 'higher', more holistic level, the apparent 'problems' are not problems at all. If millions of people suffer and die as a result of Third World famine, this is merely part of the infinite interplay between life and death which is continually carried on by the universe as a whole.

Yet is not such a view callous and uncaring? Should we not do what we can for our fellow human beings?

Perhaps it is worth bearing in mind at this point that the body as a whole is *not* uncaring about its individual body-cells. It continually feeds, nurtures and protects them to the best of its ability. But it does not make the mistake of waging an absolute war against their death, since it knows at an 'instinctive' or autonomic level that all of them must regularly die merely in order for the life of the whole body to continue. At least once every seven years, in fact, this process of death and replacement is repeated for every body-cell, with the sole exception of those of the brain.

In the case of our own vigorous rejection of Third World suffering and death at the human level, then, we might do well to ask ourselves what exactly it is that we are objecting to. Not, presumably, the suffering and death itself, since if that were so we should be much more concerned about their incidence among those who are *not* the victims of famine. There are, after all, far more of them. All of us, for that matter, are subject to such things at some time or other.

What seems to concern us, in fact, is the mass nature of the suffering and death in question, which — thanks once again to the ever-present media — recalls to us all too dramatically these inevitable features of human existence of which we would rather not be reminded.

Much the same reaction can be observed in the case of major fires, air crashes, motorway accidents, ferry disasters, earthquakes and hurricanes involving the deaths of many people at once. Far less people actually die in them than in the myriad lesser equivalents that regularly kill only one or two people at a time: yet we regularly ignore the latter, while experiencing all sorts of emotions of pity, remorse and righteous indignation about the former.

What we are objecting to, in other words, is not so much what is happening to the sufferers as what is happening to us. And the charge of callousness is — once we take the trouble to look closely at what is really involved — merely a cover, a plea on the part of our illusory ego for a further lease of supposedly independent life, for a chance to affirm its usefulness and individuality by 'helping others'.

As for doing what we can to help, we have already seen what is, and is not, likely to be appropriate. Merely operating on the same, dualistic level as the events themselves and of our immediate emotional response tends merely to make matters worse. By and large we are prepared to do anything rather than the one thing which could actually rectify the situation — namely changing the very basis of our awareness, and consequently the principles by which we live.

It has been aptly remarked that the white man will do anything for the black man except get off his back. If we in the Developed World really cared about Third World poverty and famine as much as we say we do, we should long since have reformed the whole basis of our international economic activity. We should have taken steps to see that we no longer deliberately depress the prices of the Third World's cash-crops or raise protectionist barriers at home against their cheap manufactured goods. We should have forbidden our multinationals to use aggressive Western marketing techniques to sell them foods and medicines which they do not need. We should have abandoned the idea of granting their governments financial aid only on condition that they use it to buy expensive capital goods from us, and of advancing them loans only on pain of incurring crippling burdens of interest which we know that they cannot afford. In particular we should long since have ceased applying every kind of pressure on them to buy our high-priced weaponry. And for that matter we should long since have stopped producing it even for our own use . . . .

Which means, of course, that for the sake of the rest of humanity we should willingly have accepted for ourselves higher commodity prices, a weaker economy and even higher levels of unemployment than we already have — in short, a far lower standard of living than we, as relative millionaires by world standards, currently enjoy.

But of course we show little sign of doing any of these things. For all our pretended care and indignation, duality-consciousness is rampant, and the one form of consciousness which could actually do anything about the situation remains conspicuously absent.

* * *

Perhaps a further analogy will throw more light on the true situation. My thumb and my forefinger, let us say, are at daggers drawn.

Each sees the other as its 'enemy', since it is of course directly opposed to it. Each regards the other, consequently, as a 'problem'. It is only I myself, as a whole human being, who can see not merely that their mutual opposition is useful and necessary for my continued existence, but that it is actually the means whereby I grasp whatever I grasp.

Possibly the universe uses our own dualistic oppositions in a similar way. Possibly our own conflicts, in other words, are the means whereby it grasps whatever it grasps.

Be that as it may, suppose that we now imagine that the thumb manages to overcome its feelings of antagonism to the point where it can now regard the forefinger as its brother, as another being like itself deserving of love and care. (This would of course still be a dualistic view — one not untypical, say, of modern New Agers to those about them.)

What happens now if the forefinger accidentally gets cut? No doubt the thumb becomes distressed, rails against the circumstances which caused the injury. But what can it do to help? Precious little, apart from applying temporary local pressure to staunch any bleeding. It is only I, at my level of *over-all* consciousness, who am capable of directing the thumb and fingers of the hand as a whole — as well as of the other hand — in such a way as to wash the wound, cleanse it with antiseptic and apply a suitable first aid dressing. Or indeed of deciding that some other treatment, or even none at all, would be more suitable.

And for the thumb in question the right course — indeed the only possible course — may well be to do nothing.

Once again, then, it is the 'higher', over-all view which alone is capable not only of seeing things in their true perspective, but actually of acting — or refraining from acting — appropriately.

Or even of bringing in help from other sources entirely.

* * *

Neither of my analogies is of course exact. No analogy ever is. And yet they do help to demonstrate not only the aptness, but the inherent practicality of the holistic, over-all view. No analogy, however, can be of much assistance in suggesting how to attain that view.

But then possibly this is because *it does not need to be attained*. The very idea of an individual 'me' attaining a separate 'it', in other words, is inherently dualistic and a denial of that which is to be attained.

As the Buddha always insisted, *you are* enlightened. All that is necessary is to wake up to the fact.

And certainly it may well be that in our earliest years we already know this holistic consciousness, much as we suggested in the early stages of this book. Perhaps that is why Jesus of Nazareth is said to have pointed out that only when we become like little children again are we likely to enter the final Kingdom of Heaven. Indeed, there is not one of the ancient religious traditions which sees the final Golden Age as in any sense a culmination: in every case, on the contrary, it is a *tabula rasa*, a new beginning.

In practice, however, any such consciousness that we may have is educated out of us at the first opportunity by our parental and social conditioning, so that all too few of us retain it. What then follows is a long and often painful process of working through the imposed illusions of duality-consciousness . . . until we eventually come out again on the other side.

For come out of it all again we eventually do, provided only that we conscientiously work through the illusions to the very end, never giving up the struggle and the quest — and above all never sitting back in satisfaction and saying to ourselves, 'This is it.'

For it so happens that dualistic thinking, pursued to its logical conclusion, always finishes up by exposing its own fundamental non-validity, as ancient oriental philosophy long ago demonstrated and the reductionist processes of modern scientific investigation are revealing anew in our own day.[42]

Thought destroys thought. At the basis of the enormous edifice of all our theorising and ratiocination lies . . . literally nothing.

A mere mirage. An illusion.

But this discovery, of course, spells the doom of all our hitherto most cherished beliefs. It means the total collapse of our old, familiar world (what else would you expect of a true New Age?) All that is left, if the quest has been honestly conducted, is what might be termed *appropriate uncertainty*. And the result may well be a period of black despair, or what St John of the Cross called the 'dark night of the soul'.

Eventually, however, the light dawns. For a fortunate few it seems to do so spontaneously. But for most of us some kind of catalytic agent has to be called in.

Of recent years, many of the younger generation have sought to claw themselves out of this particular Black Hole with the aid of drugs. And it is true that, under careful control and supervision, the experience of some of the less harmful so-called 'hallucinogens' such as LSD can help to reintroduce the seeker for the first time since infancy to a full-blooded experience of the universe's total oneness and wholeness in all its power and glory.[82] That one 'trip' is generally enough. Once re-experienced in adulthood, the vision remains, never again to be lost. For a good many New Agers, indeed, it has been this very experience which has provided the initial, decisive impetus for the whole of their subsequent quest.

But there is a serious snag in this approach. So overwhelming and alluring is the crucial drug experience that it tends to turn everything that follows — meditation, consciousness-expanding exercises, psychological therapies — into a kind of substitute drug experience in its own right, a continued search for 'kicks' or 'highs' (the 'Wow! That was some meditation!' syndrome, so well known in New Age circles).

Which is more than a little unfortunate, since nearly all of the techniques involved themselves turn out to be only too addictive in practice, even without any predisposing drug experience.

People who do meditation soon turn into Meditators, people who do Transactional Analysis into Transactionalists. The New Age movement is full of committed Psychosynthesisers and Rebirthers, Rajneeshists and Rosicrucians, Yogists and Anthroposophists, Sufis, Gurdjieffians and so on. Even the few techniques and approaches which seem, *a priori*, most likely to avoid this particular trap seem incapable of doing so.

Thus, Zen Buddhists, who are taught that there is no activity whatsoever that is necessary for the gaining of enlightenment, persist in 'doing Zen'. Graduates of *est* regularly attend reunions to relive their transformative experiences — thus casting doubt on whether their attitudes have really been transformed at all. Until his death in 1986, large numbers of enthusiasts for the ideas of Krishnamurti, who for over half a century vehemently rejected the very idea of teachings and authorities,[36,47] insisted on making annual pilgrimages to his various camp-meetings to be told it on his own authority all over again. Followers of Ramana Maharshi, who always insisted that truth was to be attained only through a process of self-enquiry,[55] still regularly revisit his ashram at Arunachala as though that truth were somehow to be soaked up from the lingering 'vibrations' of his own former presence there. Those who claim to have accepted the late Joel Goldsmith's *Infinite Way* paradoxically keep attending 'Joel Goldsmith' meetings as though in an effort to pick up *more* of it.

And all of them are afraid to take that one step beyond what the teachers say that would finally make the teachers unnecessary.

The acceptance of any one of these approaches, in other words, seems to imprison seekers at least as much as it frees them. It encourages a spirit of group-exclusivity, and thus of discrimination. And so — as practised, at least — it strengthens the very dualistic thinking which it is actually designed to help destroy, and so ensures that the promised New Age stays as far away as ever.

The antidote, then, would seem to be either to take on all of them at once (which is clearly next to impossible) or else to move on continually from one to the other, always asking the vital question 'What next?'

The latter approach, admittedly, does seem to be inherently healthy, in that it avoids the temptation ever to imagine that one has found in any one system or approach the 'final' answer. Yet it, too, has its built-in snag, in that the 'pilgrim' soon finds that he or she has become addicted to a new drug — one which Donald Keys has aptly described as 'nomadic sampling'.

And so the long search goes on, somehow seeming to provide its own pleasure and justification . . . .

* * *

It may take a long time before the light starts to dawn. Many, indeed, may fall by the wayside. But eventually, for those who persist long enough, the penny drops.

And it consists in the realisation that the answer does not lie, after all, in any search, approach, technique or therapy whatever. There is nothing to be done but to drop all of them, just as one has already dropped the tottering edifices built up by the more every-day forms of duality-consciousness.

The answer, indeed, is not to be *sought* at all. Instead it is there already, staring us in the face, just as it has been all along.

What, after all, have you been experiencing? What else but a series of ever-changing 'I's undertaking a series of ever-differing approaches, each reflecting whichever 'I' has currently been uppermost? The 'I', in other words, has not been constant. Neither have the approaches themselves — nor, for that matter, has the perceived universe in general.

The sole constant in the entire operation has been your own perception. Your perception, that is, both of yourself and of the universe 'out there'. And for a very good reason. For you have only to look closely into the nature of your perceiving (precisely the approach recommended, it has to be said, by both Krishnamurti and Ramana Maharshi) to realise that not one of your ever-changing 'I's is your *real* 'I'. Your real 'I' is intimately bound up with your perceptions themselves. Indeed, it is more than just bound up with them: it *is* them. You have never had a perception without an 'I', or an 'I' without a perception.

In a word, *you are* your perception. The real 'you' is nothing more or less than consciousness itself.

But the astonishing thing is that exactly the same consideration applies to the universe as a whole. For whatever 'objective' universe there may be out there, the only universe that you can ever perceive is *the universe that you perceive*. What you are actually perceiving, in other words, is nothing more or less than your own perceptions. The universe itself, it would seem, is random enough (scientific speculators currently prefer to explain this idea in terms of a theoretically infinite number of possible 'parallel universes') to permit your consciousness to model it in any way it wishes.[42]

Which has to mean, in effect, that whatever seems to you to be happening 'out there' is — strange as it may seem on first consideration — ultimately a direct result of your own state of consciousness. Eerie though the realisation may at first seem, the world's problems are actually your own problems. Its divisions merely reflect your own inner conflicts; its inhumanity your own inhumanity to yourself; its famines the extent to which you are starving large parts of your own psyche; its pollution problems your proneness to smother your own inner reality with imposed beliefs and illusions; its drug addiction your refusal to face reality; its unemployment your failure to put whole areas of your awareness to work; its anti-black racialism your rejection of your own darker side; its lawlessness your disregard of the basic laws of your own being; its AIDS — along with the breakdown of the earth's protective ozone layer — your unconscious realisation that you ultimately cannot protect yourself or cut yourself off from the rest of the universe; its global warming your participation in the fever of transformation that humanity is currently undergoing; its mass-movements and mass-disasters your increasing involvement, perhaps, in the growth of some kind of new, transhuman super-entity . . . .

In a phrase, we do not see things as they are: we see them as *we* are.

And other people, in particular, are merely particular aspects of ourselves.

As Jung himself once put it, 'The problems that are not realised within us must eventually externalise themselves and become our fate.'

And so it is not so much a matter of your head being in the universe, as of the universe being in your head. As the Australian aboriginal tradition prefers to put it, while the gods of the Dream

Time create humanity, humanity at the same time creates the gods.

Your consciousness, then, is not only the sole constant in the whole of your experience. It is the one thing which binds yourself and the universe into the single entity that it truly is. Indeed, because that consciousness is the one thing that is indubitably there, it has to be *reality itself*.

And so it follows that you have only to achieve (or possibly re-achieve) a state of pure consciousness — and not merely the partial, distorted consciousness of dualistic thinking — for the Golden Age of ultimate, holistic reality to be restored on Earth. With the dawning of the knowledge of truth (as both the Essenes and St Paul foresaw) the perceived universe is utterly transformed.

From the point of view of duality-consciousness, admittedly, it might theoretically seem as though your own change of attitude has spread to others via a kind of ripple-effect in such a way as progressively to transform the world. As perceived in *whole* consciousness, however, there are no 'others' to convert, and universal transformation is both total and immediate.

It occurs not in the past, not in the future, but now, in this instant, in the twinkling of an eye.

* * *

Yet that change comes only as we let go of our current obsession with dualistic thinking, along with its progeny of non-stop thought and language and all the apparent 'problems' to which they inevitably lead. To achieve it we must finally have done with the fruit of the Tree of the Knowledge of Good and Evil.

True, both thought and language are still needed in the limited context of daily social and occupational intercourse. But outside that context — and it follows that there needs to be a very considerable 'outside' to it — each of us needs to commit ourselves not so much to resisting dualistic thinking (which would of course merely be another manifestation of that very process), as to a life of *pure observation* — redolent, perhaps, of much earlier stages of human culture. Direct observation, uncontaminated by linguistic categories, of what is going on inside us — our emotions, our sensations, our psychological drives and tensions, even our budding ideas — as well as of what is apparently going on 'out there'. Observation of 'inner' and 'outer', in fact, as a single continuum of experience.

And then — and this is perhaps the truly crucial point — observation *of that process of observation itself*.

In this state of pure consciousness, once attained, there is no thought, no judgement, no discrimination, no idea of imperfection, no regret, no suffering, no urge to reform the world. No illusion, indeed, that there is a separate world 'out there' to reform, or anybody independent 'in here' to reform it.

You may call it watchfulness, awareness, attention, observation, mindfulness or simply Being Here Now. The dualistically-inclined sceptic may see it as merely contemplating your own navel, or accuse you of shutting your eyes to reality.

And yet, in reality, you will merely be shutting your eyes to illusion.

The illusion is that the world is imperfect and divided against itself, that the Garden of Eden has been lost to us and needs to be restored. The reality is that all is absolutely perfect as it is, and that the Garden of Eden has never ceased to be.

All (in an often quoted but rarely understood Findhornian phrase) is very well. The blessedness of the Dream Time is not past, but ever-present.

And so the reason for the failure of all the various attempts to bring about a New Age at last becomes blindingly clear. It is that there was never any need to inaugurate a New Age in the first place.

For the Kingdom of Heaven is already spread abroad in all its glory upon the earth.

... And whether or not it is clear to you,
no doubt the universe is unfolding as it should.

Max Ehrmann: 'Desiderata'

Reference-Bibliography

Except where otherwise indicated, all biblical quotations are taken from the New English Bible (Oxford & Cambridge University Presses, 1970). Wherever the Hebrew warrants it, however, the conventional English euphemism 'the LORD' is replaced by the original word 'Yahweh' in Old Testament quotations.

1. al-Sadr, Ayatullah M.M. & Mutahhery, Ayatullah M.: *The Awaited Saviour* (Islamic Seminary, 1982)
2. Annett, S.: *The Many Ways of Being* (Abacus, 1976)
3. Barlow, W.: *The Alexander Principle* (Arrow, 1975)
4. Bennet, J.G.: *Concerning Subud* (Hodder & Stoughton, 1958)
5. Blavatsky, H.P.: *The Secret Doctrine* (Quest, 1967)
6. Bronowski, J.: *The Ascent of Man* (BBC, 1976)
7. Bry, A.: *est* (Turnstone, 1977)
8. Burke, J.: *The Day the Universe Changed* (BBC,1985)
9. Burland, C.A. et al: *Mythology of the Americas* (Hamlyn, 1971)
10. Caddy, E.: *God Spoke to Me* (Findhorn Press, 1981)
11. Capra, F.: *The Turning Point* (Wildwood House, 1982)
12. Clark, K.: *Civilisation* (BBC, 1971)
13. Cooke, A.: *Alistair Cooke's America* (BBC, 1981)
14. *A Course in Miracles* (Arkana, 1985)
15. Cupitt, D.: *The Sea of Faith* (BBC, 1985)
16. Esselmont, J.E.: *Bahá'u'lláh and the New Era* (Bahá'í Publishing Trust, 1974)
17. Evans, C.: *Cults of Unreason* (Panther, 1974)
18. Fairbridge, R.W.: 'The Changing Level of the Ocean' in *Scientific American*, May 1960, Vol. 202, No. 5.
19. Ferguson, M.: *The Aquarian Conspiracy* (Paladin, 1982)
20. Gleadow, R.: *The Origin of the Zodiac* (Cape, 1968)
21. Govinda, Lama A.: *The Way of the White Clouds* (Rider, 1966)
22. Greenlees, D.: *The Gospel of Zarathustra* (Theosophical Publishing House, 1951)
23. Guillaume, A.: *Islam* (Pelican, 1956)
24. Hagen, V.W. von: *World of the Maya* (Mentor, 1960)
25. Hamel, P.M.: *Through Music to the Self* (Element, 1978)
26. Harman, W.W.: *An Incomplete Guide to the Future* (Norton, 1976)
27. Harris, T.A.: *I'm OK - You're OK* (Pan, 1973)
28. Hawken, P.: *The Magic of Findhorn* (Souvenir, 1975)
29. Hounam, P. & Hogg, A.: *Secret Cult* (Lion, 1984)
30. Humphreys, C.: *Buddhism* (Pelican, 1951)
31. Jowett, B. (tr.): *The Dialogues of Plato*, Vol.3 (Sphere, 1970)
32. Jung, C.G.: *Man and His Symbols* (Aldus, 1964)
33. Jung, C.G.: *Memories, Dreams, Reflections* (Fontana, 1967)
34. Keller, W.: *The Bible as History* (Hodder & Stoughton, 1974)
35. Knight, C.: *The Brotherhood* (Granada, 1983)
36. Krishnamurti, J.: *Freedom from the Known* (Gollancz, 1969)

37. Kryananda, Swami: *Your Sun Sign as a Spiritual Guide* (Ananda, 1971)
38. Lao-Tsu (tr. Gia-Fu-Feng & Jane English): *Tao Te Ching* (Wildwood House, 1973)
39. Leakey, R. & Lewin, R.: *Origins* (Futura, 1982)
40. Lefevre, D.N.: *Playing for the Fun of It* (Element, 1984)
41. Lemesurier, P.: *The Armageddon Script* (Element, 1981)
42. Lemesurier, P.: *Beyond All Belief* (Element, 1983)
43. Lemesurier, P.: *Gospel of the Stars* (Element, 1977)
44. Lemesurier, P.: *The Great Pyramid Decoded* (Element, 1977) and *The Great Pyramid: Your Personal Guide* (Element, 1987)
45. Lewis, C.S.: *Out of the Silent Planet* (Pan, 1952)
46. Lewis, H.R. & Streitfeld, H.S.: *Growth Games* (Abacus, 1973)
47. Lutyens, M.: Krishnamurti: *The Years of Fulfilment* (Murray, 1983)
48. Mascaró, J. (tr.): *Bhagavad Gita* (Penguin, 1962)
49. Matson, K. (ed.): *The Encyclopaedia of Reality* (Paladin, 1979)
50. McIntosh, C.: *The Rosy Cross Unveiled* (Aquarian, 1980)
51. Mehta, P.D.: *The Heart of Religion* (Element, 1976)
52. Miers, H.E.: *Lexikon des Geheimwissens* (Goldmann, 1976)
53. Moore, P.: *The A-Z of Astronomy* (Fontana, 1976)
54. Murray, M.: *Seeking the Master: A Guide to the Ashrams of India* (Spearman, 1981)
55. Osborne, A.: *Ramana Maharshi and the Path of Self-Knowledge* (Rider, 1954)
56. Ouspensky, P.D.: *In Search of the Miraculous* (Routledge & Kegan Paul, 1969)
57. Pickthall, M.M.: *The Meaning of the Glorious Koran* (Mentor)
58. Powell Davies, A.: *The Meaning of the Dead Sea Scrolls* (Mentor,   1956)
59. Prabhupada, A.C.B. Swami: *The Science of Self-Realization* (Bhaktivedanta Book Trust, 1977)
60. Preston, J. & J.: *Alternative Wales* (Orkid/Cilgwyn, 1982)
61. Priebsch, R. & Collinson, W.E.: *The German Language* (Faber & Faber, 1948)
62. Ropp, R.S. de: *The Master Game* (Picador, 1974)
63. Rudhyar, D.: *Occult Preparations for a New Age* (Quest, 1975)
64. Russell, P.: *The Awakening Earth* (Routledge & Kegan Paul, 1982)
65. Russell, P.: *The TM Technique* (Routledge & Kegan Paul, 1978)
66. Rutherford, A.: *Pyramidology*, Vols. 1-4 (Institute of Pyramidology, 1957 onwards)
67. Saunders, N.: *Alternative England and Wales* (N. Saunders, 1975)
68. Saunders, N.: *Alternative London* (Wildwood House & N. Saunders, 1974)
69. Sawtell, V.: *The Medicine of the Stars* (Essential Nutrients, 1969)
70. Schonfield, H.J.: *The Authentic New Testament* (Dobson)
71. Schonfield, H.J.: *The Essene Odyssey* (Element, 1984)
72. Schumacher, E.F.: *Small is Beautiful* (Abacus, 1974)
73. Sen, K.: *Hinduism* (Pelican, 1961)
74. Sinkler, L.: *The Spiritual Journey of Joel S. Goldsmith* (Allen & Unwin, 1974)
75. Spangler, D.: *Revelation: The Birth of a New Age* (Findhorn, 1977) and *The Rebirth of the Sacred* (Gateway, 1984)
76. Stevens, J.O.: *Gestalt Is* (Bantam, 1977)
77. Tereschenko, N.: *A Look at Fourth Way Work* (Hermetic Research Series, 1983)
78. Timms, M.: *The Six O'Clock Bus* (Turnstone, 1979)
79. Vaillant, G.C.: *Aztecs of Mexico* (Pelican, 1965)
80. Vermes, G.: *The Dead Sea Scrolls* (Collins, 1977)
81. Vermes, G.: *The Dead Sea Scrolls in English* (Penguin, 1968)
82. Watts, A.W.: *The Joyous Cosmology* (Vintage, 1962)
83. Watts, A.W.: *Myth and Ritual in Christianity* (Thames & Hudson, 1953)
84. Watts, A.W.: *The Way of Zen* (Penguin, 1970)
85. Wilson, C.: *The Occult* (Hodder & Stoughton, 1971)
86. Wright, B. & Worsley, C.: *Alternative Scotland* (Wildwood House, 1975)